The People's Roman Remains Park

Research: David Kidd assisted by Jean Stokes

Text: David Kidd

Layout: Jean Stokes

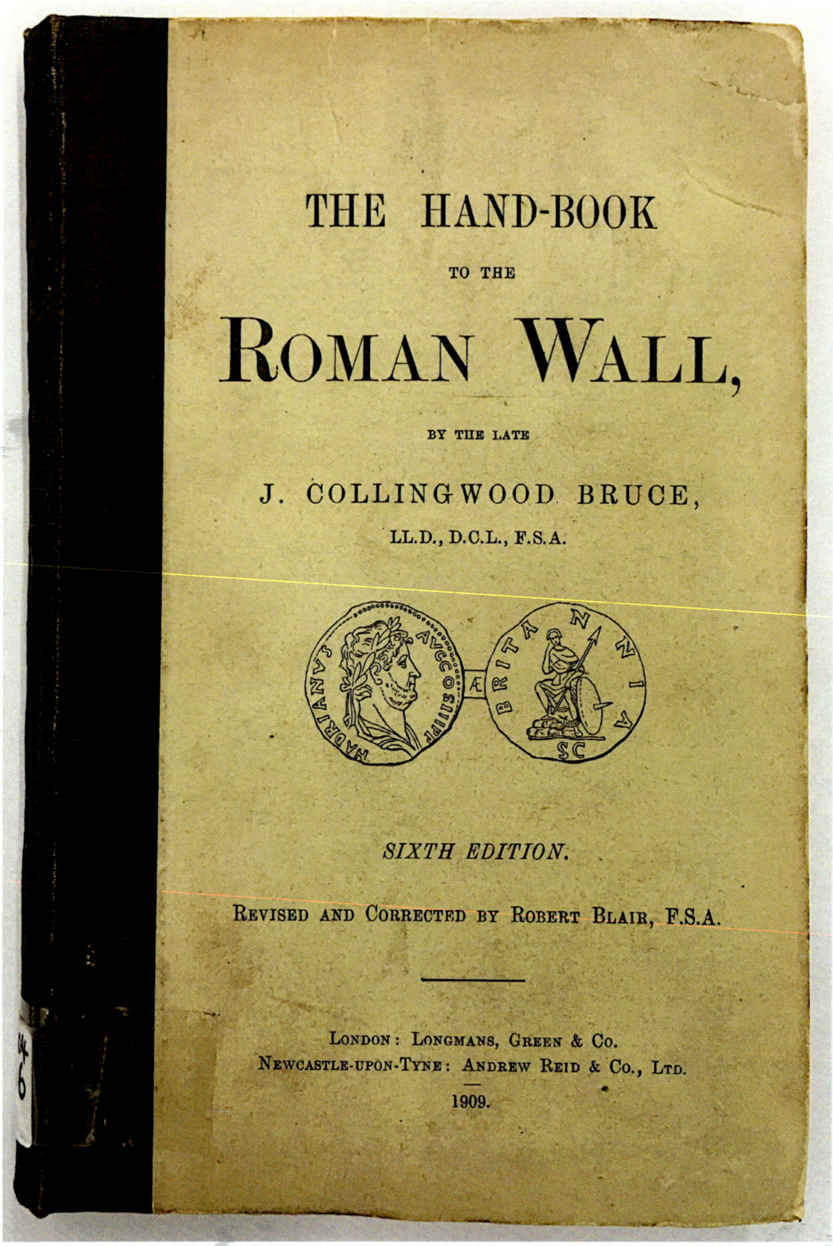

Reproduced by kind permission of the Natural History Society of Northumbria, Great North Museum: Hancock, Newcastle-upon-Tyne.

Contents

Forward		v
Preface		vii
1	The Roman Summer	1
2	The Lawe	9
3	The Campaign	31
4	The Excavation	67
5	Regina & Victor	113
6	The Scrapbook	137
7	The People's Roman Remains Park	183
8	Heritage & History	205
Index		223
Bibliography		233
Places to Visit		234

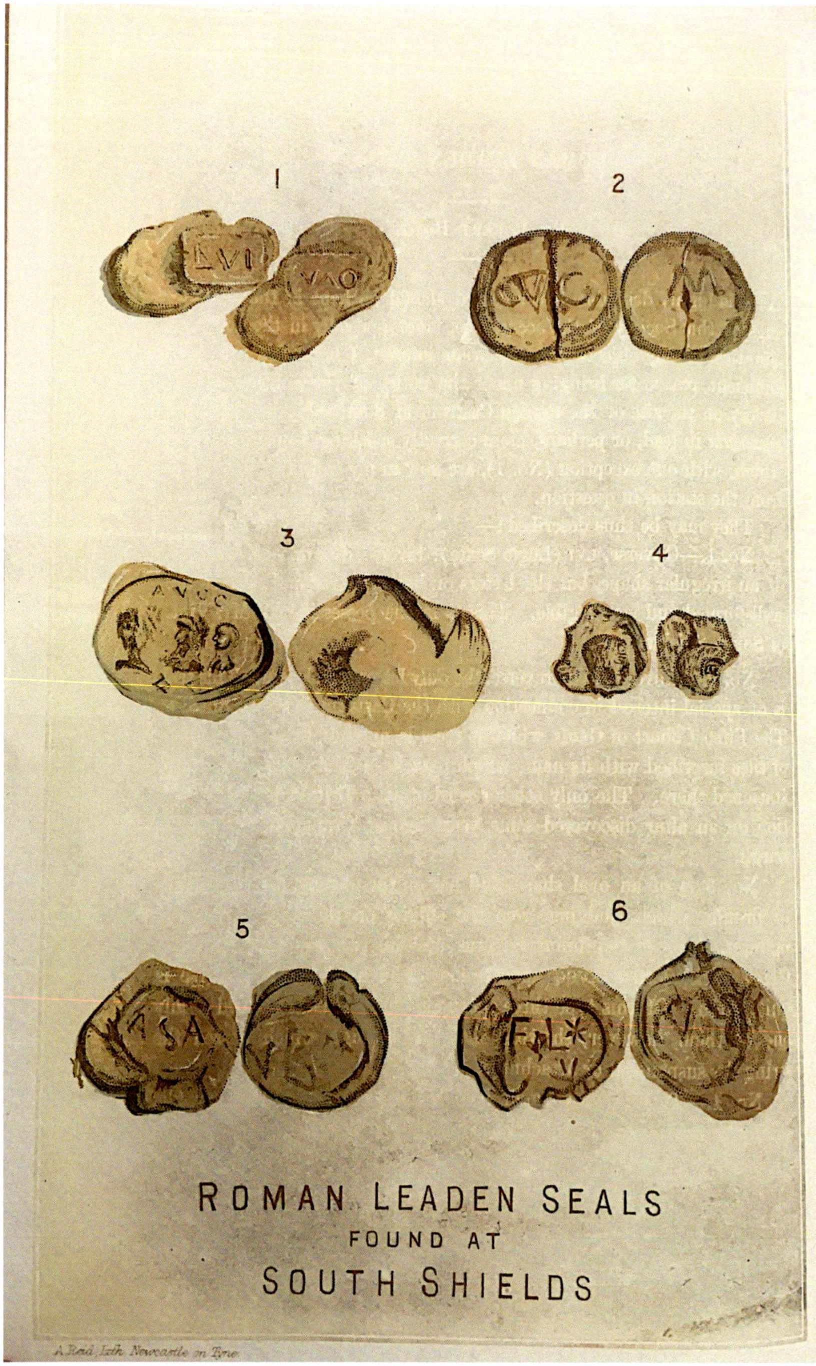

Blair Scrapbook; courtesy of South Tyneside Libraries.
These are now called** 'sealings' **rather than** 'seals' **(to distinguish them from the** 'seal' **that made the impression).

Forward

The excavations of South Shields Roman fort and its surroundings provoked great interest in 1875 and the following years, and members of the public flocked to visit the site on public holidays. This was a time when South Shields was expanding and developing, and the local inhabitants considered the presence of an important Roman settlement there in the past might be mirrored by an equal greatness of the town in the future. The interest and the pride in the site that started back then continue to this day, and the fort still welcomes large numbers of visitors.

Many of the artefacts, illustrated so carefully in Robert Blair's scrapbook preserved in The Word, National Centre for the Written Word, in South Shields, still survive in the collections of Arbeia, South Shields Roman Fort and the Great North Museum: Hancock. As part of the project Our Fort, Our Heritage, generously funded by DCMS Wolfson Museums and Galleries Improvement Fund, the National Lottery Heritage Fund and Arts Council England (ACE), I was delighted to be able to give the authors access to photographs of the objects included in this lavishly illustrated book.

Jean and David have produced a wonderful book, not only looking at the earliest excavations of the site and the remains and artefacts discovered, but also presenting many of the personalities involved. I am sure you will enjoy reading this intriguing story.

Alex Croom
Keeper of Archaeology
Arbeia, South Shields Roman Fort

A South Shields Corporation bus carrying the CU registration in King Street in 1960.
Photograph reproduced by kind permission of South Tyneside Libraries.

Preface

It has been a great pleasure for us to research the Roman heritage of South Shields for this book. The County Borough of South Shields has always been proud of its Roman past and the Roman fort has never, since its original days, looked better than it does now with its spectacular reconstructed west gate, courtyard house and barrack block.

This book tells the story of how The People's Roman Remains Park began and how the Roman fort on the Lawe became part of South Shields' identity. Jean and I remember when the letters identifying cars registered in South Shields were CU and being told with pride that they stood for Caer Urfa, making Shields the only town with Roman car number plates. The letters, a little piece of urban mythology linking past and present are now gone, and perhaps forgotten, but we hope South Shields' pride in its Roman past remains and will grow by the story we have to tell.

The book had its origins in our discovery of Robert Blair's scrapbook in the local history collections of The Word, South Shields. Blair, the son of a Tyne Pilot, was the secretary of the excavation committee, the driving force behind the preservation of the fort; his collection of newspaper cuttings, drawings and photographs is an eyewitness account that captures the excitement of the excavation in 1875 and the struggle to secure its legacy.

This book could not have been written without the help of many people: the staff at The Word, who gave us access to the scrapbook and the staff at the Great North Museum: Hancock in Newcastle, who allowed us to photograph items from Robert Blair's collection in their custody deserve a special mention, but most of all we would like to thank Alex Croom of the Arbeia South Shields Roman Fort for showing us the fantastic finds from the 1875 excavation that are held at the fort. We hope you enjoy reading this book as much as we have enjoyed writing it and also hope it will encourage you to visit, or revisit, the Roman fort on the Lawe and also the Great North Museum: Hancock to see for yourself the treasures of the Lawe and the places where they were found.

All profits from the sale of this book will be donated to Arbeia, South Shields Roman Fort to support its work.

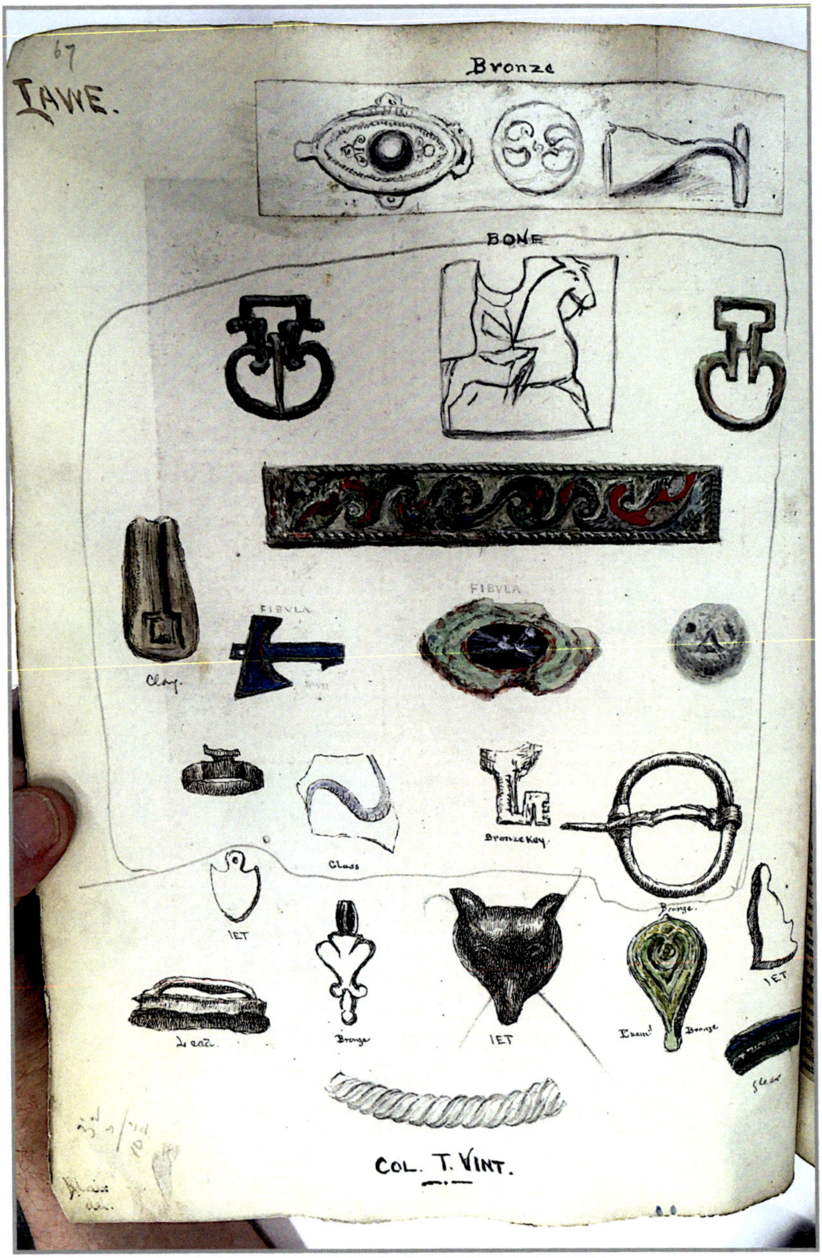

Page 67 of the Blair Scrapbook in The Word, National Centre for the Written Word, South Shields.
The illustrations are by Robert Blair and all the items were found on the Lawe but it would seem that some, if not all, of the items on this page were in the collection of Colonel T Vint.
Blair Scrapbook; courtesy of South Tyneside Libraries.

The Roman Summer

Small bronze figure of a man in a toga in the collection of the Arbeia South Shields Roman Fort.
Photograph courtesy of Tyne & Wear Archives & Museums.

1

SIDDALL'S

NEW ALHAMBRA

AND AMPHITHEATRE ROYAL,

MILL DAM, SOUTH SHIELDS.

Thousand of delighted visitors attend this, the largest and best conducted Theatre in the North. To-night, grand Shakesperian revival of

JULIUS CÆSAR.

Time. — The ROMANS in ENGLAND. The ROMANS in SHIELDS. The ROMAN REMAINS. This grand Roman Tragedy has not been performed in Shields for the past 22 years.

Brutus.......................... J. O. STEWART.

Monday 12th July 1875, Shields Gazette and Daily Telegraph.
Reproduced by kind permission of the Shields Gazette.

South Shields in 1875 from a map in Robert Blair's scrapbook.
The site of Sam Siddall's Alhambra at the Mill Dam is marked with an X, bottom left hand corner of the map.
Reproduced by kind permission of South Tyneside Libraries.

Sam Siddall, the sole proprietor of the New Alhambra and Amphitheatre Royal Music Hall, wasn't interested in antiquarian discussions about the Roman name of South Shields or the interpretation of obscure ancient texts giving details of the allocation of units of the Roman army to long forgotten forts along Hadrian's Wall but he knew a good thing when he saw one. The New Alhambra which opened on Monday 31st August 1874 was, as he never ceased to boast, the biggest and best theatre outside London and it needed an attractive and exciting programme to keep it filled so, for Sam, a *'grand revival'* of Shakespeare's Roman play *Julius Caesar* was an obvious way to cash in on the Roman fever that gripped South Shields during the summer of 1875.

The Alhambra, recently rebuilt from an earlier wooden hall, could accommodate 4000 people and had a glamour that belied its position next to the glassworks in the back streets of a northern industrial town at the Mill Dam. It had none of the architectural pretensions of its rival, South Shields' first theatre, the elegantly classical Theatre Royal in King Street, but it was more than twice the size of the Royal and a very different operation; part theatre, part music hall, part circus and wholly spectacle and entertainment. The Alhambra was a plain brick building but its grand entrance, lit by two huge lamps set in a wall of glazed white bricks that shone with reflected light on dark northern nights, promised wonders inside. Patrons at the opening night on the 31st August 1874 when 4,200 people packed into Mr. Siddall's new theatre were not disappointed. The Alhambra must have seemed like a royal palace to the crowd who had never seen such luxury: its interior was lit by six cut glass chandeliers fully seven feet long, there were private boxes supported by white Corinthian columns topped with raised figures trimmed with gold and the seats in the boxes and dress circle were upholstered with the best scarlet velvet cloth. Long mirrors on either side of the white and gold classical proscenium arch appeared to double the size of the huge hall which had its own orchestra made up, Sam Siddall claimed, of the best musicians in the North East. In many ways Sam Siddall and his grand Alhambra Theatre symbolised the growth and ambition of the *'new'* town of South Shields. Before the industrial revolution Shields was a place apart known only for its burning spoil heaps (a by-product of its historic salt panning industry) and ballast hills. A potent combination of deep coal mining, iron ship building and railways made Shields a Victorian boom town which like the Alhambra grew from nothing to massive proportions.

ALHAMBRA AND AMPHITHEATRE.—(Proprietor, Mr S. B. Siddall.)—On Monday a good audience welcomed Mr J. H. Milburn, a Shields favourite, who sang some of his highly amusing songs; Mahomed and Hassan, Arab acrobats; Mr W. Jackson, Negro comedian; Miss Etty Cowell, burlesque artist; Sisters Daisy and Lillian Ramsden, burlesque artists; Mr Will George, Negro comedian; Miss Marion Winter, serio-comic; Mr T. Walker, extempore comic; Miss Lottie Montrose, ballad vocalist; Miss Marion Drew, ballad vocalist; and Mr Mat Atkinson, comic. Mr Jos. Bartle is the conductor of the band.

24th September 1876 cutting from the ERA.
The ERA was a British weekly paper, published from 1838 to 1939. Originally a general newspaper, it became noted for its sports coverage, and later for its theatrical content.

THE CRITERION RESTAURANT AND DINING ROOMS,
Within a Few Minutes' Walk of the
SPLENDID SEA PIERS AND
ROMAN REMAINS.

J. TODHUNTER,

OWNER AND OCCUPIER OF THE

CRITERION RESTAURANT,

Extending from Fowler Street to the Free Library, South Shields, respectfully announces to the public that the Establishment, in all its Departments, is well suited to supply the wants of all Classes in the community.

THE PUBLIC ROOMS AND BAR

Are arranged with every comfort and convenience for Visitors.

THE PRIVATE ROOMS

Are fitted up in a style rarely to be seen out of London.

The rooms have also a fine Sea View, and are in close proximity to the Roman Remains, which are attracting so much attention. Strangers will find the "Criterion" unequalled as a Refreshment House.

A Bill of Fare is hung up in every room.

Saturday 17th July 1875, Shields Gazette and Daily Telegraph.
Reproduced by kind permission of the Shields Gazette.

As a boy Sam was apprenticed as a fitter in West Yorkshire before moving to South Shields to work in one of the many engineering works along the riverside. The town had few facilities for its growing population and Sam saw the chance to make his fortune by moving into show business and building his first music hall. This was a simple wooden hall which grew into the Alhambra, South Shields' biggest public building, which brought the community together and made them proud of their rather ramshackle boom town. South Shields needed to find its identity quickly, so the discovery of the Roman remains on the Lawe was a heaven-sent opportunity to build civic pride and recover thousands of years of *'lost'* history in one summer: a fact which the excavation committee led by Dr. R E Hooppell, headmaster of the new Marine School, and Robert Blair, a local solicitor, seized with both hands.

The Alhambra's production of *Julius Caesar,* the first for 22 years, had no pretensions to historical accuracy, but it was a spectacle that filled the huge hall with paying customers to the delight of Sam Siddall and his company. Shakespeare's text was heavily cut to allow for frequent changes of costume and scenery, including specially painted backcloths which were a feature of productions at the Alhambra, while the actors made loud and melodramatic speeches that captured the attention of the huge audience. There was something Roman about the design of the Alhambra as in addition to a conventional stage, it had a circus ring 40 feet in diameter in the centre of the hall and its performances regularly featured trapeze artists and circus acts together with ballets, musicals, popular farces, and novelty acts.

Sam had originally planned a season of four *'fashionable'* Shakespearean plays for the summer of 1875 – *King Lear, Macbeth, Richard III, and Othello* (listed as *Iago*) – to build the Alhambra's reputation as a serious theatre. He added *Julius Caesar* to the programme when the extent of Roman mania gripping South Shields became obvious, as this chance to place his theatre at the centre of the latest popular enthusiasm which was bringing thousands of visitors to the town was too good to miss. Admission prices at the Alhambra started at 3d (3 old pennies) rose through 6d, 9d and 1s (shilling) to the best seats at 2s. The production of *Julius Caesar* was of no financial benefit for the excavation committee as there is no evidence that a collection was taken or money received into Robert Blair's office, which was the centre of the fundraising campaign for the excavations.

A present day photograph of street name signs at the corner of Lawe Road and Vespasian Avenue, this terrace being called Flavia Terrace. The roundel explaining that Flavia was the wife of Vespasian.

A similar sign from the corner of Lawe Road and Julian Avenue.

Sam, wasn't the only businessman in South Shields who was aware of the visitors flocking to the excavations. The proprietor of the fashionable Criterion Restaurant in Ocean Road was soon advertising it as *'convenient for the Roman remains'* as were most of his competitors. Similarly without a hint of irony, the speculative builders whose developments on the Lawe threatened the destruction of Shields' Roman heritage advertised their properties as being *'near the Roman remains in the most interesting part of town'*. Approaching the much enlarged Roman site and museum on the Lawe today, the successor of the original People's Roman Remains Park, the fort still advertises its presence in neighbouring streets and terraces named after Roman Emperors and their Empresses.

Like the Roman station on the Lawe the Alhambra fell in flames only to rise again from the ashes. The huge hall was destroyed by a massive fire in the early hours of Saturday 27th April 1878. The alarm was raised by officials at the railway station just after midnight as the flames lit up the low clouds of a dark wet night like the promise of an early dawn. The building was empty after the last performance and no one was injured in the disaster, but the performers who lost all their possessions were very distressed and Sam Siddall was comforted by the crowds who gathered to watch the Alhambra's final spectacular performance. He was heard to say the building was only half-insured but his business survived and he built another hall on the site *(The Grand)* and filled it with scenery and costumes bought from the *Royal Grecian Theatre* in London, before he emigrated to New Zealand in the 1880s with his wife and family, one son and four daughters, who all appeared on the stage.

For all their achievements the Victorian excavators never found the holy grail of the dig, an inscription or artefact giving the Roman name of the fort, but in The People's Roman Remains Park it took on a life of its own and the names they used - Caer Urfa and Arbeia – became part of South Shields' core identity even after the excavation itself had been almost forgotten. Arbeia with its splendid reconstructed west gate, barrack block, and courtyard house has now grown into something that Robert Blair and Dr. Hooppell (but perhaps not Sam Siddall) could never have imagined.

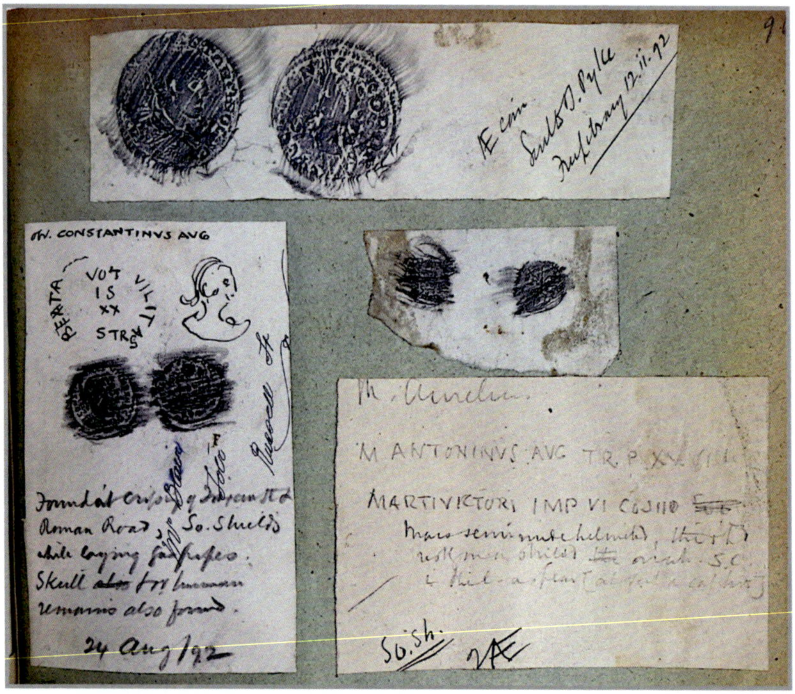

Please note in the lower section of these images from Blair's Scrapbook is an early photograph of some of the small finds, one being of a bronze crossbow brooch similar to that shown opposite; all were found on the Lawe.
Blair Scrapbook; courtesy of South Tyneside Libraries.

The Lawe

A bronze crossbow brooch in the collection of the Arbeia South Shields RomanFort.
Photograph courtesy of Tyne & Wear Archives & Museums.

2

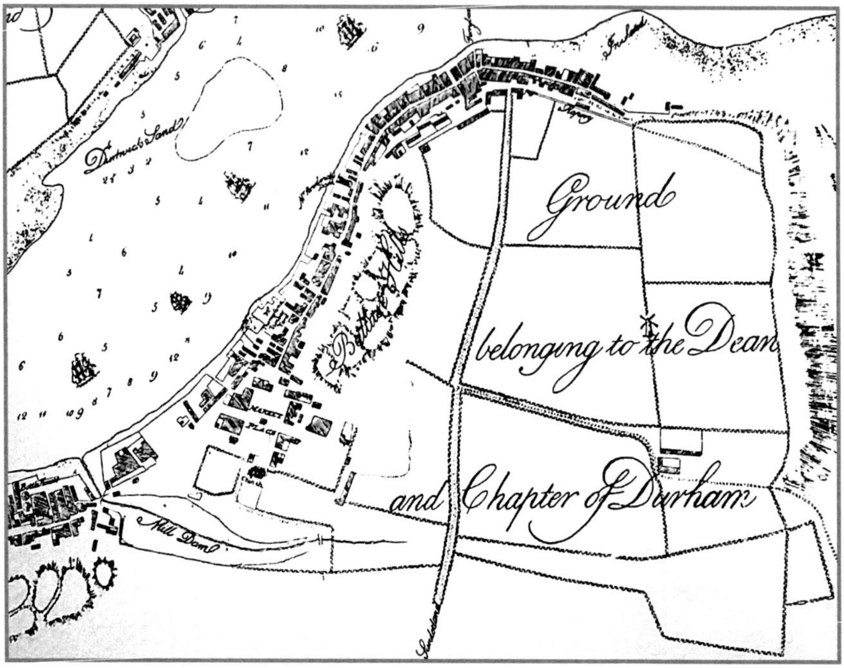

An extract from the plan of the *River Tyne* ***by John Fryer, 1773.***

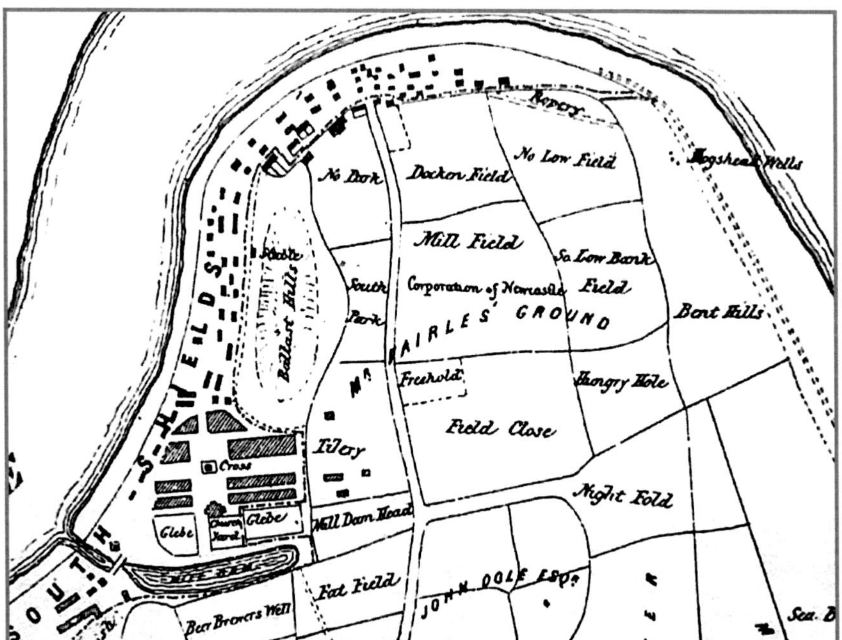

An extract from a *Plan of the Townships of South Shields and Westoe in County Durham,* ***from a survey by Mr Richardson of Darlington, 1786.***

John Leland had an exciting life for a librarian. Born in 1503 he had the patronage of Henry VIII's powerful advisor Thomas Cromwell and in 1533 he was given the King's commission to examine the libraries of all the religious houses in England. Armed with his Royal warrant Leland spent most of the next decade travelling the country against the background of the dissolution of the monasteries, making lists of the books in the libraries of abbeys and priories great and small. In his 1544 letter to the King, later published as *The Laborious Journey and Search of John Leland for England's Antiquities,* Leland outlined his ambitious plans for a new comprehensive history of England with one volume being dedicated to each county. The project was never completed but his notes, itineraries and collections were preserved and eventually donated to the Bodleian Library at Oxford in 1642 where they remain, a priceless resource for historians and antiquarians.

Leland was the discoverer of the Roman fort at South Shields, or at least the first person since the fall of Rome to write down anything of its history. His few words said nothing about the Romans but framed the fort's past in the myth of a lost city, the birthplace of a king, a story which (even if there was little hard evidence to support his claims) inspired the campaign leading to the 1875 excavations and captured the imaginations of the people of Victorian South Shields. Leland arrived at Tynemouth some time before 1542, drawn by a passage in the *Chronicles of the Monastery of St Albans* which stated that *'opposite to Tynemouth was a city ravaged by the Danes, Urfa by name, where King Oswin was born'* and he was interested to record anything that the few monks who remained there could add to the story. Tynemouth was once the shrine of Oswin and the monks repeated the *Chronicles*' story adding a little local detail to increase its credibility. Leland noted: *'They report indeed that King Oswin was born in a certain fortress anciently named Burgh, the foundations of which in part still remain on the south side of the water of Tyne, near South Shields, in territory which now belongs to the Prior of Durham'.*

If Tynemouth with its dramatic cliffs and ruined priory church still looks like a suitable place for the burial of kings (three were once buried there), South Shields in 1540 was an unlikely place for the birth of a king. The Shields Leland saw from the cliffs of Tynemouth was a small fishing village blanketed by the smoke from salt pans boiling sea water to make salt. Shields was a new but rapidly growing centre of the industry, its rise driven

A section from a map of 1801.
The supposed site of a Roman Station is marked at the tip of the peninsular which forms the southern side of the mouth of the River Tyne, an area known as the Lawe. This map was produced long before the 1875 excavations of the site and clearly shows that the ancient edifice though, indistinguishable in the grass fields of the Lawe, was well known to have existed in that place.
The town of South Shields is seen nestled on the sheltered western side of the peninsula.

by the new technology of iron tanks called *'pans'* and abundant cheap coal which was replacing the traditional wooden pans of sea water evaporated by the sun. Burning poor quality coal (the best went by sea to London) to boil water to make salt made Shields a place to be avoided. In 1725 Lord Hartley described it as *'the chief place for making salt. The houses there are poor little hovels and are in a perpetual thick nasty smoke'*. It wasn't somewhere a scholar like Leland would normally visit but it is possible he inspected the remains of Urfa although, if he did, he found little of note beyond a few stones in the rough pasture. South Shields, with the advantage of being at the mouth of the River Tyne, was an obvious centre for the lucrative coal trade, nationally important even in 1540; however its growth was stunted by a Royal Charter granted to the burgesses of Newcastle giving them a monopoly on the trading of all goods landed or exported from the River Tyne between Spar Hawk (a rock on the Black Middens at Tynemouth) and Hedwin Streams (the tidal limit of navigation on the river, west of Newcastle). Newcastle prospered on the growth of the coal trade but South Shields, despite the power of the Bishops of Durham who promoted the new town on the riverside by the Mill Dam as a rival, had to be content with the crumbs that fell from Newcastle's table, or rather the salt pans and ballast dumps that Newcastle didn't want.

King Oswin might have been born in South Shields, according to Leland, and he was once buried at Tynemouth but after death his body travelled the country on an odyssey second only to the wanderings of St Cuthbert of Durham. The story of Oswin's life, even if he is almost unknown in the town of his birth, seems strangely familiar containing, as it does, common elements of many pious histories. Oswin was of royal birth; he was unjustly forced into exile and then returned to usher in a period of peace and prosperity, only to be betrayed by a trusted courtier and murdered on the orders of an ambitious rival. Much of the story, like Leland's, is unsupported by any hard evidence but what is known for certain is that he was killed at Gilling in North Yorkshire on the 20th August 651 and buried in a monastery nearby, built by the wife of his penitent rival. Gilling became a place of pilgrimage after reports of miracles at Oswin's tomb but, threatened by the rising power of the pagan Danes, his body was moved north and reburied at Tynemouth. Later, possibly following the destruction of the first priory by the Danes in 875, Tynemouth was abandoned and the site of Oswin's grave was lost until, according to legend, the King himself appeared to a young

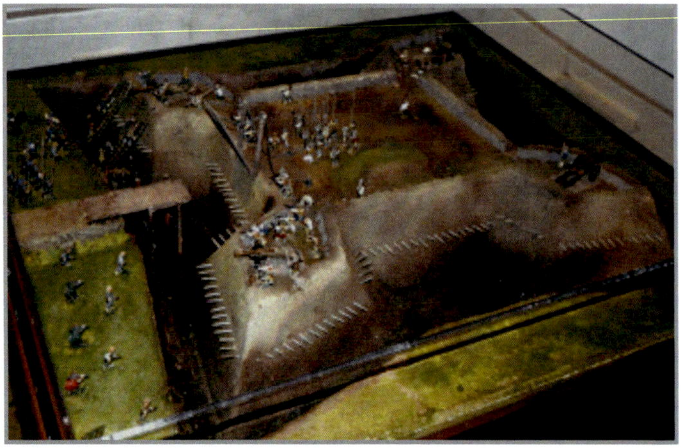

A model of a Civil War Fort on display at South Shields in the west gate at Arbeia South Shields Roman Fort.
Photograph courtesy of Tyne & Wear Archives & Museums.

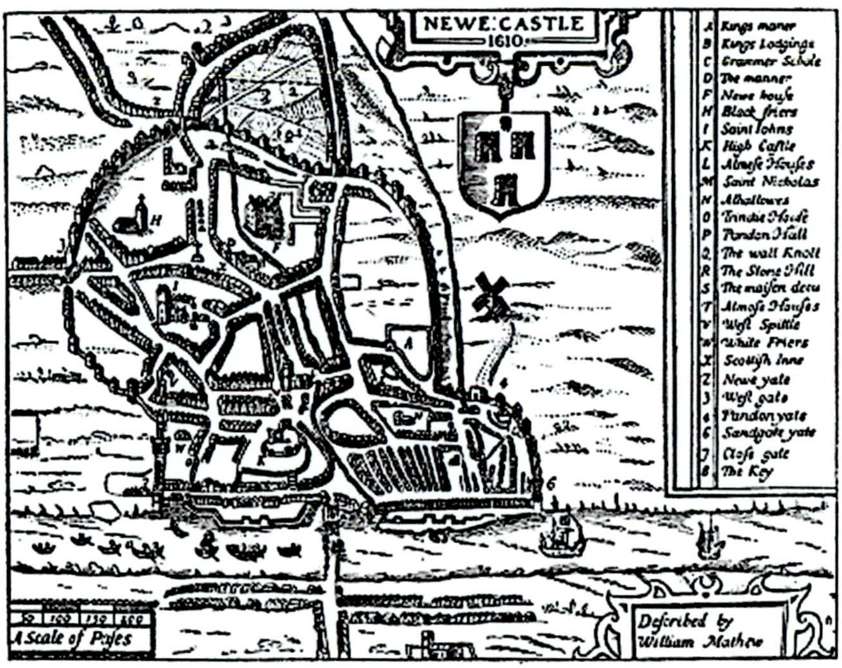

A map of the walled city of Newcastle upon Tyne published in William Gray's** Chorographia **published in 1649. The capture of the sconce on the Lawe at South Shields was part of a campaign by the Scottish Covenanters who supported the Parliamentary forces to take Newcastle. The City fell on 27th October 1644 after a lengthy siege, an event still commemorated in the City's coat of arms and motto** Fortiter Defendit Triumphans **which were granted after the Restoration in recognition of its loyalty to the Crown.

hermit and revealed the location of his body. When the grave was opened his body was found to have decayed, disappointing the faithful who expected it to be uncorrupted. Oswin's bones were interred in a purpose built oratory in 1065, but plans for a grand new church came to nothing and his bones may have spent some time at Jarrow before being finally taken to St Albans, mother house of the new Tynemouth Priory, in 1103. After almost 500 years of wandering Oswin was finally at rest.

The new town of South Shields, which appeared as an appendage to the Prior of Durham's village of Westoe sometime before 1150, had no connection with Leland's Urfa. Forsaking Oswin it had its own saint, Hilda, later famous as the abbess of the great joint monastery at Whitby, who Bede reported in 685 was given a grant of land in a district north of the Wear to found a nunnery where she lived for a year before moving to Hartlepool. Traditionally the nunnery was believed to be on the site of St Hilda's Church which was founded as a chapel in the parish of Jarrow before 1200 and received its first regular curate in 1321. By the time Leland came to Tynemouth St Hilda's Church probably had a nave and a south aisle reflecting its importance to the life of the growing town; its first record of a burial dates from 1565. The Church was rebuilt and extended in 1812 largely obliterating the medieval building although some fragments are said to survive in the tower arch and lower part of the west wall.

Despite the growth of the salt trade (by 1663 the accounts of the chapel wardens counted 121 iron pans each employing three people) South Shields remained an obscure backwater although the Lawe enjoyed a revival of its ancient strategic importance during the English Civil War when Royalist and Scots armies supporting Parliament fought for its possession. Newcastle was a Royalist stronghold and a small fort was built on the Lawe on the orders of Marquis of Newcastle to hold 100 men and 5 cannon to command the Tyne estuary. The sconce, a standard fortification in the shape of a star, had walls 9 feet high surrounded by a ditch 12 feet wide and 11 feet deep. It was on the crest of the hill near the Lawe beacons where its guns could control the Tyne. The Scots laid siege to the sconce on the 15th March 1544. The Royalists commanded by Captain Chapman of South Shields put up a brave defence but were greatly outnumbered and the sconce fell on the 20th March 1644 with 16 men killed, 5 captured and

An Edwardian postcard and a contemporary photograph of the Jubilee Memorial, also known as the Wouldhave Memorial, in Ocean Road, South Shields.
From the collection of E Lewthwaite.

A photograph of the east facing side of the memorial, displaying its dedication and date of inauguration.

the rest escaping to the river, prompting claims that some of the defenders had deserted their posts. Nine Scotsmen were killed and many more wounded in the final assault but they took possession of 5 guns, 7 barrels of powder and 70 muskets and, with the sconce gone, Newcastle was cut off and its end was inevitable.

The famous walled city eventually fell to the Parliamentary forces after a siege of 10 weeks on 19th October 1644 when the Scots, exasperated by the Mayor's refusal to negotiate terms with vastly superior forces, blew down a section of the wall, and the starving townsfolk surrendered: an event still commemorated by Newcastle's city motto and coat of arms. No trace of the sconce remained by the time the Lawe was developed in 1875 but musket balls and one possible skeleton from the Civil War battle were found during the 1875 excavations.

Even within the isolated town of South Shields, the Lawe, before the housebuilding boom of 1875, was a place apart. Shields found its identity in the nineteenth century through the lifeboat, placing it at the centre of the new municipal borough's coat of arms in 1850 and celebrating Queen Victoria's Jubilee by building a clock tower in Ocean Road as a memorial to the *'inventors'.* However the real story of the lifeboat can be found on the Lawe. The success of the South Shields lifeboat depended on the pilots, a close knit community who handed down their profession as a birth right from father to son, who manned the boats as volunteers and without whom there would have been no lifeboat.

St Stephen's Church on Mile End Road, built in 1846 and now within sight of Arbeia Roman Fort, was their church and it contains a sad memorial to the darkest day in their history when the death of 20 lifeboat men led to the creation of the modern lifeboat service. On 4th December 1849 the lifeboat *Providence* capsized, throwing her crew of 24 into the raging seas while attempting to rescue the crew of the brig *Betsy* of Littlehampton, which was aground on Herd Sand. Three managed to cling to the upturned hull of the *Providence* and were picked up by another lifeboat, while one escaped to the *Betsy* and was rescued with the ship's crew, but 20 pilots were lost. The *Providence's* men drowned in front of their distraught families and within sight of their homes but the tight community of pilots on the Lawe kept their grief to themselves.

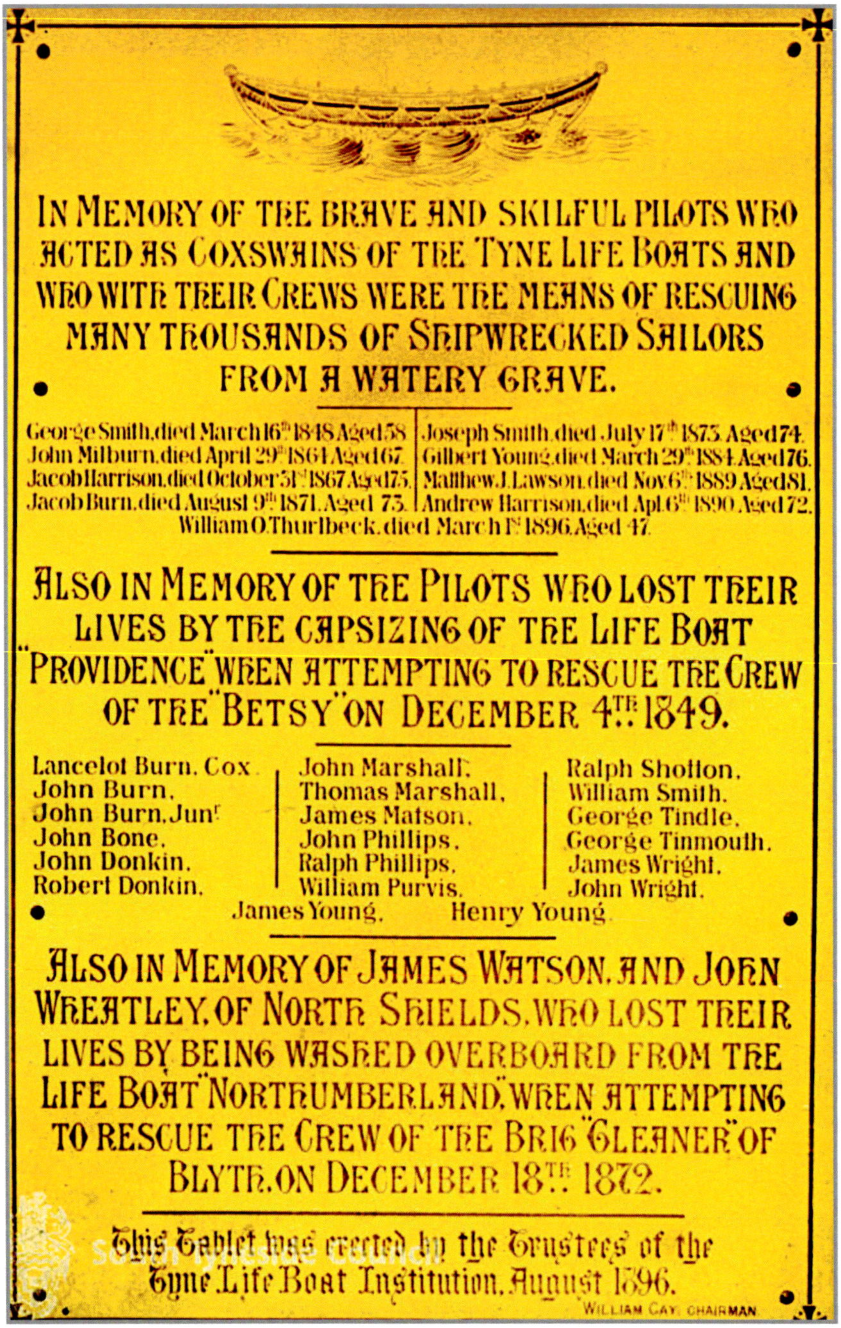

Plaque in St Stephen's Church.
Reproduced by kind permission of the Churchwardens of St Stephen's Church, The Lawe, South Shields.

To the town's shame, there was (as the Shields' Gazette put it) no memorial to the disaster until 1896 when the Trustees of the Tyne Lifeboat Society erected a plaque in St Stephen's Church listing the names of the lost crew of the *Providence,* but the disaster left a lasting legacy. The Duke of Northumberland, whose family had long been patrons of the Tyne lifeboats, offered a prize of one hundred guineas for the best model which could improve on the design of the *Providence,* which, despite being unsinkable, was not self-righting.

Two hundred and eighty models and sets of plans were sent to Somerset House and displayed at the Great Exhibition, including five from South Shields and one from Robert Blair, the father of the secretary of the excavation committee. Blair senior's model scored well, being placed in the short list of 36 with 63 points, the winner being James Beeching of Yarmouth's design which won with 84 points and was adopted as the RNLI National Lifeboat.

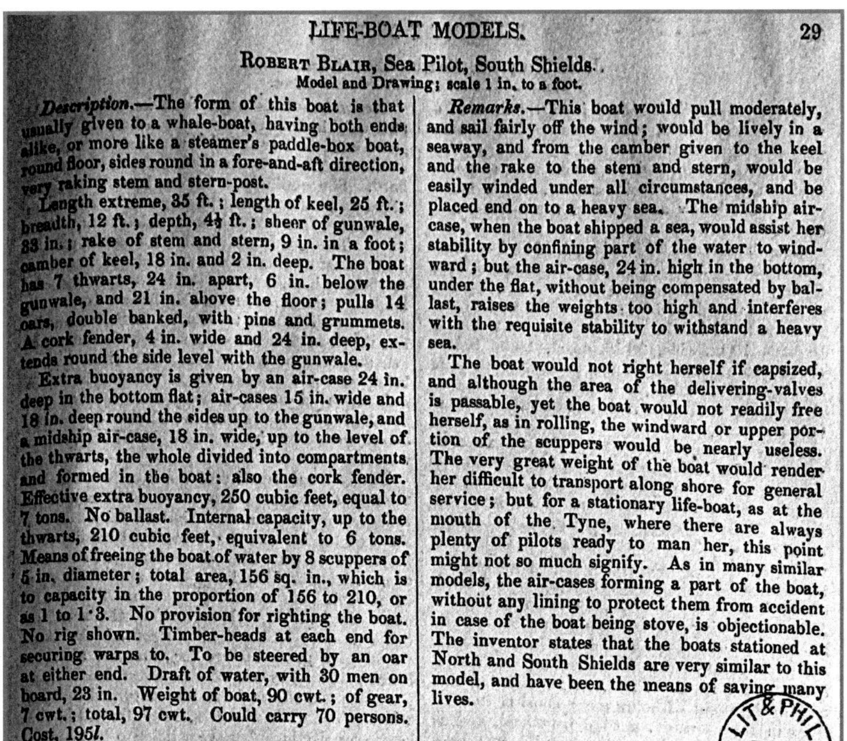

LIFE-BOAT MODELS. 29

ROBERT BLAIR, Sea Pilot, South Shields.

Model and Drawing; scale 1 in. to a foot.

Description.—The form of this boat is that usually given to a whale-boat, having both ends alike, or more like a steamer's paddle-box boat, round floor, sides round in a fore-and-aft direction, very raking stem and stern-post.

Length extreme, 35 ft.; length of keel, 25 ft.; breadth, 12 ft.; depth, 4½ ft.; sheer of gunwale, 33 in.; rake of stem and stern, 9 in. in a foot; camber of keel, 18 in. and 2 in. deep. The boat has 7 thwarts, 24 in. apart, 6 in. below the gunwale, and 21 in. above the floor; pulls 14 oars, double banked, with pins and grummets. A cork fender, 4 in. wide and 24 in. deep, extends round the side level with the gunwale.

Extra buoyancy is given by an air-case 24 in. deep in the bottom flat; air-cases 15 in. wide and 18 in. deep round the sides up to the gunwale, and a midship air-case, 18 in. wide, up to the level of the thwarts, the whole divided into compartments and formed in the boat: also the cork fender. Effective extra buoyancy, 250 cubic feet, equal to 7 tons. No ballast. Internal capacity, up to the thwarts, 210 cubic feet, equivalent to 6 tons. Means of freeing the boat of water by 8 scuppers of 5 in. diameter; total area, 156 sq. in., which is to capacity in the proportion of 156 to 210, or as 1 to 1·3. No provision for righting the boat. No rig shown. Timber-heads at each end for securing warps to. To be steered by an oar at either end. Draft of water, with 30 men on board, 23 in. Weight of boat, 90 cwt.; of gear, 7 cwt.; total, 97 cwt. Could carry 70 persons. Cost, 195*l*.

Remarks.—This boat would pull moderately, and sail fairly off the wind; would be lively in a seaway, and from the camber given to the keel and the rake to the stem and stern, would be easily winded under all circumstances, and be placed end on to a heavy sea. The midship air-case, when the boat shipped a sea, would assist her stability by confining part of the water to windward; but the air-case, 24 in. high in the bottom, under the flat, without being compensated by ballast, raises the weights too high and interferes with the requisite stability to withstand a heavy sea.

The boat would not right herself if capsized, and although the area of the delivering-valves is passable, yet the boat would not readily free herself, as in rolling, the windward or upper portion of the scuppers would be nearly useless. The very great weight of the boat would render her difficult to transport along shore for general service; but for a stationary life-boat, as at the mouth of the Tyne, where there are always plenty of pilots ready to man her, this point might not so much signify. As in many similar models, the air-cases forming a part of the boat, without any lining to protect them from accident in case of the boat being stove, is objectionable. The inventor states that the boats stationed at North and South Shields are very similar to this model, and have been the means of saving many lives.

Taken from the report of the Committee for the Northumberland Prize 1851.
Reproduced by kind permission of the Literary and Philosophical Society, Newcastle.

An engraving from a pamphlet by William Hails, *An enquiry concerning the invention of the lifeboat 1806.*
Reproduced by kind permission of the Literary and Philosophical Society, Newcastle.

Stephen Laverick's Lifeboat Model in St Hilda's Church, South Shields.
Reproduced by kind permission of the Churchwardens of St Hilda's Church, The Market Place, South Shields.

Blair's design, as might be expected from a Tyne pilot, was an improved version of the traditional Shields lifeboat, a larger version of the *Tyne* which can still be seen preserved in its shelter on Ocean Road but, unlike Beeching's, it wasn't self-righting and couldn't set a sail. The Shields pilots were notoriously conservative and despite the *Providence* disaster they still had confidence in their boats. The *Providence* was recovered undamaged after the disaster and less than two weeks later she was launched again in one of the worst gales ever seen on the east coast, with John Milburn one of the four survivors of the disaster as her coxswain. *Providence* remained in service until 1872 when she was sold by auction to Mr. Purvis of South Shields. Purvis was a common name on the Lawe, William Purvis was drowned in the *Providence* in the 1849 disaster, but his family obviously didn't hold any grudges against the boat and she continued to work as a salvage and diving boat on the river for many years.

The confidence of the pilots in the traditional Shields lifeboat was understandable because the Lawe was its birthplace. Famously in 1789, following the wreck of the *Adventure* on Herd Sand, the Gentlemen of Lawe House, a group of ship owners led by Nicholas Fairles who frequented a reading room on the Lawe, placed an advert in the *Newcastle Courant* offering a reward of two guineas for the best plan for a boat capable of holding 24 persons and going through very heavy broken seas *'the intention being to preserve the lives of seamen from ships going ashore in hard gales of wind'*.

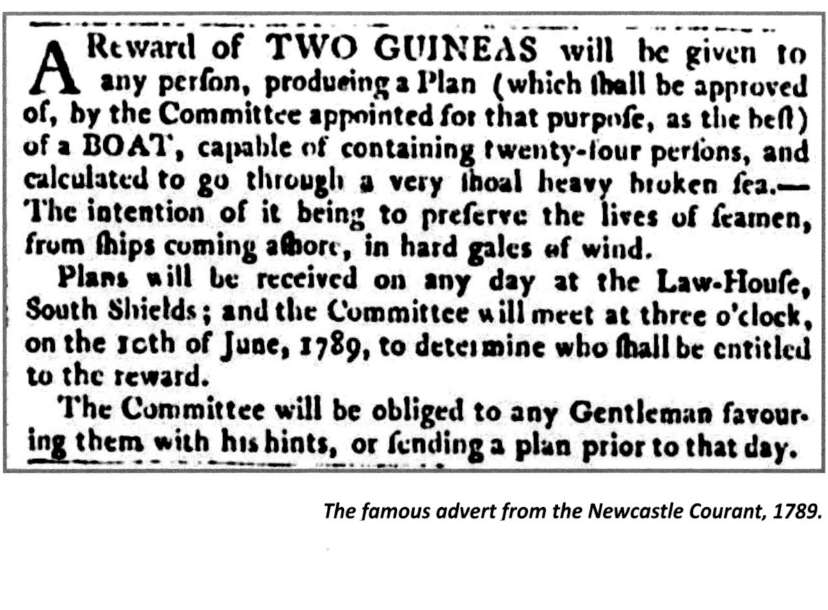

A Reward of TWO GUINEAS will be given to any perſon, producing a Plan (which ſhall be approved of, by the Committee appointed for that purpoſe, as the beſt) of a BOAT, capable of containing twenty-four perſons, and calculated to go through a very ſhoal heavy broken ſea.— The intention of it being to preſerve the lives of ſeamen, from ſhips coming aſhore, in hard gales of wind.

Plans will be received on any day at the Law-Houſe, South Shields; and the Committee will meet at three o'clock, on the 10th of June, 1789, to determine who ſhall be entitled to the reward.

The Committee will be obliged to any Gentleman favouring them with his hints, or ſending a plan prior to that day.

The famous advert from the Newcastle Courant, 1789.

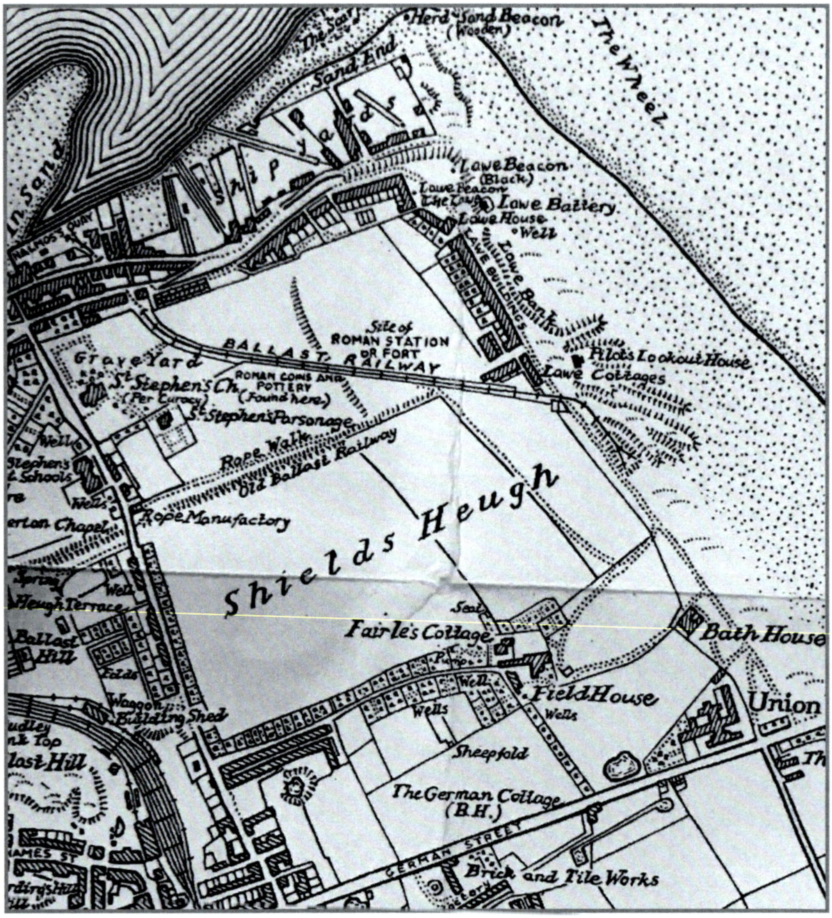

A section from an 1856 map of South Shields.

South Shields Roman Station was a place known from myth and legend long before the excavations of 1875 led by Rev. Hooppell and Robert Blair took it from the pages of antiquarian speculation to the headlines of the national press.

In the early Victorian period locals, such as Robert Blair's uncle, often found Roman coins and other small items on the open pasture area which until the 1870s comprised the Lawe. Note the comment just below the ballast railway at the opposite side to the supposed site of the Roman Station where is states; *'Roman coins and pottery found here.'*

The map names among other places of note; St Stephen's Church, Lawe House, Field House and Fairles' Cottage as well as German Street which was later renamed Ocean Road.
Section reproduced by kind permission of Heritage Cartography, Victorian Town Maps.

The project was regarded with some skepticism in the town and only two sets of models and plans were submitted by the deadline of the 10th of June: one was a raft like boat submitted by Henry Greathead, a relative newcomer to the town who was inevitably viewed with some suspicion as an outsider, and the other was a tin model of a boat to be constructed of copper made by the local eccentric William (Willie) Wouldhave. It's not difficult to imagine what the pilots thought of these designs but the Fairles' committee having secured funding from local ship owners went ahead with their plan and employed Henry Greathead, the only boatbuilder interested in the project, to build the first lifeboat.

The origins of the boat that emerged from Greathead's yard are mired in controversy: both Wouldhave and Greathead claimed to be the inventor and the controversy grew when Greathead successfully petitioned Parliament for a reward of £1,200 for his *invention*. In truth the first lifeboat, *the Original*, bore little resemblance to either of their designs and the debate between their supporters, which has now raged for more than 200 years without showing any signs of reaching any conclusion, has surely missed the point. The key to the success of the rescue service was the crew, the Tyne Pilots who would be required to take the life saver's boat out in seas where no other boat could survive. The design of the *Original* reflected their experience based on the highly regarded Norway Yawl with the addition of cork around the gunwales to make it unsinkable. Nicholas Fairles always said the *Original* was designed by his committee and significantly refused to back Henry Greathead's petition to Parliament for a reward, but the boat did follow Wouldhave's use of cork floatation and in Shields the first lifeboat was always locally referred to as *Willie Wouldhave's cork boat*.

The Coat of Arms of the County Borough of South Shields, with a lifeboat and crew depicted in the centre.

Two early twentieth century photographs of Lawe House, one showing the front, north elevation, the other the rear, south elevation. The building was demolished in 1972.
Both photograph reproduced by kind permission of South Tyneside Libraries.

Lawe House or Cross House as it was also known was used as a barracks during the Napoleonic Wars. It subsequently became the meeting place of the group of ship-owners who founded the Tyne Lifeboat Society. Standing on the summit of the Lawe it had a commanding view over the Tyne estuary. The remains of the Roman fort is near by to the west and the Civil War fort was likely to have been to the north east, in front of the building, as seen on Fairles' plan on the next page. A modern block of flats now stands on this site.

Lawe House, or Cross House because of its position across the top of Lawe Road (the meeting place of the gentlemen who founded the world's first lifeboat service) was a large, solid building that stood near the Lawe Beacons until 1972. Its origins are obscure and it was used as a barracks during the Napoleonic Wars, but its role as a reading room suggests it may once have been an inn.

The Gentlemen of Lawe House was a relatively short lived group; it was founded on 20th February 1788 with 43 subscribers and wound up in 1802 with 24, but it reflected the aspirations of the town. Nicholas Fairles, just 28 years old in 1789 and a member of an old South Shields family which rented much of the land on the Lawe from the Dean and Chapter of Durham Cathedral, was the leading light of the club. In time he would make his fortune as a speculative ship builder and owner of the largest dock in South Shields and, as a member of the Literary and Philosophical Society of Newcastle, he was in the circle of the intellectual elite of Newcastle which had coalesced around William Turner celebrating discovery and innovation. Fairles himself patented an improved anchor winch for ships in 1808 and promoted it through a series of newspaper adverts so, with his background, it is no surprise that he was the first to document the physical Roman remains on the Lawe. In 1798 Fairles' workmen unearthed a supposed Roman hypocaust on the summit of the Lawe, probably part of a bath house as it was outside the walls of the fort.

dispatch it later.

Discovery of Relics.—The workmen employ-ed in excavating the railroad by Thomas Salmon, Esq., at South Shields, for the conveyance of ballast from his wharf at the Tyne, to the place of deposit at the Lawe, have struck upon what is believed to be the ancient military way, called Wreken Dyke, leading from the Roman station, discovered in the same field, near the Lawe, by the late Nicholas Fairles, Esq., in 1758. The bones and antlers of deer have also now been dug out. Mr Fairles, when the former discovery of a Hypocaust or Sudatory took place, became possessed of a beautiful gold coin of Marcus Aurelius, and several of brass, from Claudius Gothicus to Valentinian; but the only coin which has now been discovered is a Danish one of brass.

A report of Roman remains discovered on the Lawe during the building of the ballast railway, Newcastle Courant, October 24th 1845.

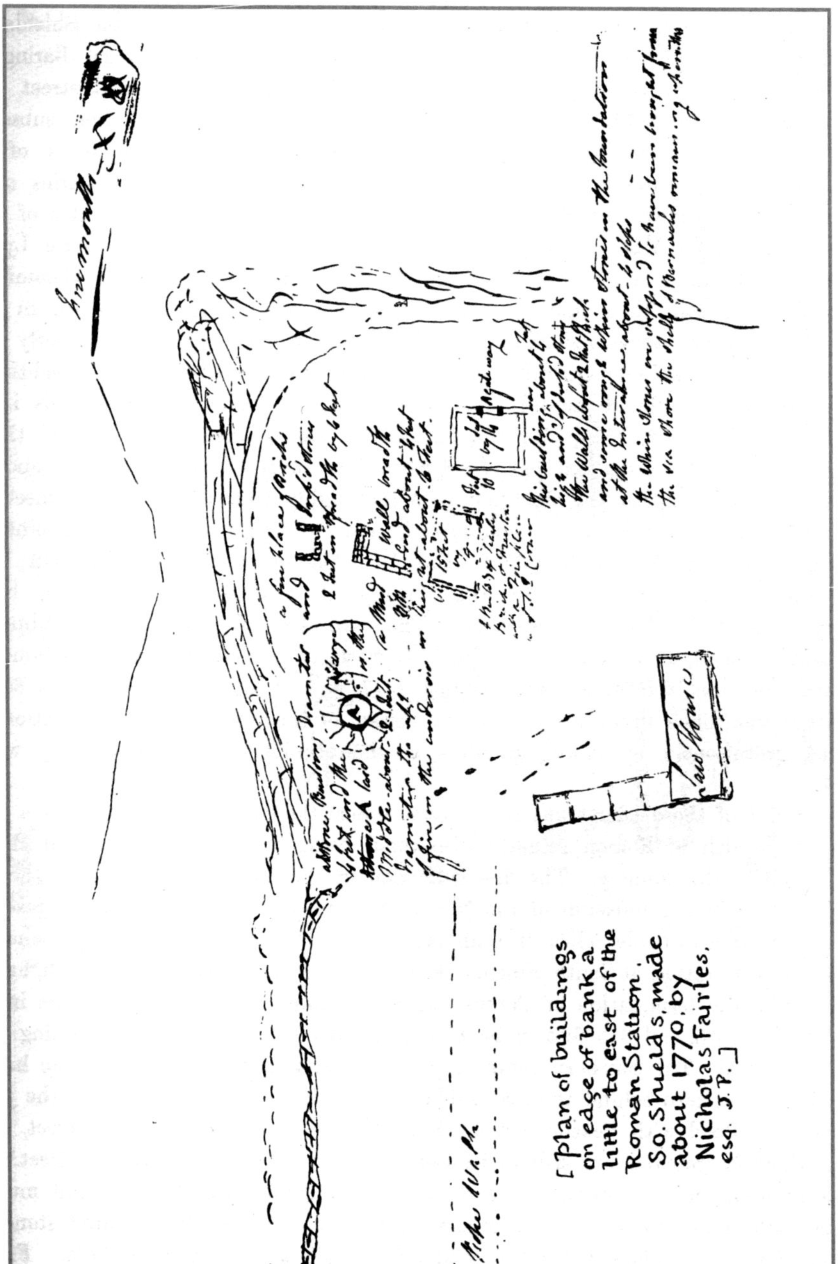

A plan drawn by Nicholas Fairles in the late eighteenth century of buildings on the edge of the Lawe, possibly the remains of the Civil War Fortifications.

The plan came into the ownership of Robert Blair, now in his Scrapbook in The Word. Reproduced by kind permission of South Tyneside Libraries.

They may have been looking for treasure, as a Medieval or Tudor gold coin had been found on the site and, in the papers given to Robert Blair by Fairles' son William Watson Fairles, there is a copy of the lettering on the gold coin found on the Lawe many years earlier in addition to a sketch plan. (shown opposite) Fairles' finds weren't the first Roman objects found on the Lawe; altars had been found built into quay walls or recovered from the river and ended up in places as diverse as the Chapter House at Durham Cathedral and the Bodleian Library Oxford (see pages 78 & 79). They were however the most important because they brought the Roman remains to the attention of the town so that when the builders of a railway came across Roman remains on the Lawe in 1845 Nicholas Fairles was referred to as the discoverer of the fort. Perhaps Fairles also inspired Robert Blair, born the son of a pilot on the Lawe top, so that when the fort was threatened by the apparently irresistible advance of a new housing development, it was easy to convince the town that the remains should be excavated and their secrets revealed. That's why Fairles' plan, annotated in pencil, became very valuable, had pride of place in Robert Blair's collection and was preserved in his scrapbook.

Nicholas Fairles had a tragic death that made national news in 1832 when he was murdered by a Jarrow pitman in the middle of a bitter strike. As a magistrate Fairles was awarded a silver cup for his part in suppressing a riot in 1815, but he was generally trusted by the pitmen and had acted as a mediator in the 1825 strike at Jarrow so it seems likely that his death was an accident, the result of a petty skirmish fuelled by drink that got out of hand. The actual murderer, a Jarrow pitman called Ralph Armstrong, escaped to Australia before he could be arrested so, William Jobling who was there and known to Fairles as his wife was Fairles's servant, was executed for the crime under the law of common purpose. Jobling's body was then hung in irons on a gibbet on Jarrow Slake as a warning to the rebellious pitmen, a grisly spectacle and a miscarriage of justice that was sadly linked to the end of the life of a great Shieldsman, Nicholas Fairles.

Nicholas Fairles had lived at Field House on the Lawe which surprisingly survived the urbanisation of the area until 1897 when it was finally demolished for new housing. Fairles' son William Watson Fairles lived at Field House until his death on 13th September 1890. Unlike his father, William Watson Fairles shunned public office and lived as a recluse behind

Two photographs of Field House taken in 1890s. The lower photograph was taken in the garden of Field House.

The former home of South Shields magistrate and land owner Nicholas Fairles. The building was demolished in 1898 to make way for; Fairles Street, Salmon Street, Henry Nelson Street, George Scott Street.

Both photographs reproduced by kind permission of South Tyneside Libraries.

the high walls of Field House, besieged by encroaching housing on all sides just as the Roman fort and the sconce were besieged by invading Scots. Field House remained an oasis of calm in the middle of the busy life of the town for a while after William Watson Fairles' death and for a time the garden was let out but eventually the land was bought by the Corporation under the powers given to it by Parliament and the house was demolished.

The Corporation wanted to build new model houses, on the site, for workers displaced by the demolition of some riverside slums but the development was controversial with residents complaining that it would lower property values in the area. There was a public enquiry in 1900 which approved the scheme after the Corporation assured the Commissioner that they were not proposing a municipal housing scheme and agreed that the land would be sold to private developers. The land was auctioned at the Golden Lion Hotel at 8pm in the evening on Monday 7th April 1902 with strict conditions imposed on the developers who were required to build what would now be called *'affordable housing'*. Thus the last part of the Lawe disappeared under bricks and mortar, except of course for The People's Roman Remains Park, a memorial to both the 1875 excavation whose story will now be told and to Robert Blair, son of a Lawe pilot who led the campaign for the preservation of the Roman remains it unearthed.

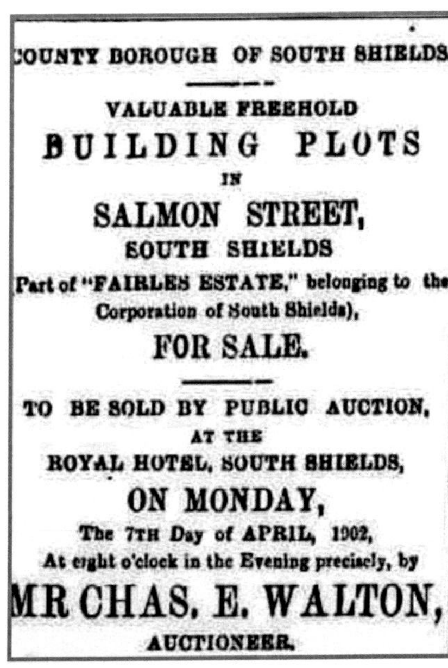
COUNTY BOROUGH OF SOUTH SHIELDS.

VALUABLE FREEHOLD
BUILDING PLOTS
IN
SALMON STREET,
SOUTH SHIELDS
Part of "FAIRLES ESTATE," belonging to the Corporation of South Shields),
FOR SALE.

TO BE SOLD BY PUBLIC AUCTION,
AT THE
ROYAL HOTEL, SOUTH SHIELDS,
ON MONDAY,
The 7TH Day of APRIL, 1902,
At eight o'clock in the Evening precisely, by
MR CHAS. E. WALTON,
AUCTIONEER.

An advert from the *Shields Daily News,* ***29th March 1902, announcing the last part of the historic Lawe Estate to be sold.***

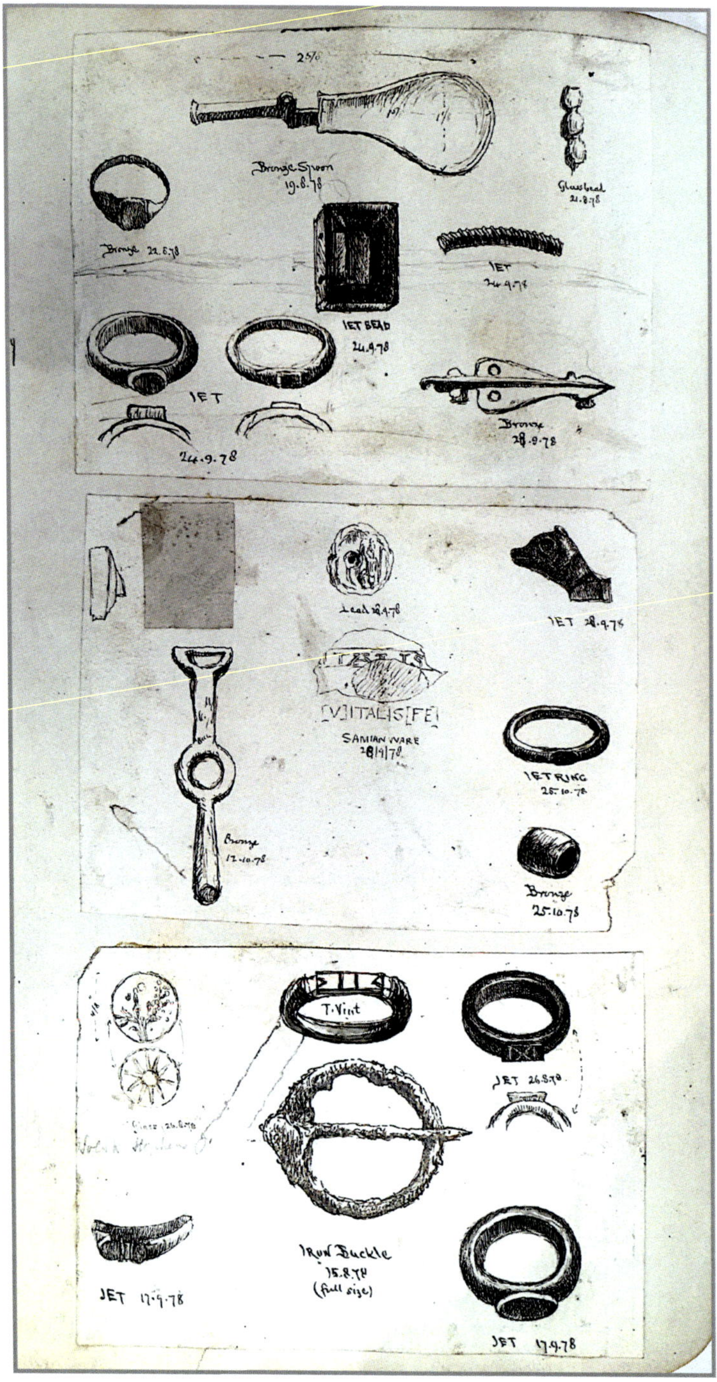

Page 108 of the Blair Scrapbook. Note the date when each item was discovered is written beside its illustration.
Blair Scrapbook; courtesy of South Tyneside Libraries.

The Campaign

A small bronze figure of Jupiter from Robert Blair's collection found on the site of Baring Street School now in the collection of the Great North Museum: Hancock, Newcastle.
Photograph courtesy of Tyne & Wear Archives & Museums.

3

A photograph and an engraved picture of Rev. Dr. R E Hooppell (1833 – 1895)

An early photograph of the Winterbottom Marine School in Ocean Road, opened in 1869, with Ocean Road Board's Schools seen on the next block east (to the right in this image).
Reproduced by kind permission of South Tyneside Libraries.

The appointment on 17th January 1861 of the radical clergyman the Reverend Dr. Robert Eli Hooppell as the first headmaster of the Marine School, which was to become the heart of South Shields' maritime community, must have seemed strange to the pilots of the Lawe who were the traditional carriers of town's maritime heritage. Dr. Hooppell had no seagoing experience and he wasn't even from South Shields but his appointment as the first principal of Thomas Winterbottom's charitable foundation was a clear sign of the ambition of the new venture.

Dr. Hooppell stood out from the many unqualified teachers providing mathematical instruction to ambitious officers of the growing mercantile marine community of the town through his impressive academic record, which included a degree in mathematics from St John's College, Cambridge and a post at a charitable school on Anglesey that prepared pupils for fellowships at Oxford.

Celebrating the opening of the impressive new building for his school on 12th January 1869 Dr. Hooppell must have been confident that he had fulfilled or even exceeded the founder's expectations but, while he was respected, he was not a popular man in the town. Dr. Hooppell's commitment to education was matched by his commitment to abstention from alcohol, radical social reform in general and the repeal of the Contagious Diseases Acts in particular. In addition to his mathematical qualifications Dr. Hooppell had also graduated first class from Cambridge in 1856 in the new Moral Science Tripos, an interdisciplinary examination which included moral philosophy, political economy, modern history and mental philosophy; an unusual choice for a mathematician but an obvious one for a social reformer.

The college was at the centre of the intellectual life of South Shields. Dr. Winterbottom's will stipulated that public lectures should be included in the curriculum and even before the College had its own premises free public lectures were given in the Mechanic's Institute, quickly rising to four a week. Subjects ranged from astronomy to physical geography, pneumatics to hydrostatics. Dr. Hooppell, the only master until 1869, was the evening lecturer as well as being the sole teacher of the day school and this post where he had a high degree of autonomy suited his wide ranging academic interests and personality.

Two photographs of Albion Terrace, Fowler Street, South Shields which is now completely built out as shop fronts. The top photograph is dated 1886 and the lower one is from the 1950s.

Number 14 Albion Terrace most probably stood at the top of the terrace, the southern end, and if so appears to have been replaced or added to after 1886 by the amazing decorative three storied building (Victoria Buildings) we see in the lower photograph.
Reproduced by kind permission of South Tyneside Libraries.

Early in 1869 Dr.Hooppell pointed out that as there was a need for him to be close to the school he should live nearby and asked the Trustees to provide him with a local property and in 1871 he moved from his lodgings to 14 Albion Terrace, Fowler Street in the heart of the town with his wife and five children.

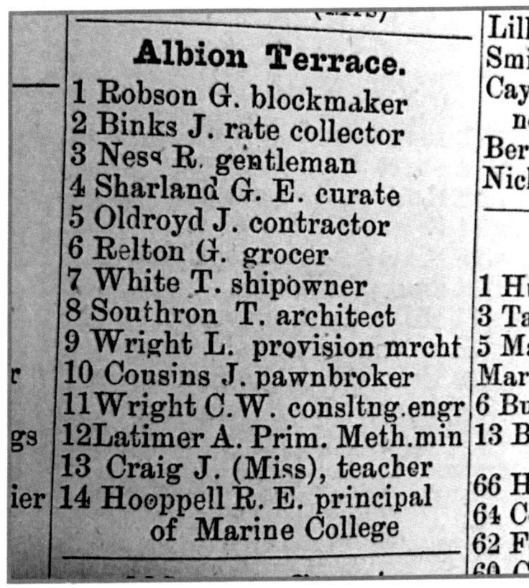

Albion Terrace.

1 Robson G. blockmaker
2 Binks J. rate collector
3 Ness R. gentleman
4 Sharland G. E. curate
5 Oldroyd J. contractor
6 Relton G. grocer
7 White T. shipowner
8 Southron T. architect
9 Wright L. provision mrcht
10 Cousins J. pawnbroker
11 Wright C.W. consltng.engr
12 Latimer A. Prim. Meth.min
13 Craig J. (Miss), teacher
14 Hooppell R. E. principal of Marine College

A small section from Ward's Directory of 1874, listing the streets alphabetically in the town and the names of the residents and their occupations.
Reproduced by kind permission of South Tyneside Libraries.

Settled in South Shields, Dr. Hooppell found himself at the centre of a political storm which pushed the limits of what was reasonable debate in Victorian society. He achieved notoriety as a result of his outspoken campaign against the Contagious Diseases Acts, a public health measure that required women identified as prostitutes to undergo compulsory medical checks for venereal disease and be confined in secure locked hospitals if found to be infected. The Acts originally applied to a few selected naval ports and army towns, but after 1866 it was proposed to extend them to the civilian population in the North of England as a means of regulating prostitution.

Prostitutes certainly plied their trade in the back streets of the busy port of South Shields with its large population of transient seamen but there was little support for the heavy handed methods of the Acts and unfortunately Dr. Hooppell's approach alienated people who might otherwise have been his supporters. He held public meetings for working class men, warning them that their wives could be forced to undergo intimate physical examinations and demonstrated the use of a speculum to reinforce his point.

A twenty first century photograph and one dating from 1900, of Cleadon water tower and water works.
Reproduced by kind permission of South Tyneside Libraries.

The Opening of Tyne Dock. A painting by Mark Thompson dated 1850.
Reproduced by courtesy of Tyne & Wear Archives & Museums.

At first he was an influential figure in the women's movement against the Act, and in March 1870 he started a weekly journal *The Shield* which declared *'the system of these acts is a conspiracy, of the foulest kind, against the womanhood of the realm'* but by 1872 he was effectively side-lined by leaders like Josephine Butler who were deeply uncomfortable with his approach.

The controversy inflicted lasting damage on his reputation and might explain his move from the centre of public life in South Shields to the relative obscurity of the position of Rector in the rural backwater of Byers Green near Bishop Auckland in County Durham.

For a '*social scientist'* like Dr. Hooppell, South Shields was like a great experiment in the building of a new society. For men like Hooppell the symbols of the age weren't the coal mines and ironworks that roared with power on a scale that dwarfed human beings but the schools and the public utilities that opened new opportunities for the residents of the new industrial towns and kept them healthy. The collieries, foundries, shipyards, and staithes of that heroic age are now long gone but a potent reminder of the drive to improve the lives of ordinary people that inspired social reformers like Dr. Hooppell remains in the waterworks chimney on Cleadon Hills which still stands high and proud on the edge of the town. The chimney looks like the detached bell tower of an Italian church and the waterworks with its impressive gothic architecture (which opened in 1863 supplying a million gallons of pure water a day to the town) is truly a secular cathedral of public health rich with the promise of a better life for all.

The opening of Tyne Dock on 3rd March 1859 was the most important single event in the history of South Shields since the fall of Rome more than thirteen hundred years earlier. The town had left behind its unpromising beginnings as a centre of salt panning and ballast dumping long before the North Eastern Railway opened this great dock, a spectacular example of the latest technology for coal shipment. The sheer size and ambition of Tyne Dock made South Shields the biggest coal port in the world and shaped the future of the town. It grew up quickly from a dirty slum on the fringe of Tyneside to a world power in the coal trade in just one generation based on the trinity of coal, steam and iron that made Britain the workshop of the world in the nineteenth century.

A section of an 1849 map showing the town of South Shields clinging to the south bank of the river. The dark line is the Stanhope and Tyne Railway.
Reproduced by kind permission of South Tyneside Libraries.

A photograph from about 1900 showing the Mill Dam Ferry Landing with the Customs House behind. The building is now a theatre.
Reproduced by kind permission of South Tyneside Libraries.

The first public railway on Tyneside, the Stanhope and Tyne, came to South Shields on 15th May 1834 to carry coal and limestone from west Durham to ships at the mouth of the Tyne. It wasn't a financial success, but it pointed the way for others to follow, using the new technology of steam railways to deliver coal direct from the pit to steam colliers at the quay, which revolutionised the historic coal trade that had previously made Newcastle's fortune.

The industrial revolution broke Newcastle's monopoly of the coal trade and increased the demand for coal around the world exponentially. South Shields was both free to take advantage of its privileged position at the estuary and well placed to serve the growing international market for Durham coal. The opening of the Customs House at the Mill Dam in 1865 marked the town's coming of age as it had grown to such an extent that its trade could no longer practically be administered from Newcastle and had to be finally recognised as port in its own right.

Local hero Ralph Gardner of North Shields, the author of *England's Grievance Discovered in Relation to the Coal Trade*, a rant published in 1655 which blamed most of the ills of the North on the Corporation of Newcastle, was surely present in spirit at the inauguration of the new building. Its classical architecture reflects South Shields' overwhelming sense of its own importance, something which lay at the centre of the town's identity and culture at the end of the nineteenth century.

The actual shipment of coal was just one of the driving forces of Shields' prosperity for with the ships came shipbuilding, ship repair, and all the services associated with the business of a great port. The massive increase in trade after the opening of Tyne Dock created jobs at all levels, so South Shields' population grew rapidly after 1860 especially in the riverside district of Holborn, between the market place and Tyne Dock, where poor quality housing was thrown up to house the new industrial labourers. Homes were also needed for the clerks and craftsmen in the engineering and shipping industries that were the foundation of South Shields' wealth, so it wasn't a surprise that by 1875 speculative builders saw the Lawe as a prime site for development to meet the needs of the growing town.

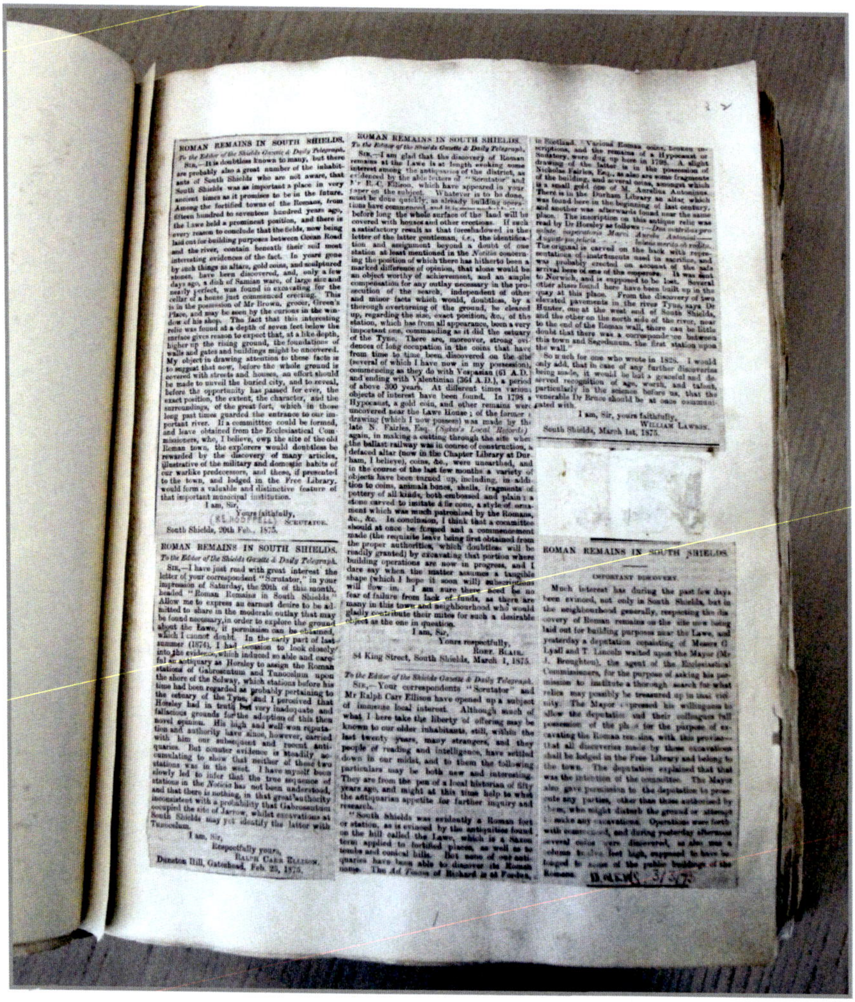
ROMAN REMAINS IN SOUTH SHIELDS.

ROMAN REMAINS IN SOUTH SHIELDS.

ROMAN REMAINS IN SOUTH SHIELDS.

ROMAN REMAINS IN SOUTH SHIELDS.

A page of cuttings from the** Shields Gazette and Telegraph **from 1875 preserved by Robert Blair in his Scrapbook which is now in The Word, South Shields.

The Scrutator's letter on the top left column is followed by Ralph Carr Ellison's of the 25th February 1875 and then the letter from Robert Blair, published on 1st March 1875, and another supportive letter from William Lawson was also published on 1st March. The last cutting reports on the important discovery of the 3rd March, by which time the campaign, short as it had been was won.

Blair Scrapbook; courtesy of South Tyneside Libraries.

The Lawe was, as any estate agent will confirm, an ideal location for the new middle class of the town to enjoy their new prosperity and advertise their status as members of respectable society. They were far away from the crowded riverside slums, seamen's boarding houses, and drinking dens of the old town, which had become a dangerous and dirty warren of narrow streets where outsiders rarely ventured. Wealthy professionals like Robert Blair, the excavator of the Roman fort, an amateur antiquarian and a solicitor by occupation, moved to rural villages like Harton or Westoe but the middle classes went to the Lawe, close to the town centre, but separate from the industrial districts and the port, and with the added benefit of healthy sea air. South Shields had been hit hard by cholera (which first came to the North East in Sunderland in 1831) at that time popularly believed to be caused by bad air. The attraction of clean sea air was an additional selling point, if one was needed, for the new houses being built on the Lawe.

So if South Shields desperately needed new houses and the Lawe was ripe for development how could the remains of an obscure Roman fort, which even antiquarians believed to have been robbed out for building stone long ago, possibly stand in the way of progress? After all, this was the age which drove the railway through the castle at Newcastle and demolished large sections of the city's famous walls which were once compared, admittedly with a large dose of local patriotism, to those of Jerusalem. South Shields however grasped the opportunity to underpin its civic pride in the town's early history and its link to the era of the Roman Empire.

Against this background the two Roberts, Hooppell and Blair, ran a brilliant campaign. There is little doubt that Dr. Hooppell was the brains behind it: he wrote the first anonymous letter to the *Shields Gazette* on 20th February 1875 calling for the remains to be explored with any discoveries being placed in the free library for the benefit of the town, and he then orchestrated a series of letters from supporters to keep the issue in the public eye. If Hooppell was the man behind the campaign Blair on the other hand was the public face, a Shields-man born and bred who unlike Hooppell was not mired in controversy, and an administrator with a solicitor's eye for detail.

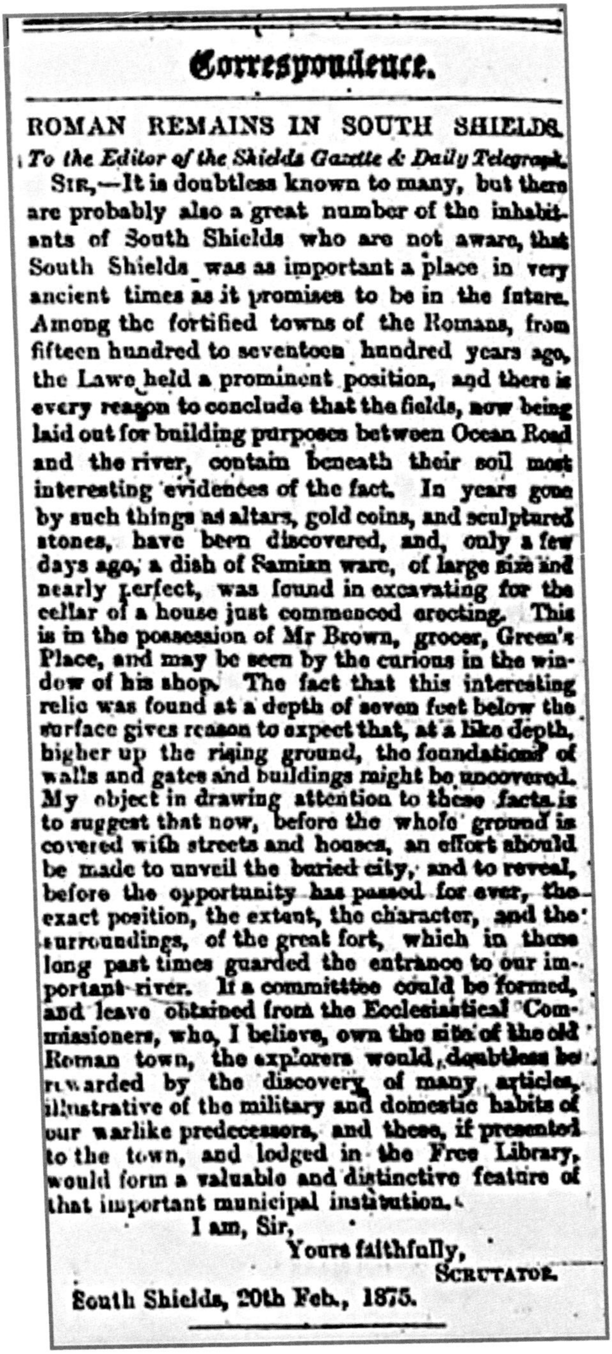

Correspondence.

ROMAN REMAINS IN SOUTH SHIELDS.

To the Editor of the Shields Gazette & Daily Telegraph.

SIR,—It is doubtless known to many, but there are probably also a great number of the inhabitants of South Shields who are not aware, that South Shields was as important a place in very ancient times as it promises to be in the future. Among the fortified towns of the Romans, from fifteen hundred to seventeen hundred years ago, the Lawe held a prominent position, and there is every reason to conclude that the fields, now being laid out for building purposes between Ocean Road and the river, contain beneath their soil most interesting evidences of the fact. In years gone by such things as altars, gold coins, and sculptured stones, have been discovered, and, only a few days ago, a dish of Samian ware, of large size and nearly perfect, was found in excavating for the cellar of a house just commenced erecting. This is in the possession of Mr Brown, grocer, Green's Place, and may be seen by the curious in the window of his shop. The fact that this interesting relic was found at a depth of seven feet below the surface gives reason to expect that, at a like depth, higher up the rising ground, the foundations of walls and gates and buildings might be uncovered. My object in drawing attention to these facts is to suggest that now, before the whole ground is covered with streets and houses, an effort should be made to unveil the buried city, and to reveal, before the opportunity has passed for ever, the exact position, the extent, the character, and the surroundings, of the great fort, which in those long past times guarded the entrance to our important river. If a committee could be formed, and leave obtained from the Ecclesiastical Commissioners, who, I believe, own the site of the old Roman town, the explorers would doubtless be rewarded by the discovery of many articles, illustrative of the military and domestic habits of our warlike predecessors, and these, if presented to the town, and lodged in the Free Library, would form a valuable and distinctive feature of that important municipal institution.

I am, Sir,

Yours faithfully,

SCRUTATOR.

South Shields, 20th Feb., 1875.

On Saturday the 20th February 1875 this letter appeared in the Shields Gazette and Daily Telegraph, transcribed opposite.

Reproduced by kind permission of the Shields Gazette.

ROMAN REMAINS IN SOUTH SHIELDS
To the Editor of the Shields Gazette & Daily Telegraph

Sir, —It is doubtless known to many, but there are probably also a great number of the inhabitants of South Shields who are not aware, that South Shields was as important a place in very ancient times as it promises to be in the future. Among the fortified towns of the Romans, from fifteen hundred to seventeen hundred years ago, the Lawe held prominent position, and there is every reason to conclude that the fields, now being laid out for building purposes between Ocean Road and the river, contain beneath their soil most interesting evidences of the fact. In years gone such things as altars, gold coins, and sculptured atones, have been discovered, and, only a few days ago, a dish of Samian Ware, of large size nearly perfect, was found in excavating for the cellar of a house just commenced erecting. This is in the possession of Mr. Brown, grocer, Green's Place, and may be seen by the curious in the window of his shop. The fact that this interesting relic was found at depth seven feet below the surface gives reason to expect that, at a like depth, the walls and gates might be uncovered.

My object in drawing attention these facts is to suggest that now, before the whole ground is covered with streets and houses, an effort should be made to unveil the buried city, and reveal, before the opportunity has passed for ever, the exact position, the extent, the character, and the surroundings, of the great fort, which those long past times guarded the entrance to our important river. If a committee could be formed, and leave obtained from the Ecclesiastical Commissioners, who, I believe, own the site of the old Roman town, the explorers would doubtless be rewarded by the discovery of many articles, illustrative of the military and domestic habits of our warlike predecessors, and these, if presented to the town, and lodged in the Free Library, would form a valuable and distinctive feature of that important municipal institution.

I am, Sir,
Yours faithfully,
Scrutator.

South Shields, 20th. Feb., 1875.

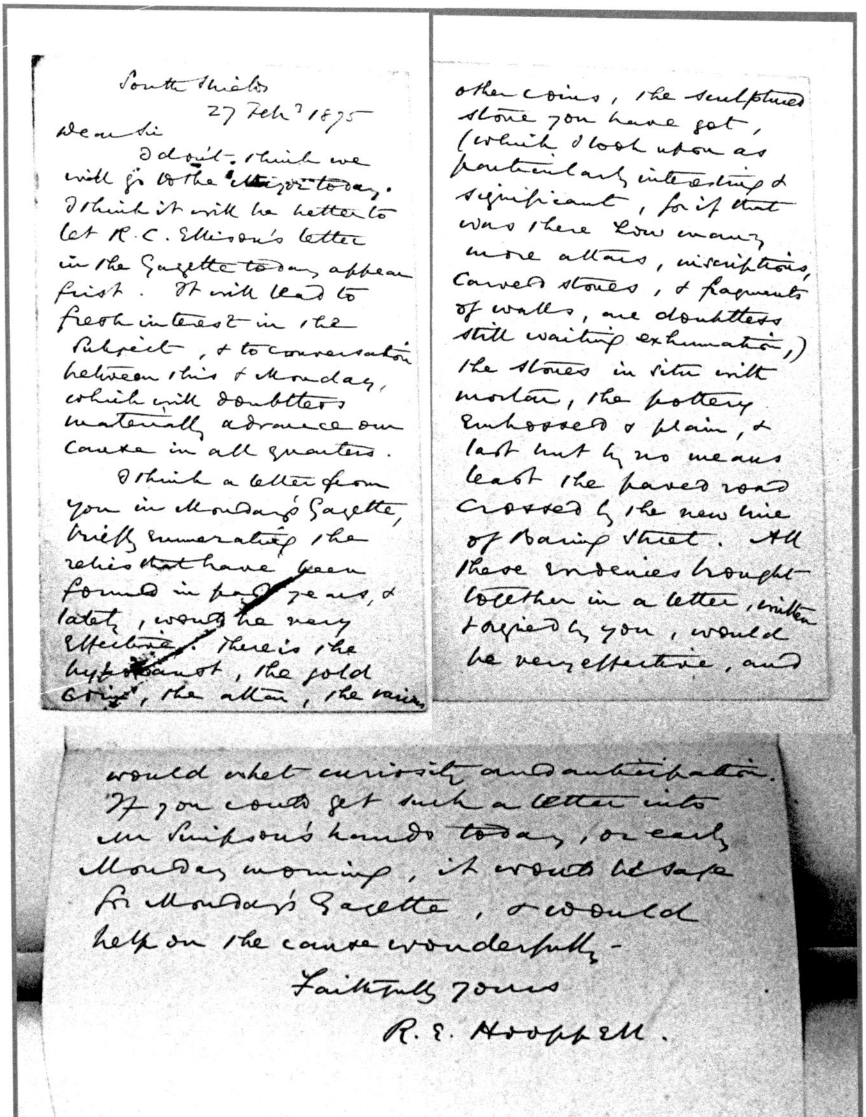

South Shields
27 Feb 1875

Dear Sir

I don't think we will go to the [illegible] today. I think it will be better to let R.C. Ellison's letter in the Gazette today appear first. It will lead to fresh interest in the subject, & to conversation between this & Monday, which will doubtless materially advance our cause in all quarters.

I think a letter from you in Monday's Gazette, briefly enumerating the relics that have been found in past years, & lately, would be very effective. There is the hypocaust, the gold coin, the altar, the various other coins, the sculptured stone you have got, (which I look upon as particularly interesting & significant, for if that was there how many more altars, inscriptions, carved stones, & fragments of walls, are doubtless still waiting exhumation,) the stones in situ with mortar, the pottery embossed & plain, & last but by no means least the paved road crossed by the new line of Baring Street. All these evidences brought together in a letter, written & signed by you, would be very effective, and would whet curiosity and anticipation. If you could get such a letter into Mr Simpson's hands today, or early Monday morning, it would be safe for Monday's Gazette, & would help on the cause wonderfully -

Faithfully yours

R. E. Hooppell.

The Scrutator was the Reverend Dr. Hooppell. In the scrapbook of the excavations that Robert Blair kept, this letter which Hooppell wrote to Blair is preserved, showing clearly the strategy of the campaigners which aimed to keep the issue in the public eye, give the impression of growing popular support and culminate in a meeting where an excavation committee could be formally established.

The letter is transcribed opposite. (Additional punctuation has been added for ease of reading.)
Blair Scrapbook; courtesy of South Shields Libraries.

South Shields

27th Feb 1875

Dear Sir;

I don't think we will go to the Mayor today. I think it will be better to let R. C. Ellison's letter in the Gazette today appear first. It will lead to fresh interest in the subject, and to conversation between this and Monday which will doubtless materially advance our cause in all quarters.

I think a letter from you in Monday's Gazette briefly summarising the relics that have been found in the past years & lately, would be very effective. There is the hypocaust, the gold coin, the altar, the various other coins, the sculptured stone you have got, (which I look upon as particularly interesting & significant, for if that was there how many more altars, inscriptions, carved stones, & fragments of walls, are doubtless still waiting exhumation,) the stones in situ with mortar, the pottery embossed and plain, & last but by no means least the paved road crossed by the new line of Baring Street. All these ingenies brought together in a letter, written and argued by you, would be very effective, and would whet curiosity and anticipation.

If you could get such letter into Mr Simpson's hands today, or early Monday morning, it would be safe for Monday's Gazette, and would help on the cause wonderfully.

Faithfully yours

R. E. Hooppell.

As planned a week after Dr. Hooppell's letter another was published in the *Shields Gazette* by Ralph Carr Ellison. Then Robert Blair's lengthy letter appeared on 1st March, as Hooppell had suggested, mentioning the recent finds on the Lawe.

Pine cone sculpture found on the Lawe and on display at Arbeia, South Shields Roman Fort (95cm high).
Photograph by kind permission of Tyne & Wear Archives & Museums.

This large pine cone sculpture, probably found in the fort's cemetery near what is now Coston Drive, was one of the most important early discoveries made on the Lawe before the start of the formal excavations in 1875. Pine cones as the seed of an evergreen tree were symbols of fertility in ancient religion and in this case represented the eternal cycle of life, death and rebirth together with a belief in immortality.
A similar sculpture found at Carlisle has a snake coiled round the cone reinforcing the idea of a cycle of rebirth and renewal as the snake is a creature which grows by shedding its skin but doesn't die.

The monuments to Regina and Victor the Moor (see later chapters) were also found in this area which was outside of the formal excavations.

Pine cone and snake sculpture (90cm high)
Tullie House Museum, Carlisle.
Photograph courtesy the Tullie House Museum.

To the Editor of the Shields Gazette & Daily Telegraph

Dear Sir,

I am glad that the discovery of Roman remains at the Lawe is at length evoking some interest among the antiquaries of the district, as evidenced by the able letters of 'Scrutator ' and Mr. R. C. Ellison which have appeared in your paper on the subject. Whatever is to be done, it must be done quickly, as already building operations have commenced, and it is very probable that before long the whole surface of the land will be covered with houses and other erections. If such a satisfactory result as that foreshadowed in the letter of the latter gentleman, i.e. the identification and assignment beyond a doubt of one station at least mentioned the Notitia concerning the position of which there has hitherto been marked difference of opinion, that alone would be an object worthy of achievement, and an ample compensation for any outlay necessary in the prosecution of the search, independent of other and minor facts which would, doubtless, by thorough overturning the ground, be cleared up, regarding the size, exact position, etc. of the station, which has from all appearance, been a very important one, commanding as it did the estuary of the Tyne.

There are, moreover, strong evidences of long occupation in the coins that have from time to time been discovered on the site (several of which I have now in my possession), commencing as they do with Vespasian (61AD) and ending with Valentinian (364AD), a period of above 300 years. At different times various objects of interest have been found. In 1798 a Hypocaust, a gold coin, and other remains were uncovered near the Lawe House; of the former a drawing (which I now possess) was made by the late N. Fairles, Esq. (Sykes Local Records) again, in making a cutting through the site when the ballast railway was in course of construction, a defaced altar (now in the Chapter Library at Durham, I believe), coins, etc. were unearthed, and in the course of the last few months a variety of objects have been turned up including, in addition to coins, animals' bones, shells, all kinds of fragments of pottery, both embossed and plain, a stone carved to imitate a fir cone, a style ornament which was much patronized by the Romans, etc. etc..

In conclusion, I think that a committee should at once be formed and a commencement made (the requisite leave being first obtained from the

A photograph of the columns after they had been removed to the grounds of the Winterbottom Marine College on Ocean Road for safe storage.
Blair Scrapbook; courtesy of South Tyneside Libraries.

The present day South Shields Museum in Ocean Road incorporates the old free library building which hosted the packed public meetings that launched the campaign to save the Roman remains and also displayed the finds from the excavation in the summer of 1875.

proper authorities, which doubtless will be readily granted) by excavating that portion where building operations are now in progress, and I dare say when the matter assumes tangible shape (which I hope it soon will) subscriptions will flow in. I am sure there need be no fear of failure from lack of funds, as there are many in this town and neighbourhood who would gladly contribute their mites for such a desirable object as the one in question.
I am, Sir,
Yours respectfully,
Robert Blair
South Shields, March 1, 1875

Ten days after the Scrutator's letter this article appeared in the *Shields Gazette and Telegraph* and the campaign, short as it had been, was won.

Shields Gazette and Daily Telegraph, Wednesday 3rd March 1875

ROMAN, REMAINS SOUTH SHIELDS. IMPORTANT DISCOVERY
Much interest has during the past few days been evinced, not only in South Shields, but in the neighbourhood generally, respecting the discovery of remains on the site now being laid out for building purposes near the Lawe, and yesterday a deputation consisting Messrs. G. Lyall and T. Lincoln waited upon the Mayor (Mr. J. Broughton), the agent of the Ecclesiastical Commissioners, for the purpose of asking his permission to institute a thorough search for what relics may possibly be treasured in that vicinity.

The Mayor expressed his willingness to allow the deputation and their colleagues full possession of the place for the purpose of excavating the Roman remains, with this proviso— that all discoveries made by those excavations shall be lodged in the Free Library and belong to the town. The deputation explained that was the intention of the committee. The Mayor also gave permission to the deputation to prosecute any parties, other than those authorised by them, who might disturb the ground or attempt to make any excavations. Operations were forthwith commenced, and during yesterday afternoon several coins were discovered, as also was a column twelve feet high, supposed to have belonged to some of the public buildings of the Romans.

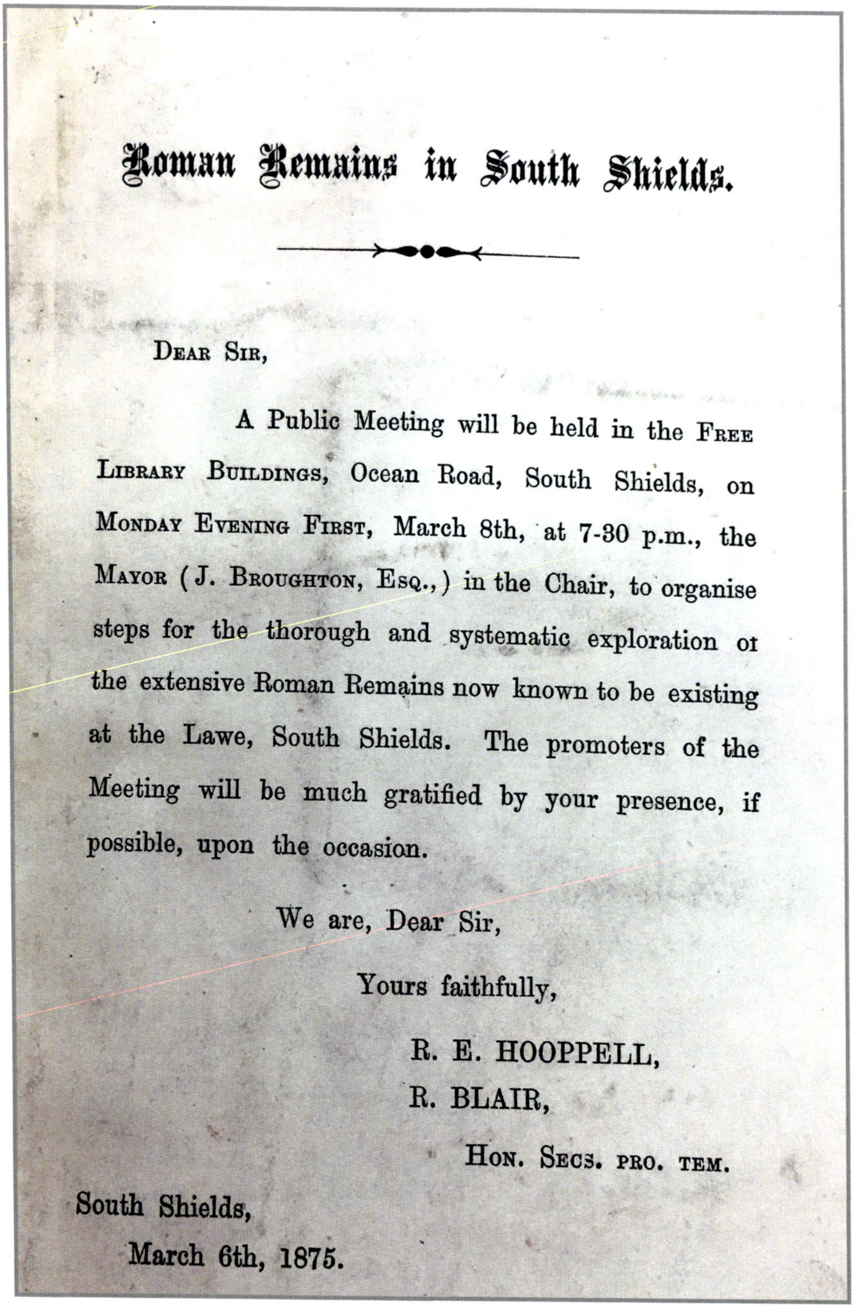

Roman Remains in South Shields.

DEAR SIR,

A Public Meeting will be held in the FREE LIBRARY BUILDINGS, Ocean Road, South Shields, on MONDAY EVENING FIRST, March 8th, at 7-30 p.m., the MAYOR (J. BROUGHTON, ESQ.,) in the Chair, to organise steps for the thorough and systematic exploration of the extensive Roman Remains now known to be existing at the Lawe, South Shields. The promoters of the Meeting will be much gratified by your presence, if possible, upon the occasion.

We are, Dear Sir,

Yours faithfully,

R. E. HOOPPELL,

R. BLAIR,

HON. SECS. PRO. TEM.

South Shields,

March 6th, 1875.

The hand bill advertising the public meeting of March 8th 1875.
Blair Scrapbook; courtesy of South Tyneside Libraries.

The discovery of these columns (see photograph on page 48) on Tuesday 2nd March 1875 along with numerous minor finds of coins and pottery captured the public's imagination and a treasure hunt began to recover as much as possible before the site was lost under new housing. Dr. Collingwood Bruce was an early enthusiastic supporter of the campaign to excavate the site but even he, the foremost authority on the antiquities of the Roman Wall, had no idea of the true riches; the remains of a buried city as Dr. Hooppell memorably called it, an important Roman Station that was waiting to be discovered in the wind blown fields of the Lawe.

Upon the 3rd March Hooppell and Blair spoke to the Society of Antiquaries of Newcastle upon Tyne probably at the invitation of Dr. Collingwood Bruce. Their account of the finds to date and the potential of the site convinced the Society, though with Collingwood Bruce's support they needed little convincing, to form a small committee to co-operate with them. On Friday of the same week they had a meeting after work with members of the South Shields Council in the then Town Hall that still stands in the centre of the Market Place and the stage was set for a dramatic finale – the public meeting which would appoint a committee, authorise it to raise funds and allow the formal excavation of the remains to begin.

Shields Gazette and Daily Telegraph, Friday 5th March 1875

ROMAN REMAINS IN SOUTH SHIELDS.

At a meeting of the gentlemen who have recently taken an active part in the promotion of researches into the relics of Roman occupation at the Lawe, South Shields, held yesterday evening, it was resolved to hold a public meeting on an early day, notice should shortly be given by advertisement under the presidency of the Mayor of the Borough (J. Broughton, Esq.), to organise publicly a movement for the thorough and systematic exploration of the site. No further excavation will be made by the preliminary committee during the few days that must elapse till this is done.

Mr. John Clayton and Mr. Ralph Carr Ellison visited the ground yesterday, and expressed their strong opinion of the importance of exploring the site, and the probability of finding many objects of great archaeological interest.

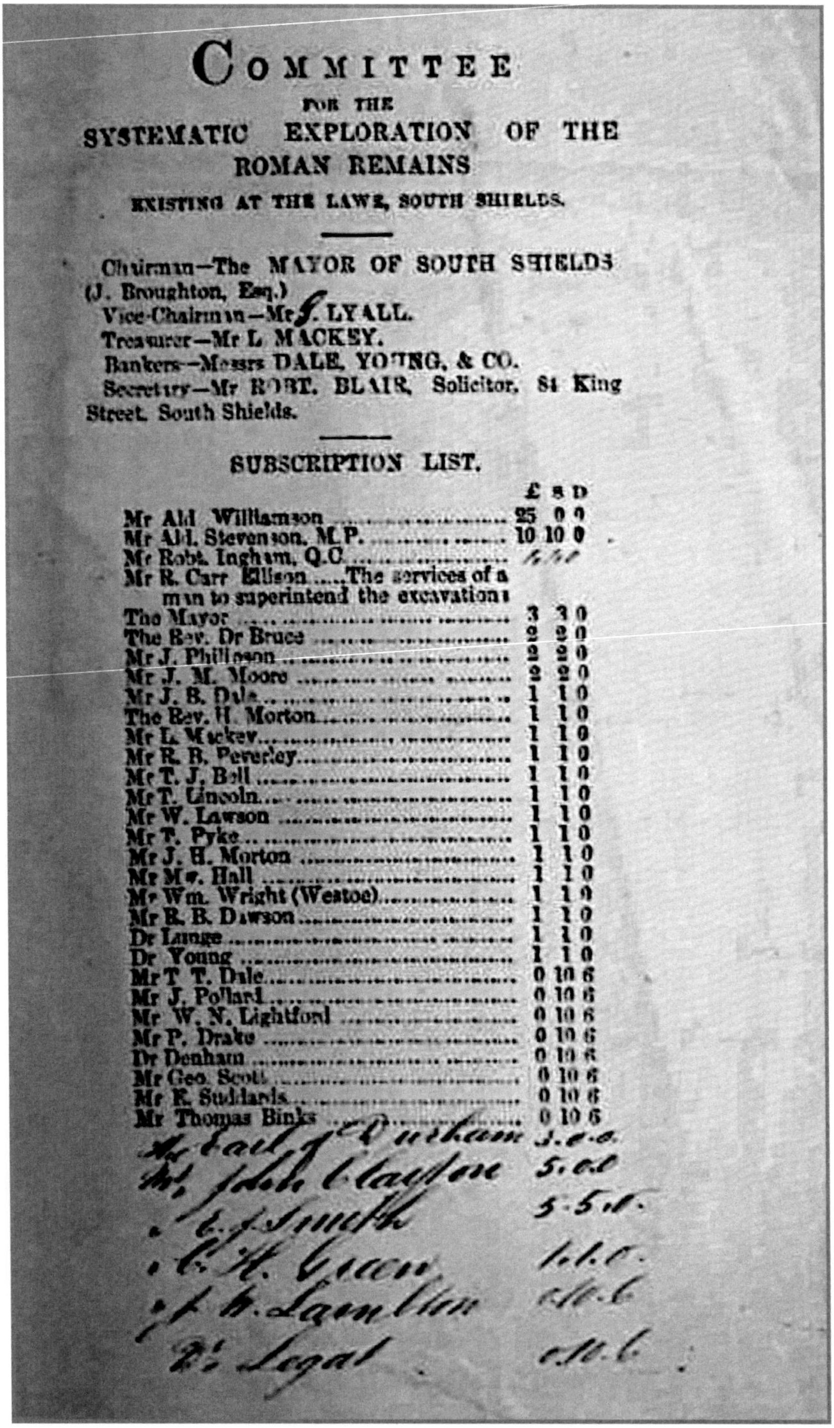

COMMITTEE

FOR THE

SYSTEMATIC EXPLORATION OF THE ROMAN REMAINS

EXISTING AT THE LAWE, SOUTH SHIELDS.

Chairman—The MAYOR OF SOUTH SHIELDS (J. Broughton, Esq.)
Vice-Chairman—Mr J. LYALL.
Treasurer—Mr L. MACKEY.
Bankers—Messrs DALE, YOUNG, & CO.
Secretary—Mr ROBT. BLAIR, Solicitor, 84 King Street, South Shields.

SUBSCRIPTION LIST.

	£	S	D
Mr Ald. Williamson	25	0	0
Mr Ald. Stevenson, M.P.	10	10	0
Mr Robt. Ingham, Q.C.	1.	1.	0
Mr R. Carr Ellison .....The services of a man to superintend the excavations			
The Mayor	3	3	0
The Rev. Dr Bruce	2	2	0
Mr J. Phillipson	2	2	0
Mr J. M. Moore	2	2	0
Mr J. B. Dale	1	1	0
The Rev. H. Morton	1	1	0
Mr L. Mackey	1	1	0
Mr R. B. Peverley	1	1	0
Mr T. J. Bell	1	1	0
Mr T. Lincoln	1	1	0
Mr W. Lawson	1	1	0
Mr T. Pyke	1	1	0
Mr J. H. Morton	1	1	0
Mr Mw. Hall	1	1	0
Mr Wm. Wright (Westoe)	1	1	0
Mr R. B. Dawson	1	1	0
Dr Lange	1	1	0
Dr Young	1	1	0
Mr T. T. Dale	0	10	6
Mr J. Pollard	0	10	6
Mr W. N. Lightfoot	0	10	6
Mr P. Drake	0	10	6
Dr Denham	0	10	6
Mr Geo. Scott	0	10	6
Mr E. Suddards	0	10	6
Mr Thomas Binks	0	10	6
The Earl of Durham	5.	0.	0.
Mr John Clayton	5.	0.	0
E. J. Smith	5.	5.	0.
C. H. Green	1.	1.	0.
J. W. Lambton	0.	10.	6
Dr Legat	0.	10.	6

Blair Scrapbook; courtesy of South Tyneside Libraries.

> It is expected that Collingwood Bruce, the well-known historian of the Roman Wall, will visit the site on the day of the public meeting, and be present and speak at the latter. The member for the borough (J. Stevenson, Esq.), Mr. John Williamson, and other gentlemen have promised their hearty cooperation on the work. The honorary secretaries pro tem are the Rev. Dr. Hooppell and Mr. Robert Blair, solicitor.

A public meeting was arranged for the Monday 8th March by Robert Blair and Dr. Hooppell, notice (see illustration on page 50) having quickly gone to the printers so it could be displayed by 6th March. The meeting was presided over by the Mayor and addressed by Dr Collingwood Bruce and others. At this meeting an excavations fund was started and a working committee elected to watch and guide operations. Robert Blair was appointed secretary and work was to begin immediately. A transcript of the meeting published in the *Shields Gazette and Telegraph* on 10th March 1875 (follows on page 55) captures the drama and excitement of a unique moment in the town's history which confirmed Shields folks' fundamental article of faith that their town really was somewhere special.

Perhaps they were surprised by the success of the campaign which appealed to Shields' sense of its own importance supplemented by an attractive narrative of a glorious Roman one but I think they expected to succeed. Robert Blair, the relatively unknown but respectable local solicitor, wrote letters appealing for funds and canvassed for academic support through Dr. Collingwood Bruce at the Society of Antiquaries to put the project on a sound financial and academic foundation.

Robert Blair was an active secretary and sought contributions from neighbours and friends in Harton Village where he lived (Mr. J M Moore of Harton Hall and Mr. M Hall of Harton Grange), colleagues who like himself had premises on King Street in South Shields (Mr. J B Dale a banker on King Street and Mr. J H Morton an architect whose offices were 50 King Street) and also the great and good who might be willing to contribute. His scrapbook contains this initial printed list of Committee Members together (see opposite page) with the first subscriptions received and others added by hand to the bottom of the page.

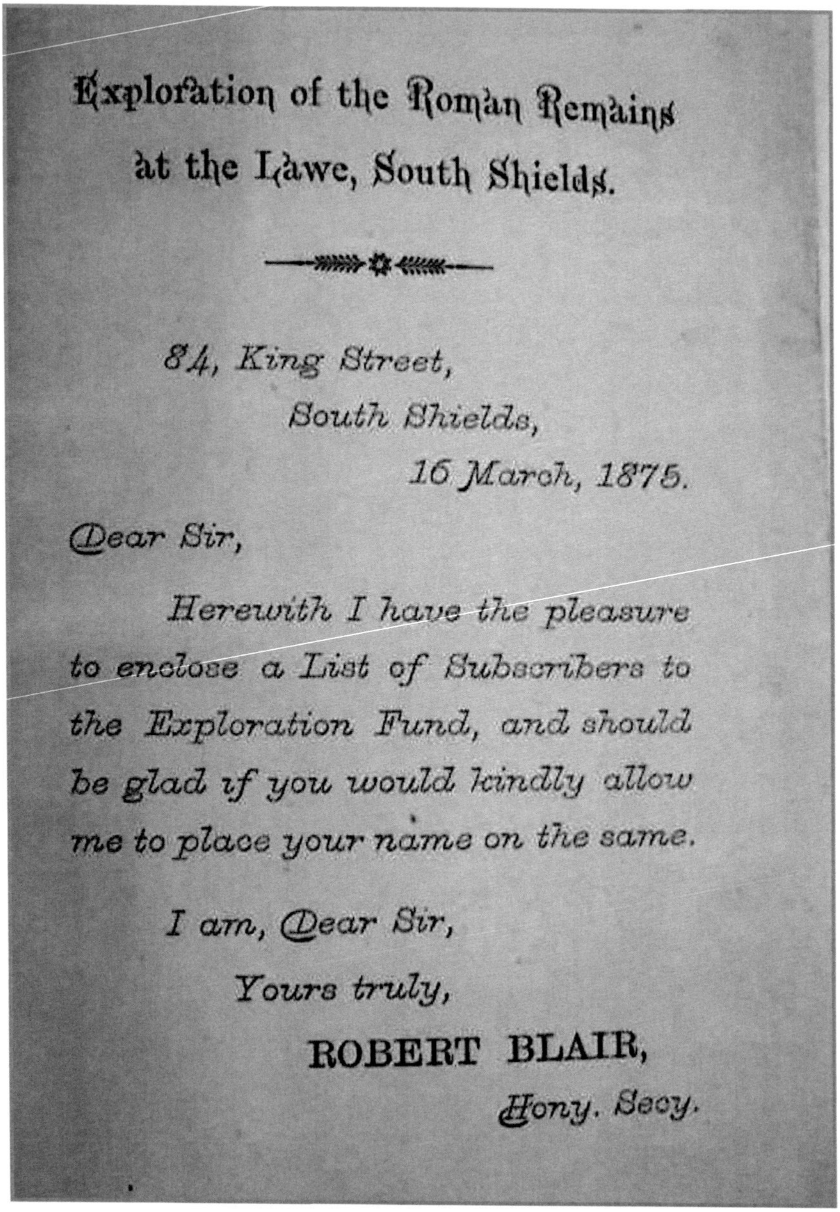

Exploration of the Roman Remains
at the Lawe, South Shields.

84, King Street,
South Shields,
16 March, 1875.

Dear Sir,

Herewith I have the pleasure to enclose a List of Subscribers to the Exploration Fund, and should be glad if you would kindly allow me to place your name on the same.

I am, Dear Sir,
Yours truly,
ROBERT BLAIR,
Hony. Secy.

Blair had a letter printed, this copy being preserved in his scrapbook, subtly asking for recipients to become subscribers to the Exploration Fund.
Blair Scrapbook; courtesy of South Tyneside Libraries.

The following pages contain a few of the letters Blair received; he kept them all in his scrapbook.

Shields Gazette and Daily Telegraph, Wednesday 10th March 1875

ROMAN REMAINS SOUTH SHIELDS

A largely-attended meeting was held Monday night in the Free Library Buildings, South Shields, for the purpose of promoting a thorough and systematic exploration of the site where the Roman remains have recently been discovered at the Lawe. The Mayor (Ald. J. Broughton) presided, and amongst those present were the Rev. Dr. C Bruce, Newcastle; R. H. Morton, P. H. Moore, T. N. Roberts, T. Leyland, Dr. Lunge, Ald. Williamson, Messrs. J. M. Moore, G. Lyall, T. Lincoln, R. Blair, L. Mackey, T. Barker, J. Lincoln, Jos. Reed, P. Drake, W. N. Lightford, S. Fletcher, W. Glover, Malcolm G. Scott, E. Suddards, M. Hall, T. T. Dale, etc..

The Chairman, opening the proceedings, said the object of the meeting was for the purpose of devising some means for excavating the very important Roman remains which had recently been discovered in South Shields, and added that the proceeds of the excavations were to be presented to the Free Library. They would materially assist in educational purposes, and he hoped the gentlemen who took interest in the Free Library and in education generally, would subscribe the means for carrying out such work.

(Applause)

Rev. Dr. Hooppell then rose to propose the first resolution. Before he read two letters which he had received in reply to invitations to attend the meeting. The first was from the Rev. T. H. Cheater, who was unable to attend the meeting, but who stated that it would give him pleasure every way to co-operate with those interested in the work. The other was from Mr. W. Lawson, who enclosed a guinea towards the exploration fund. He (Dr. Hooppell) said he need not say much about the work that had thus far been done at the Lawe, because the correspondents of the various newspapers had details during the last week or so, but he might say there was no doubt that extensive Roman remains did exist in their midst. The certainty of remains had been shown by what had been found years ago and during the last few days. He attached very great importance to the exploration of the site, as it would advance learning generally. There could be no question that great light had been thrown upon the manners, customs, arts, and modes of government of those who held sway in part of

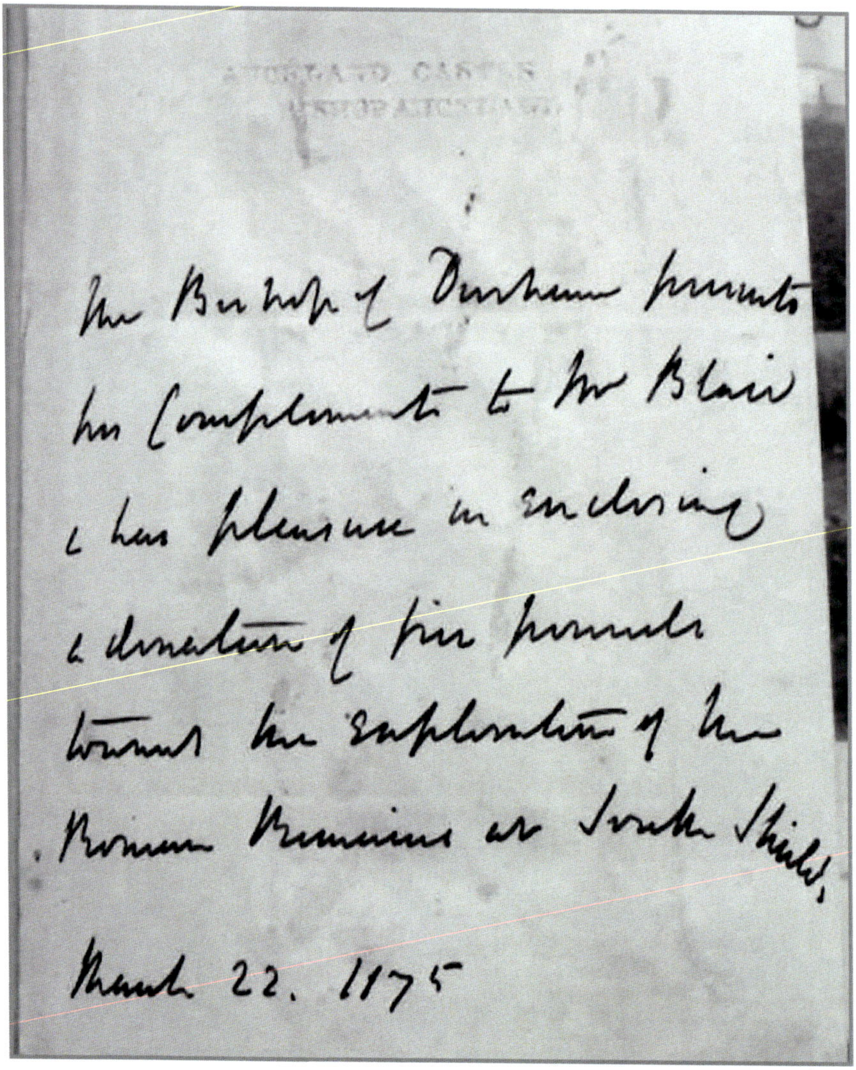

The Bishop of Durham presents his Compliments to Mr Blair & has pleasure in enclosing a donation of five pounds towards the exploration of the Roman Remains at South Shields.

March 22. 1875

The Bishop of Durham presents his compliments to Mr Blair & has pleasure in enclosing a donation of five pounds towards the exploration of the Roman Remains in South Shields.
March 22 1875

Charles Thomas Baring, Bishop of Durham 1861-1879

the world nearly 2,000 years ago, the extensive excavations which had been made into the remains which they had so abundantly left behind them. The Roman stations hitherto explored had been inland stations, and he did not recollect any station so thoroughly maritime as the one at the Lawe. If they explored the site thoroughly, and if the remains were excavated they should find their mode of fortifying maritime stations, which would throw much light upon what they did not find in inland stations. He also thought the name of the station might be decided, and they might also possibly find indications of how the station was "wrecked" or ruined, when the Romans were forced to abandon this part of the country. The result of the exploration might also be valuable to the students of Holy Scripture. If the remains of antiquity were studied they would throw light upon a great many passages of Scripture, and so enable them to realise more vividly the historical truths they read of.

He then proposed the following resolution :—"That a thorough and systematic exploration of the Roman remains now known with certainty to be existing at the Lawe, South Shields, be made, with the consent of the owners of the land, and that the relics, etc., obtained in the progress of the same, be, with the consent of the owners, presented to the borough of South Shields and lodged in the Free Library, and that the following gentlemen be a committee, with power to add to their number, to carry out this resolution : The Mayor (J. Broughton, Esq.), and J. C. Stevenson, J. Williamson, J. B. Dale, P. H. Moore, J. M. Moore, G. Lyall, L. Mackey, T. J. Bell, R. Blair, J. Hutchinson Sen., T. Lincoln, W. Marshall, R. Peverley, T. Pyke, T. Vint, J. Wright, Rev. H. Morton, Rev. T. N. Roberts, Mr. John Clayton, Mr. R. Ellison, Dr. Bruce and Dr. Hooppell. That the Mayor be chairman of the committee, Mr. G. Lyall vice-chairman, Mr. L. Mackey treasurer, Mr. R. Blair secretary and Messrs. Dale, Young and Co. bankers to the committee."

Ald. Williamson said he had very great pleasure in seconding the resolution, and remarked that he thought they were greatly indebted to those gentlemen who initiated the movement which appealed entirely to the sympathies of the community. There was probability that the town might come to be known all over the world as a spot where ancient remains would be found. He then referred to his having had the privilege of going over the buried city of Pompeii. It was covered in a light bed of ashes and the exploration there was wonderfully simple.

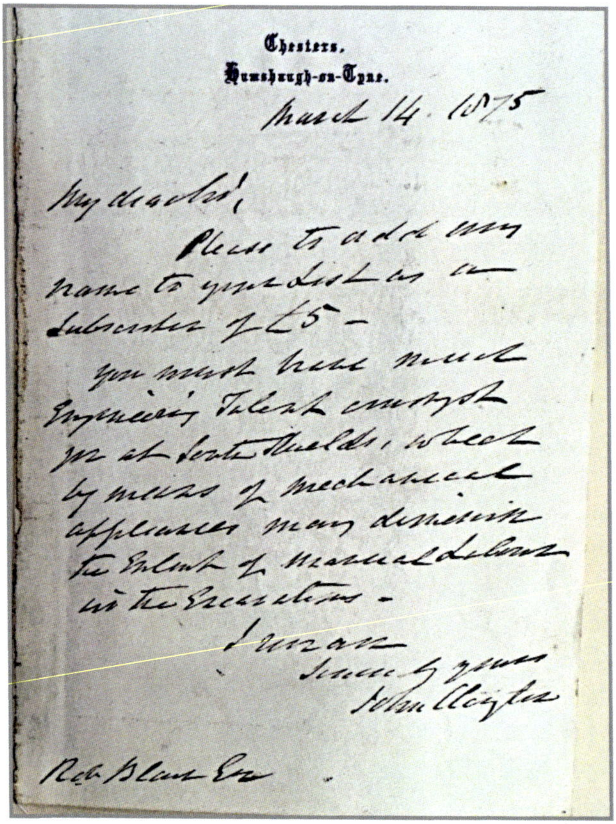

Chesters.
Humshaugh-on-Tyne.
March 14. 1875

My dear Sir,
Please to add my name to your list as a subscriber of £5 -
You must have much Engineering Talent amongst you at South Shields, which by means of mechanical appliances may diminish the extent of manual labour in the Excavations -
I remain
Sincerely yours
John Clayton

Robt Blair Esq

Chesters, Humshaugh-on-Tyne
March 14 1875
My dear Sir,
Please to add my name to your list as a subscriber of £5.
You must have much engineering talent amongst you at South Shields which by means of mechanical appliances may diminish the extent of manual labour in the excavations.
I remain sincerely yours
John Clayton

John Clayton 1792-1890, long serving Town Clerk of Newcastle-upon-Tyne and Vice President of the Society of Antiquaries 1843-1890.

He expressed a hope that the exertions of the committee would be the means of enriching the museum of the Free Library, and concluded by humorous reference to the underground fire, hoping the result of the explorations of the underground treasures would be something to compensate for the unfortunate results of the underground burning of combustible matter.

(Laughter and applause)

The motion was then put and carried unanimously.

The Rev. Dr. Bruce, who was received with applause, then proposed the second resolution, namely, "That the Sum of £100 be raised in the first instance to carry out the exploration, and that a subscription list for that amount be immediately commenced." Every Englishman, he said, liked to trace the history of his ancestors, and they wanted to know, not only something about the men who lived now, but those who lived long ago : they wanted to know something of that wonderful people who first all brought civilisation to this part of the world. Some people shut themselves up with their studies and read book after book in search of knowledge; others again mingled largely in society and sucked the brains of other people; others travelled to secure wisdom and experience as they went but there was another mode, and one with which he had been a good deal acquainted during the last twenty years, and that was taking the spade and shovel and wheel barrow and digging into the ground, and they must do that if they would get the history of their Roman ancestors.

He then referred at considerable length to the occupation of this country by the Romans, commencing with the landing of Agricola in the year 50AD. They knew from stones which they had dug up that the Emperor Hadrian came here about the year 120AD, bringing, it was believed, his wife Sabina with him. He also alluded to the Roman Wall and described its construction and the manner in which the ramparts were garrisoned. The Romans had a camp at Tynemouth, another at South Shields, another at Jarrow, and another in North Shields at Blake Chesters, to prevent the enemy getting by the river inside the wall which was brought as far into the water as they could build.

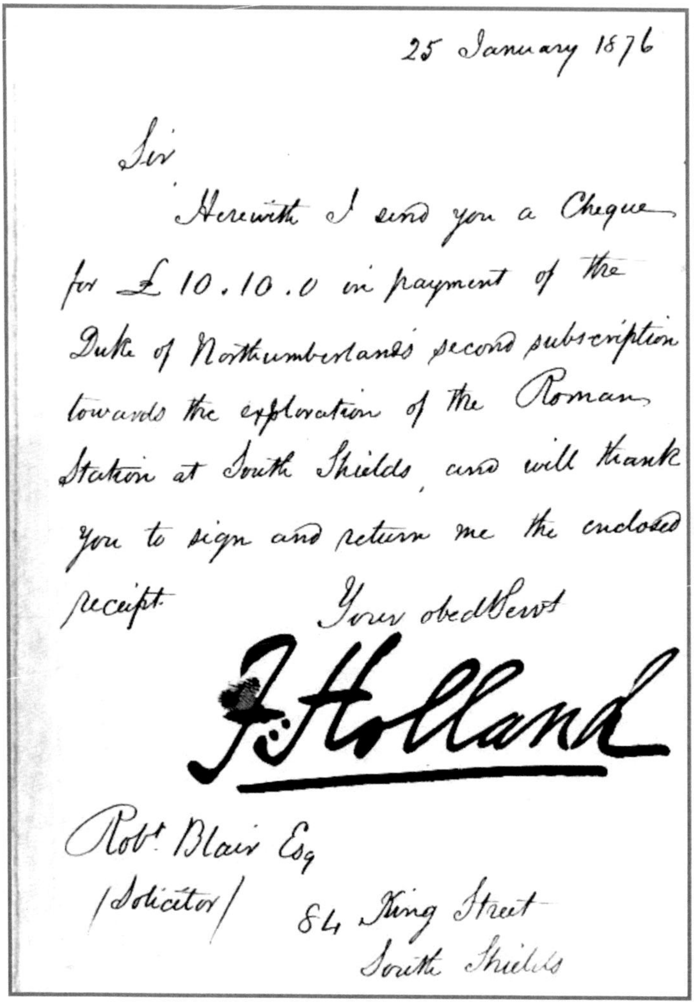

25 January 1876

Sir

Herewith I send you a Cheque for £10.10.0 in payment of the Duke of Northumberland's second subscription towards the exploration of the Roman Station at South Shields, and will thank you to sign and return me the enclosed receipt.

Your obedt Servt

F Holland

Robt. Blair Esq
(Solicitor)
84 King Street
South Shields

25 January 1876

Sir; Herewith I send you a cheque for £10.10.0 in payment of the Duke of Northumberland's second subscription towards the exploration of the Roman Station at South Shields and will thank you to sign and return me the enclosed receipt.

EARL PERCY.
(From a Photograph by Samuel A. Walker, 230, Regent-street, W.)

A letter signed by F Holland the Duke of Northumberland's agent.
Photograph of Henry George Percy, 7th Duke of Northumberland, 1846-1918.

He then proceeded to notice various discoveries of stones and coins in different parts of the country which gave ample proofs of Roman occupation. In all the stations yet discovered they had found traces of at least three periods of destruction, notwithstanding the strength of the garrison stationed on the wall (15,000 men), the good roads, and the facility with which the troops could be brought from one end of the Wall to the other. He next pointed out that the English people of the present day were indebted to the Romans for the alphabet they used every day, and concluded an instructive and interesting address, which at times was relieved by humorous and witty remarks, allusion to religion and the downfall of idolatry. He never visited the stations here or elsewhere without having his mind impressed and his courage raised by what he saw. Think, said, he, of the Romans coming from sunny Italy, think them penetrating these distant parts, and think of them, when once they had planted their foot here resolving not to leave it! They took a firm hold of the country, and from the days of Hadrian to the beginning of the fifth century they held good their possession. After some further concluding remarks the Rev. gentleman resumed his seat. Mr. J. M. Moore seconded the resolution, which was put and unanimously adopted.

The Rev. H. Morton then proposed "That the cordial thanks of this meeting be given to Dr. Bruce for his able address, and to the Mayor for his kindness in presiding on this occasion." Mr. G. Lyall seconded the proposition and said they had especially to thank the Mayor for the cordial manner in which he acceded to their request to excavate the ground. He thought they were deeply indebted to Dr. Bruce for the very instructive address he delivered, and in which he had afforded them great information which might be practically adopted in prosecuting their exploration at the Lawe. He then produced a Roman celt, which was found at the Trow Rocks some years ago, and handed it round for inspection. The motion was carried with acclamation. The Mayor and Dr. Bruce briefly acknowledged the compliment and the proceedings terminated. The subscription list was opened at the conclusion of the meeting and a good sum of money was promised, Ald. Williamson heading the list with £25, and Bruce and his son-in-law, Mr. John Philipson of Newcastle, each contributing two guineas.

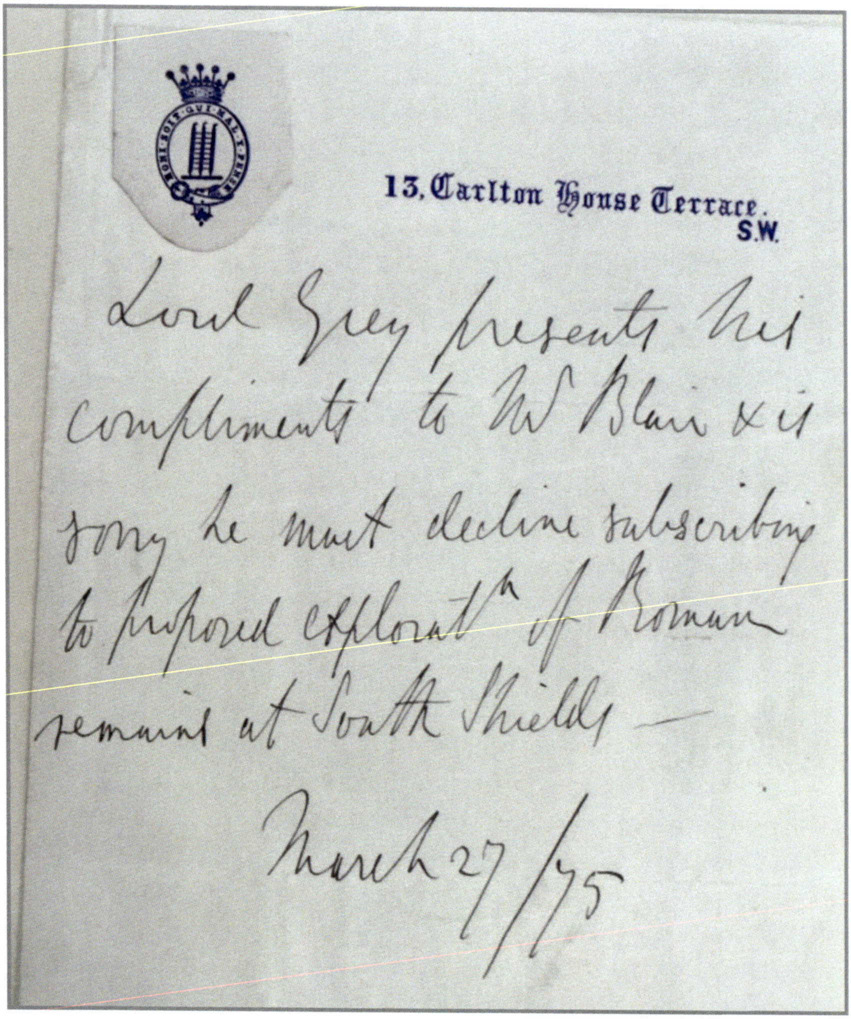

13, Carlton House Terrace.
S.W.

Lord Grey presents his compliments to Mr Blair & is sorry he must decline subscribing to proposed explorat^n of Roman remains at South Shields —

March 27/75

Lord Grey presents his compliments to Mr Blair and is sorry he must decline subscribing to proposed exploration of Roman remains at South Shields.

March 27/75

Rejection letter from Lord Grey.
Photograph of Henry George, 3rd Earl Grey 1802-1894.

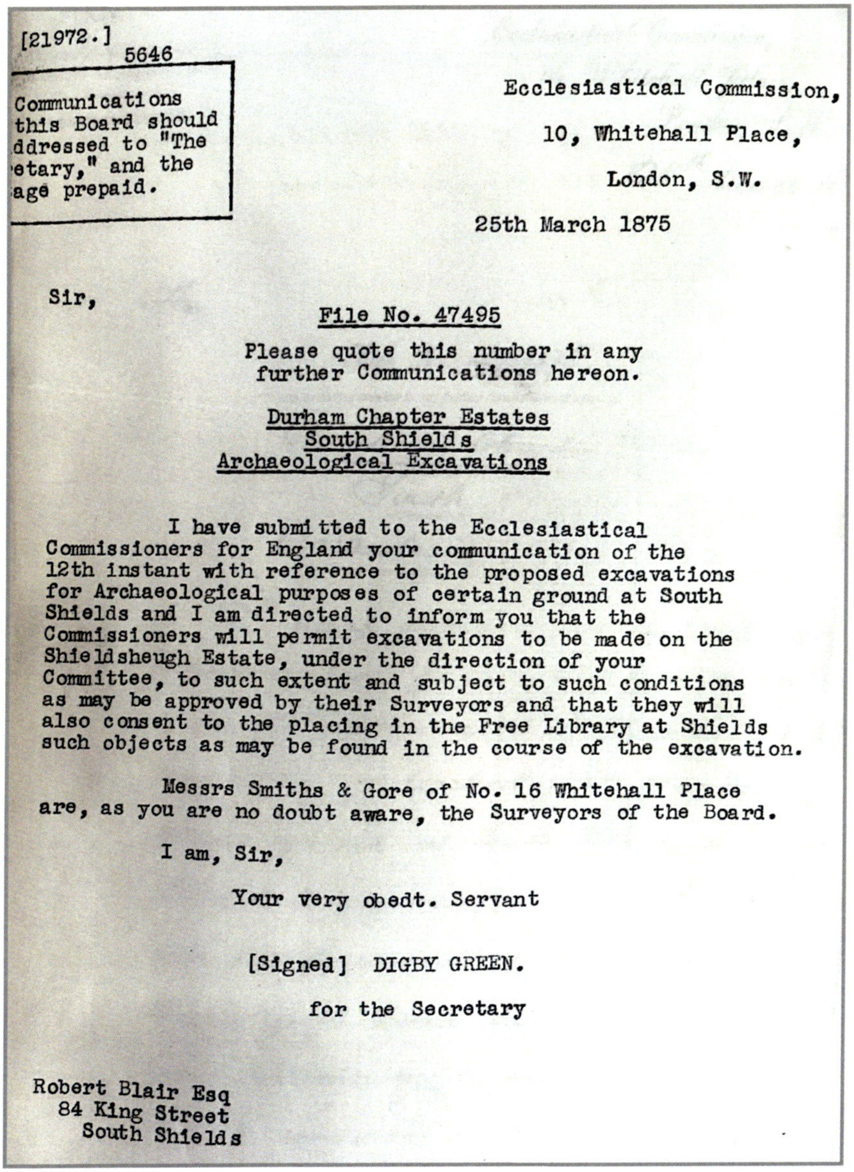

[21972.]
5646

Communications
this Board should
ddressed to "The
etary," and the
age prepaid.

Ecclesiastical Commission,
10, Whitehall Place,
London, S.W.

25th March 1875

Sir,

File No. 47495

Please quote this number in any further Communications hereon.

Durham Chapter Estates
South Shields
Archaeological Excavations

I have submitted to the Ecclesiastical Commissioners for England your communication of the 12th instant with reference to the proposed excavations for Archaeological purposes of certain ground at South Shields and I am directed to inform you that the Commissioners will permit excavations to be made on the Shieldsheugh Estate, under the direction of your Committee, to such extent and subject to such conditions as may be approved by their Surveyors and that they will also consent to the placing in the Free Library at Shields such objects as may be found in the course of the excavation.

Messrs Smiths & Gore of No. 16 Whitehall Place are, as you are no doubt aware, the Surveyors of the Board.

I am, Sir,

Your very obedt. Servant

[Signed] DIGBY GREEN.

for the Secretary

Robert Blair Esq
84 King Street
South Shields

Above is a letter preserved in Robert Blair's scrapbook from the Ecclesiastical Commissioners granting permission for the excavations to go ahead and consent for any finds to be kept in the Free Library in South Shields. The adventure had begun...

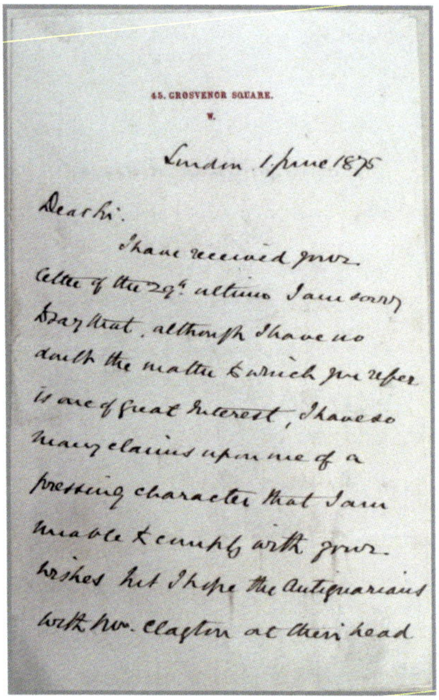

45. GROSVENOR SQUARE.
W.

London 1 June 1875

Dear Sir:

I have received your letter of the 29th ultimo I am sorry to say that, although I have no doubt the matter to which you refer is one of great interest, I have so many claims upon me of a pressing character that I am unable to comply with your wishes but I hope the antiquarians with Mr. Clayton at their head

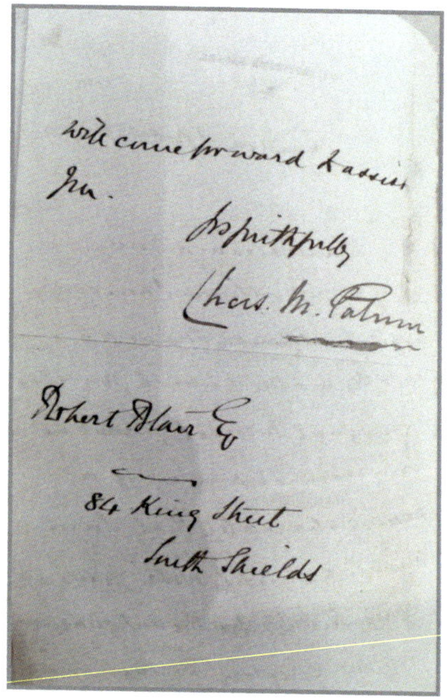

will come forward to assist you.

Yrs faithfully

Chas. M. Palmer

Robert Blair Esq

84 King Street

South Shields

London 1 June 1875

Dear Sir,

I have received your letter of the 29th ultimo. I am sorry to say that, although I have no doubt the matter to which you refer is one of great interest, I have so many claims upon me of a pressing character that I am unable to comply with your wishes but I hope the antiquarians with Mr Clayton at their head will come forward to assist you.

Yours faithfully

Chas M Palmer.

Rejection letter from Sir Charles Mark Palmer, 1st Baronet, a local shipbuilder.
Sir Charles Mark Palmer, 1822-1907, coal owner, shipbuilder and ironmaster, born in King Street, South Shields.

The committee quickly raised the £100 they needed to fund the initial excavations but, as the size and potential of the site became clear, more was needed. Blair was ambitious in his search for subscribers and wrote to leading figures locally and nationally requesting donations. The Duke of Northumberland was a generous supporter with a second gift of £10 nine months into the project. Others like Lord Grey and Sir Charles Mark Palmer, owner of the famous Jarrow shipyard, were less forthcoming.

Blair's energy and enthusiasm and the support of the local newspaper, the *Shields Gazette*, ensured the campaign caught the imagination of the townsfolk even before the finds made national news. Amazingly at the moment of triumph Dr. Hooppell left to take up a new position as the rector of the Anglican Parish Church at Byers Green. It was hardly a step up from his role as headmaster of the Marine School but it did make his name as an antiquarian. He did write a paper on the excavations at South Shields and returned to give well received lectures on the history of the fort but he is remembered now as the excavator of the Roman Fort at Binchester, in his parish of Byers Green, which he documented in his book *Vinovia: A Buried Roman City in the County of Durham,* published in 1891.

Dr. Robert Hooppell the aspiring antiquarian in 1875 had two outstanding Roman sites to choose from when he sought a new path away from the damaging battles over the Contagious Diseases Acts. Either place could have made his reputation as an antiquarian but Binchester was the better choice at the time as its rural site was safe from development, and substantial remains were known to exist in the form of a large buried chamber thought to be part of a bath house. The remains at South Shields on the other hand were in imminent danger of destruction and probably the best that could be expected was a rushed rescue dig before the few surviving Roman stones were buried under the streets and houses of the new housing development. Unsurprisingly Dr. Hooppell went to Byers Green and didn't spend too much time looking back as he found plenty there to attract his attention.

The excavation at South Shields was, after all, in the safe hands of his prodigy Robert Blair and it is from Blair's scrapbook that the following account of the excavation is drawn.

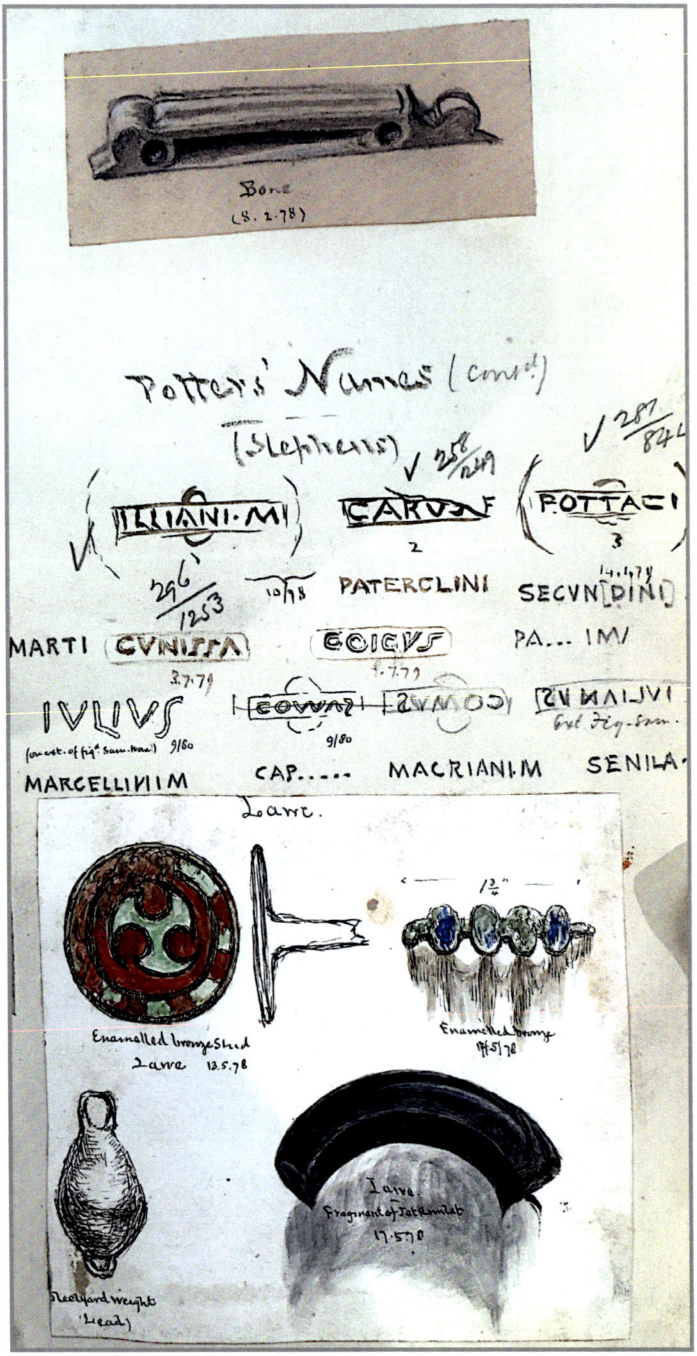

Blair made an intense study of potter's names found on pottery at the Lawe as well as coins and lead sealings from the site, as this page from his scrapbook demonstrates.
Blair Scrapbook; courtesy of South Tyneside Libraries.

The Excavation

Robert Blair's sketch of a large bronze key found on the Lawe.
Blair Scrapbook; courtesy of South Tyneside Libraries.

4

Photograph showing visitors examining the progress of the excavations, 1875.
Reproduced by kind permission of South Tyneside Libraries.

Easter 1875 was one of the most memorable in the history of South Shields. Easter fell early that year, on 28th March, but the weather was fine and crowds flocked to view the excavations on the Lawe although they were less than two weeks old. The *Shields Gazette* reported they were *'a striking sight many feet below the surface, in a field which appears to have been subjected to the plough for centuries, vast walls a dozen feet thick, with buttresses at every five feet, and massive portals.'*

Work had started on 15th March at the place where the fallen columns were found by pilots prospecting for treasure but no one knew what to expect as the excavators had little to guide them and the standard layout of Roman Forts was at the time only poorly understood. Small finds from the excavation were on display at the Marine School courtesy of Dr. Hooppell, the Headmaster, and restaurants in Ocean Road prospered as they provided refreshments to the holiday crowds. The excavation at Shields was unique; a Roman fort being uncovered in the centre of an industrial town. Especially as it came at a time when Roman enthusiasm was sweeping the North due, at least in part, to the publication of a guide to the Roman Wall by Rev. Dr. John Collingwood Bruce; a prominent supporter of the exploration of the fort and a member of the excavation committee. When Dr. Collingwood Bruce rose to speak at a public meeting in the Free Library at South Shields on the 10th March 1875, to propose that a fund of £100 be established (see pages 55, 57, 59 & 61 for a transcript of this meeting) to excavate the Roman remains on the Lawe he was greeted with prolonged applause and, with his support, the appeal was destined to reach its target.

Dr. Collingwood Bruce was the leading light of the Society of Antiquaries Newcastle-upon-Tyne, the foremost authority on the history and archaeology of the Roman Wall, and a massive local celebrity. The *Newcastle Daily Chronicle* devoted a full page to his obituary on the announcement of his death on 6th April 1892, and while the glowing account of his life gave prominence to his achievements as a schoolmaster, preacher and antiquarian, the eulogy was somehow rather greater than the sum of its parts. Dr. Collingwood Bruce was acclaimed as a personification of the character of the city itself and a symbol of its rise from obscurity to wealth and power. He, the *Chronicle* reported, saw the first steamboat on the Tyne, he remembered the first screw steamer in the port and, as a young child, he visited George Stephenson in his cottage at Killingworth and saw Stephenson's locomotive in its cradle.

Dr. Collingwood Bruce's tomb in the south quire aisle of Newcastle Cathedral.

Coal and Iron ***painted by William Bell Scott, 1861. Wallington Hall, Northumberland.***
Image courtesy of National Trust Images.

It seems strange for someone described as an antiquarian to be celebrated as an apostle of industrialisation but Dr. Collingwood Bruce's influence went far beyond the limits of antiquarian research and he was associated with some of the pillars of nineteenth century Newcastle society. He was educated in his father's school, the famed Percy Street Academy (alongside Robert Stephenson) graduated from Glasgow University with a degree in Classics and Theology and was ordained as a Presbyterian Minister, although he didn't seek the call of a congregation and instead returned to Newcastle to teach at the Academy of which he became sole proprietor in 1834. The school taught a wide curriculum in addition to the usual classics which, according to the *Chronicle,* was of the kind '*needed by boys about to embark on the actual business of life as it exists in this town and neighbourhood,*' including mathematics, even navigation, astronomy and geography and boasted a stellar collection of *old boys*. Dr. Collingwood Bruce retired from teaching in 1863 and his work as a schoolmaster is now a footnote to his career as an antiquarian which flourished during his long and productive retirement, but the contribution of his pupils to the wealth and power of Newcastle cannot be overestimated.

A course of five lectures on *The Roman Wall and its Antiquarian Remains* delivered at the Literary and Philosophical Society of Newcastle in 1848 marked the beginnings of a change in the direction of Dr. Collingwood Bruce's career which culminated in the publication in 1863 of his famous *Wallet Book* or *Handbook of the Roman Wall,* (see illustration on page ii) which is still in print. Unlike Edward Gibbon whose epic *The History of the Decline and Fall of the Roman Empire* described the end of an empire weakened by corruption and eroded from within by Christianity, Dr. Collingwood Bruce saw Rome as the foundation and origin of the new industrial civilisation of the north centred on Newcastle. With an antiquarian's eye to the past nothing illustrates his pride in the history of what he called Northumbria better than the series of eight large murals with life-size figures completed by the Head of the Government School of Design in Newcastle upon Tyne, William Bell Scott, between 1855 and 1861 at Wallington Hall. Wallington, the stately home where the intellectual Trevelyan family hosted visitors, including members of the Pre-Raphaelite Brotherhood, was something of a cultural centre for the north and the murals aimed to capture the essential spirit of the region. William Bell Scott visualised its history as a triumph of the people; beginning with a centurion

The Romans Cause a Wall to Be Built for the Protection of the South ***by William Bell Scott 1857. Wallington Hall, Northumberland.***
Image courtesy of National Trust Images.

John Clayton 1792-1890

Part of Clayton Street, built in the neo-classical style between 1824-1841.
The street was designed by John Dobson and built by Richard Grainger, whose family home was at 36 Clayton Street West from 1842 -1861.

supervising the building of the Roman Wall and ending with a fantastic celebration of the industrial workers of Newcastle in *Coal and Iron*, as though the spirit that drove the rise of industry somehow had its origin in the building of the Wall over the wild crags of Northumberland. Dr. Collingwood Bruce documented the physical remains of the Wall marking the boundary (as he constantly reminded his readers) of the Empire of Rome and which he believed created the unique identity of Northumbria as a frontier; a place in all ages where history was made. He called his visits to the Wall pilgrimages, expeditions which he thought every true Northumbrian should undertake to understand what we would now call their heritage, and look upon the glory of ancient Rome which had been recreated in the magnificent classical architecture of Newcastle.

Dr. Collingwood Bruce's friend and colleague from the Society of Antiquaries, John Clayton, wasn't at the public meeting but he was nevertheless voted onto the committee. He visited South Shields with Ralph Carr Ellison on 4th March to view the site and he was, after Dr. Collingwood Bruce, the most influential backer of the excavation committee. Clayton was Town Clerk of Newcastle and, along with John Dobson the architect and Richard Grainger the builder, he was responsible for rebuilding the centre of Newcastle in the grand neo-classical style epitomised by the majestic sweep of Grey Street down the former valley of the Lort Burn to the quayside. He was also the owner of the Chesters Estate which included the Roman fort of Cilurnum, and since 1834 had been buying land along the line of the Wall, notably the fort at Housesteads and the dramatic section of the Wall; along the nearby crags. He was the equal of Dr. Collingwood Bruce as an authority on the Wall.

Clayton indeed is credited with saving the Wall from destruction in a guide published by the National Trust who now owns most of his property, but the most eloquent tribute to his key role - its preservation - is more subtle and yet more powerful. The Centurion in the first picture of William Bell Scott's Wallington murals, the builder of the Wall, is Clayton, a recognition of his achievements both in the preservation of the past and the creation of the future. John Clayton was also an experienced excavator of the Roman forts along the line of the wall and his knowledge shaped the committee's plan for the excavation of the fort and their interpretation of what they found.

Photographs of the excavations, 1875.
Reproduced by kind permission of South Tyneside Libraries.

The excavation continued after Easter through the spring, but the effort was scaled back as the site was gradually covered by new buildings until only the central portion which became The People's Roman Remains Park was left. While Dr. Collingwood Bruce called upon Shields folk to take up the spade most of the digging was done by workmen loaned by Mr. Ralph Carr Ellison, a landowner, naturalist and member of the Newcastle Society of Antiquarians of Newcastle who had an estate in upper Coquetdale. Sometimes in the early days when supervision was available it was supplemented in the evenings and holidays by volunteers from the local community, often pilots with whom Robert Blair had a family connection.

The archaeology can hardly be called scientific by today's standards, but the work did proceed systematically, records were kept, and the excavation was a model for its time. Photographs were taken and a plan was drawn by a professional surveyor as the main features of what was obviously a large and important fort were gradually revealed. Robert Blair, who was also a member of the Society of Antiquarians of Newcastle-upon-Tyne, wrote an account of the finds in his diary (unfortunately now lost) and made many drawings of objects after they were removed from the site, but for the majority regrettably even the basic information is missing. The most substantial building found was the strong room or treasure chamber whose remains included a flight of five stone steps worn by the feet of Roman soldiers over the hundreds of years the fort was occupied, and the sill of a window some three feet from the floor, a remarkable survival in a place thought to have been robbed out long ago for building stone.

Dramatically the diggers also found evidence of the fort's destruction by fire confirming in their opinion Leland's story of the destruction of Caer Urfa by the Danes at the end of the Empire. Sadly as activity declined public interest inevitably waned. T Lincoln, a member of the excavation committee, complained in a letter to the *Shields Gazette* in September 1875 that some people saw the remains only as old walls broken and despoiled, hardly an attraction when better could be seen any day, and suggested that the critics should use their imagination to see the history of the town in the stones. Finds continued to be made as the building work progressed and the exposed remains were threatened by treasure hunters searching for valuables, but somehow they survived and were saved after a second campaign led by Robert Blair about which more will be said later.

A panorama of Arbeia Roman Fort and Museum today, showing the reconstructed West Gate, Barrack Block and Courtyard House.

A contemporary photograph of the '**treasure chamber**' discovered in 1875 with Barrack Block and Courtyard House behind.

The interior of the Courtyard House at the Arbeia Roman Fort and Museum South Shields.
Images courtesy of Tyne & Wear Archives & Museums.

Today it is not difficult to imagine the excitement that a major archaeological dig led by celebrity archaeologists in the middle of an industrial town would generate interest, even with the counter attractions of sport, shopping, and media, but in the summer of 1875 the archaeology really was the best show in town. In 2005 the popular archaeological television programme Time Team came to the Lawe drawn by the possibility that despite well over a century of excavation and treasure hunting there was still much to be found. They targeted the fort's cemetery which although not excavated in 1875 was the source of some spectacular finds during the Victorian building boom. Celebrity archaeologists Phil Harding and Carenza Lewis were optimistic that more Roman graves could be located, perhaps even monuments like the famous Regina and Victor stones might be found, by excavating the green spaces between the new houses that covered the site, but they struggled to make progress despite the use of the latest technology. Frustrated by a complex array of utility pipes and poor soil conditions in what was a mini re-run of 1875, they confirmed that the cemetery existed but found little of interest and disappointed both the television audience and live audience on the ground although the event did have some of the spirit of 1875 about it.

Working against time in front of an expectant audience is a challenge even in ideal circumstances, and the obvious explanation for the lack of finds would be that the site was exhausted, but there is no reason to be pessimistic about the future of archaeology on the Lawe. Watching the programme it is easy to see how the area has changed over the years: much of the housing that threatened the fort has gone, some replaced by a new estate, the pioneering People's Roman Remains Park has expanded to cover most of the fort, and the impressive reconstruction of the west gate sits on the foundations of the original, first excavated in 1875. The Lawe still hides some of its secrets though, as the location of the port is unknown and the large civilian settlement outside the walls remains unexplored; so a latter day Hooppell, Blair or Collingwood Bruce would have no difficulty in making a case for further excavation should the opportunity arise.

The big question left unanswered by the 1875 excavation though has been answered. The Roman name of South Shields was Lugudunum. Ironically it is inscribed on the earliest artefact from South Shields, an altar recovered from the River Tyne by David Lister in 1682. The inscription records that it was erected by the residents of Lugudunum to mark the safe return of the

An altar found in 1682, whose worn inscription was eventually read in 2009, giving the name of the fort at South Shields as Lugudunum. It was given to the Ashmolean Museum in Oxford in the 17th century but since the early 1980s has been returned on permanent loan to Arbeia, South Shields Roman Fort.
Reproduced by kind permission of Tyne & Wear Archives & Museums.

co-emperors Caracalla and Geta to Rome in 211 following the death of their father Septimius Severus at York. The inscription had been defaced following Caracalla's murder of his brother in Rome in 212 to become sole emperor and was unreadable in its entirety until it was scanned in 2009.

Lugudunum, the fortress of the god Lugus, seems an appropriate name for a place occupied by the Fifth Cohort of Gauls. He was a Celtic god, identified in Roman times with Mercury, worshipped in Gaul and present in many place names including the modern city of Lyon. The planet Mercury would have been easily visible from the fort at sunrise giving the garrison the reassurance that their god was watching over them even in this remote northern outpost. On the 11th of August 1875, an appropriate marker of the end of Shield's Roman summer, there was an unusually close conjunction of Venus and Mercury in the dawn sky, so that the two planets appeared as one bright star; an event both Robert Hooppell (who was an astronomer) and a cavalryman of the Fifth Cohort of Gauls would have thought worth getting up early to view.

Above is an engraving from the 19th century and opposite a current photograph of the altar stone discovered in 1682.

Photograph and engraving of the eastern rampart, 1875. (See page 82 for information on the engraving.)
Photograph reproduced by kind permission of South Tyneside Libraries.

The 1875 excavations were well covered by local newspapers and photographers who captured some of the atmosphere of the Roman summer on the Lawe. The following section contains a selection of newspaper cuttings and photographs from Robert Blair's scrapbook showing how the excitement grew as the diggers discovered that much more of the fort had survived than anyone expected.

Shields Gazette and Daily Telegraph, Tuesday 16th March 1875

THE ROMAN REMAINS IN SOUTH SHIELDS.

The committee commenced active operations at the Lawe yesterday morning. They have five men engaged, four digging and one superintending. The excavations are watched by numerous persons with the greatest interest. The progress of the work thus far has been very encouraging.

The committee are driving a trench five feet broad from the spot where the columns were found westward, in the expectation of finding remains of the western rampart of the station. In the course of the work they have already cleared three walls and two paved chambers. The walls run parallel, in a north and south direction, and one of them is perfect. It is no less than four feet eight inches wide, at its widest part, for the trench has crossed it at a point where a regular buttress appears to have been placed, and three feet two inches at its narrowest, and there are four courses of stones remaining in perfect order and position. These were the four lowest courses of the wall, for under them is a bed of concrete of lime, gravel and irregular masses of stone. After reaching the rampart the committee will follow the direction of this wall and the direction of the rampart northwards, and expect it will not be long before they come to a street running east and west.

It appears, from passages in the works of the antiquaries Brand and Leland that after the Romans left South Shields a British town existed at that place called Caer Urfa, at which Oswin, King of Northumberland, was born, and which suffered destruction at the hands of Danish rovers. The discovery of the interesting Roman remains has stirred up a lively spirit of research among local antiquaries, and more light will probably be ere long thrown upon the many passages of the ancient history of the seaside borough.

Above and on the previous page are engravings based on a photograph taken, at the direction of the Ecclesiastical Commissioners, by Mr. Haggitt and engraved by John Storey in 1877, published in Dr. Hooppell's paper *On the discovery and Exploration of Roman Remains at South Shields in the Years 1875-6.*
Published in Natural History Transactions of Northumberland, Durham & Newcastle upon Tyne, 1879, (Vol VII).
Reproduced by kind permission of the Natural History Society of Northumbria, Great North Museum: Hancock.

Dr. Hooppell described this chamber as being at the south-west of the great building (bottom photograph). When found it was quite full of clay and stones from the shore. It had been filled with arches which supported the floor above. One perfect arch remained and piers of six or seven more.

Shields Gazette and Daily Telegraph, Wednesday 17th March 1875

THE ROMAN REMAINS IN SOUTH SHIELDS.
We gave account yesterday of the progress of the excavation up to the time of our going to press. Since then the exploration has been continued with further very interesting results.

At the time of writing a chamber has been reached at a depth of six feet below the surface. Three sides of it are exposed. Its length is eight feet and the thickness of the easternmost wall is two feet two inches. The thickness of the other walls is not yet determined. Indeed, it is thought quite possible that it is one of the guard chambers of the western gate of the station, and that the westernmost wall may prove to have been the rampart of the station, that is to say of the station in its earlier days, for the chamber just discovered evidently formed a portion of building erected, long anterior to the walls and paved chambers to the walls discovered yesterday and on Monday. It is at a much lower level, and other walls and paved passages cross it at each end, showing that there had been a destruction of the station and then a rebuilding. Moreover, the space now being excavated between the walls was found filled with clay which had been puddled in. We may remark, also, that the work of the chamber is of a rougher and more irregular character than the later work to the eastward, which was uncovered yesterday. This may be taken as a further proof of its antiquity, or, at any rate, of its having been built in 'troublesome times'.

Shields Gazette and Daily Telegraph, Thursday 18th March 1875

THE ROMAN REMAINS IN SOUTH SHIELDS.
DISCOVERY OF THE WESTERN RAMPART OF THE STATION.
Since yesterday the workmen engaged in excavating the Roman remains at the Lawe have reached, with what appears to be complete certainty, the western rampart of the station. The foundation of it is at a great depth below the present surface of the ground. At the lowest course of stones the wall is of the remarkable thickness of thirteen feet four inches. This is a much greater thickness than that adopted in the ordinary Roman stations "per lineam valli'" and shows the great importance the Romans must have attached to the commanding position of the Lawe at the mouth of the Tyne, and the immense strength with which they fortified it.

Photographs of visitors and a workman at the excavations, 1875.
Reproduced by kind permission of South Tyneside Libraries.

The chamber which we described in our last impression has been further excavated and has proved very singular and interesting. It is completely exposed, the four sides being shown. It is eight feet four inches in depth, eight feet nine inches in length but only two feet broad. In each side it has an arch, two feet six inches in height, and one foot eight inches in breadth. How far the vaulted passages, to which these arches lead, may penetrate, or what use this singular erection served in the station, are at present only matters of conjecture.

The workmen are busy following up the western rampart in the northerly direction, and the committee hope ere long to come upon the western gateway of the station. It is not quite certain, however, whether the gateway will be found to the north or south of the portion of the rampart already excavated.

Shields Gazette and Daily Telegraph, Monday 22nd March 1875

THE ROMAN REMAINS AT SOUTH SHIELDS.
On Saturday afternoon, when the regular workmen left off excavating at the Lawe, a number of the pilots who live in the neighbourhood expressed their willingness and desire to carry on the work till evening as volunteers. Under the direction of the committee they proceeded to the central portion of the station—the point at which the exploration began a few weeks ago,—and were soon rewarded by the discovery of a third column. The whole of it, with the exception, apparently, of the pedestal, was there originally in one piece, fractured, no doubt, by a fall. The column was carefully unearthed, and removed to the garden of the Marine School, where those formerly discovered and many other curious stones from the station have been placed.

After the exhumation of the column, the volunteers discovered a mass of masonry which puzzled every one present. It consisted of a great quantity of stones regularly fixed with mortar, but placed edgewise in such a manner that persons conversant with building, who were present, declared they must belong to a vast underground arch; others thought that they were the paving of an erection built long after the destruction of Caer Urfa, when arts and appliances had fallen into a state of primitive rudeness.

Stones and tile on display in the museum at Arbeia, South Shields Roman Fort.
Reproduced by kind permission of Tyne & Wear Archives & Museums.

> Further explorations to-day (when a greater force of men is being employed will doubtless throw more light upon this singular section. What renders it the most remarkable is that at a level only a few inches beneath this mass of stonework the workers came upon what appears with certainty to have been a street, well paved, and with a channel which would do credit to our modern road-makers, running the whole length of the portion they uncovered—a distance of perhaps thirty feet - with a well-built wall upon the other side having every appearance of belonging to one of the principal buildings in the station. It is suggested that this building may have been the Forum or market-place, which always forms an important feature in every Roman camp. In making these excavations the workers came upon some stags' horns and - what they consider more remarkable - some large bones of whales. These were embedded in the earth, an inch or two above the floor of the building, at a depth of three feet six inches below the surface.
>
> Several stones, with curious holes in them, have been found, but only one, thus far, with letters upon it. This was a loose stone, from near the western rampart, and the letters upon it are 'A. C.' Among the bones uncovered has been a portion of a human skull.
>
> The excavations continue to afford the greatest interest to the people of South Shields and visitors to the town, great numbers of whom surround the workmen. Yesterday, the camp was visited by thousands of persons.

Annoyingly for Dr. Collingwood Bruce, despite the spectacular success of the excavation and the number of objects that were recovered from the site, it failed in what he thought was its main objective. The primary aim of the excavation from an antiquarian point of view was to discover the Roman name of South Shields and place the fort firmly on the map of Roman Britain. There was a written list of forts and their garrisons at the end of the Roman Empire, the famous *Notitia Dignitatum*, but without the evidence of inscriptions giving the actual names of places or seals giving the names of units at a site, assigning names to places was a matter of endless speculation and debate. Speaking at the public meeting of the 10th March Dr. Collingwood Bruce had mocked antiquarians who *'shut themselves up in their studies and search book after book for knowledge'*, or *'mingle and suck the brains of others'*, confident that the excavation would be a triumph for his approach of *'taking up the shovel and the wheel barrow and digging the ground'*.

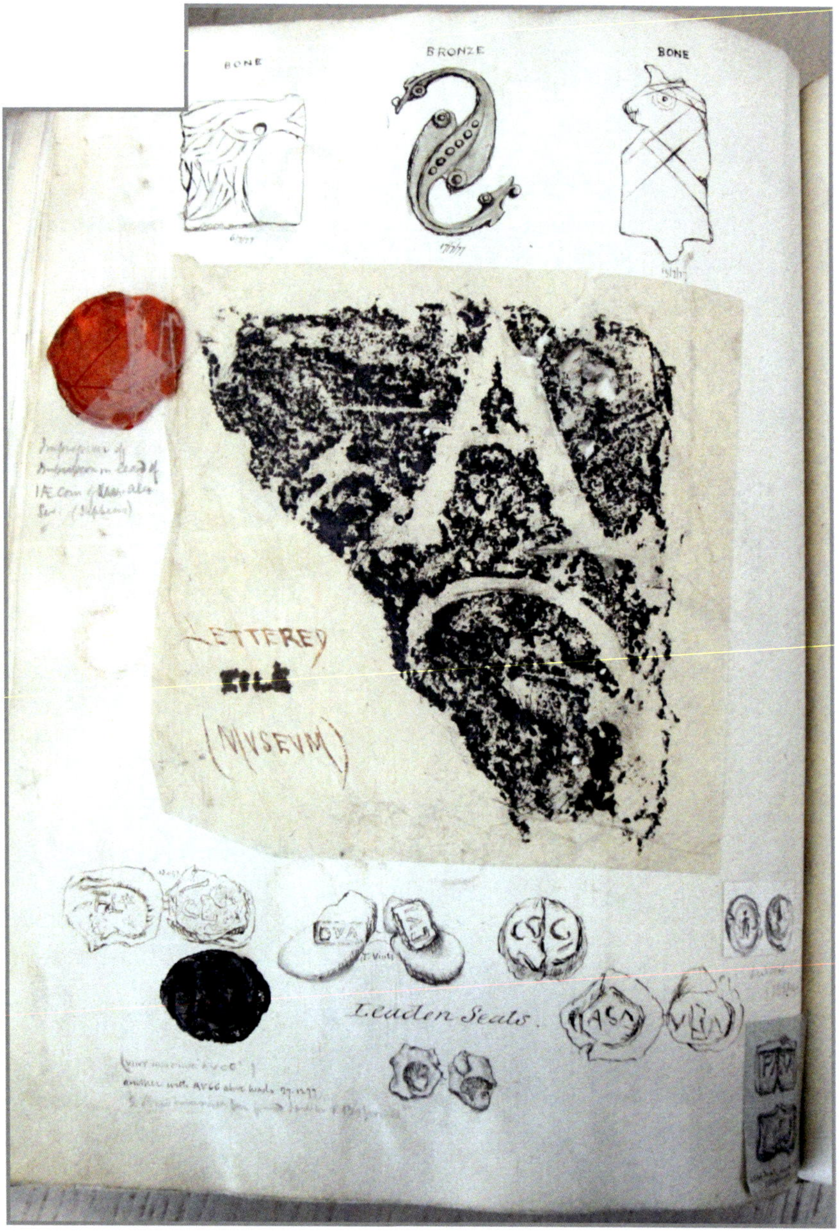

A page from the Blair's scrapbook featuring a rubbing of the tile, with the inscription A C on it, most probably taken using a wax crayon.

Other finds are recorded on this page and beneath the tile are Blair's meticulous drawings of various lead sealings (he made the study of these seals one of his passions) one shows the initials CVG.
Blair Scrapbook; courtesy of South Tyneside Libraries.

He hoped to quickly confirm that South Shields was the Tunnocelum of the *Notitia*, home to the First Cohort of Hadrian's Own Marines (*Aeliae Classicae*) the only appropriate garrison for what was thought to be a port for the Wall. Hopes were briefly raised when a fragment of a tile marked with the letters A C was found early in the excavations near the west gate, but were soon dashed by the unwanted discovery of large numbers of lead sealings marked CVG which confirmed that the garrison was the Fifth Cohort of Gauls, a unit absent from the *Notitia* whose presence gave no clue to the fort's name.

Shields Gazette and Daily Telegraph, Tuesday 23rd March 1875

THE ROMAN REMAINS IN SOUTH SHIELDS.
Since yesterday the work has been proceeding very vigorously at the Lawe, and the workmen are coming upon many indications of more massive remains at a greater depth. In the eastern part of the excavations some very large stones have been discovered, one the vonssoir of an arch apparently of large span. The four sides of the face of the stone are respectively 14, 19, 18, and 21 inches in length, and the thickness about 18 inches. Every side is carefully dressed but one. Close by it, was lying a massive stone with one side elaborately fluted with numerous mouldings. This stone, apparently, formed a portion of the entablature of some important erection. At the western end of the excavations, the workmen, who are pursuing the rampart southwards, have come upon the western gateway of the station. They are engaged in uncovering it to-day. It is of large size, double, with a massive stone in the centre, upon which gates doubtless closed. In another part of the station a tiled floor has been reached. Altogether the excavations today have a most promising appearance.

Shields Gazette and Daily Telegraph, Wednesday 24th March 1875

THE ROMAN REMAINS IN SOUTH SHIELDS.
The western gateway of the station is being uncovered to-day. Owing to the massive thickness of the rampart and the depth at which it lies beneath the present surface of the ground, the work is one requiring much time and labour. But it is one full of interest. It is a striking sight to see, many feet below the surface, in a field which appears to have been subjected to

Photograph of the important visitor to the site, May 1875. Dr. Collingwood Bruce is the central seated figure.
Reproduced by kind permission of South Tyneside Libraries.

Rev. Dr. John Collingwood Bruce, 1805-1892.

the plough for centuries, vast walls dozen feet thick, with buttresses at every five feet and massive portals.

And it adds to the remarkable character the fact to see running all along upon this rampart, a paved street, evidently the work of another generation of man ages later, yet removed from the present more than a thousand years. Further to the eastward again a most singular aspect is presented. There the workmen yesterday uncovered much larger space of what certainly appears to have been the forum or market place of the station and lying flat upon large portion of its area is what was evidently once the lofty wall of a neighbouring building. This wall, after the destruction, or one of the destructions of the fortress, must have fallen bodily across the forum. No less than twenty two feet of it in length is yet unbroken. The workmen are busy today (Wednesday), in laying it bare, and cleaning the earth away on all sides of it, in order that the place from which it fell, the character of the building to which it belonged, and the circumstances attending its overthrow, may be discovered as fully as possible. Mr. Carr Ellison of Dunston Hill visited the ground on Monday, and Dr. Bruce of Newcastle, is expected to-day.
The Duke Northumberland has expressed to the latter gentleman his intention of contributing to the exploration fund.

Shields Gazette and Daily Telegraph, Tuesday 25th March 1875

THE ROMAN REMAINS IN SOUTH SHIELDS.
Yesterday, a considerable portion more of the western rampart and gateway was uncovered, and a wall running at right angles to the rampart inside the gateway was exposed. Five courses of stones remain in position. It was probably the wall of a guard chamber. Nearby is a wall of a single stone in thickness, apparently the work of a later and ruder time! This occupies what must have been the central portion of the roadway from the gate into the town.

The further exploration of the whole of this part of the fortress will be awaited with much interest. More knowledge can be gained of the military importance of a Roman Station by thoroughly uncovering its gateway, guard chambers, and contiguous ramparts, than by any other means. It is important in a historical point of view, that the real position of South Shields as a Roman border and seaside fortress should be fully disclosed.

Describing Mr. Storey's engraving of the Forum (see above) at South Shields in 1879, Dr. Hooppell explained that,

'the immediate foreground is unexcavated. To the right are seen the massive stones forming the outer margin of the Forum. The deep depressions caused by innumerable footsteps are very visible in a stone right in the front. Just behind is a gap, whence huge stones have been taken in early times. Behind that is seen the Channel, which carried off the rain from the footpaths. Its continuation is seen turning the angle at the right hand edge of the plate. Filling the middle of the plate is the prostrate wall, blown down in some gale from its foundations, which are extending in a long line to the left of the Plate. The entrance to the Praetorium is about where the man with the pickaxe in his hand is standing, and on that man's left is seen a large extent of the original pavement of the Forum, and beyond that again the altar table, and the remains of its encompassing wall. The depth of the Remains below the present surface of the ground is shown by the high bank of unexcavated earth behind the table-altar.'

Dr. Hooppell continues his account by discussing the drainage of the forum, which he was pleased to be present to witness when,

'the first time this ancient pavement was directly exposed to violent rain after the lapse of more than a thousand years ...the flood disappeared from the old Roman market-place, throughout its entire extent, as completely and as rapidly as it does from a modern street'.

Note the table stone (shown in the opposite photograph) is upper centre of the engraving beneath the group of three standing figures.

Reproduced by kind permission of the Natural History Society of Northumbria, Great North Museum: Hancock.

The workmen are not engaged upon the rampart and gateway today. Those who were at work upon it yesterday and the two preceding days were kindly lent by Mr. Myers, the contractor, who is at present engaged in laying out the new streets on the estate, Baring Street, Roman Street and Fort Street and who liberally gave, as his contribution to the Exploration Fund, the labour of a number of men under his own supervision for half a week.

Another gratifying contribution to the fund was made yesterday by the Duke of Northumberland, who sent a cheque for £10 by the Rev. Dr. Collingwood Bruce, of Newcastle, who visited the ground yesterday. Dr. Bruce appeared to consider the excavations of a most interesting and promising character. He spent a long time upon the ground, minutely examining every feature that had been brought to light. He considered the wall which had fallen prostrate upon the forum, from a neighbouring building, most remarkably important. He was understood to say that he had never seen a similar ruin in any of the other Roman Stations in the North of England, and that it threw light upon the question of the construction of their buildings.

A photograph taken from Blair's scrapbook. of the *altar table* ***referred to by Dr. Hooppell, which was soon acknowledged to be of a post Roman date.***
Blair Scrapbook; courtesy of South Tyneside Libraries.

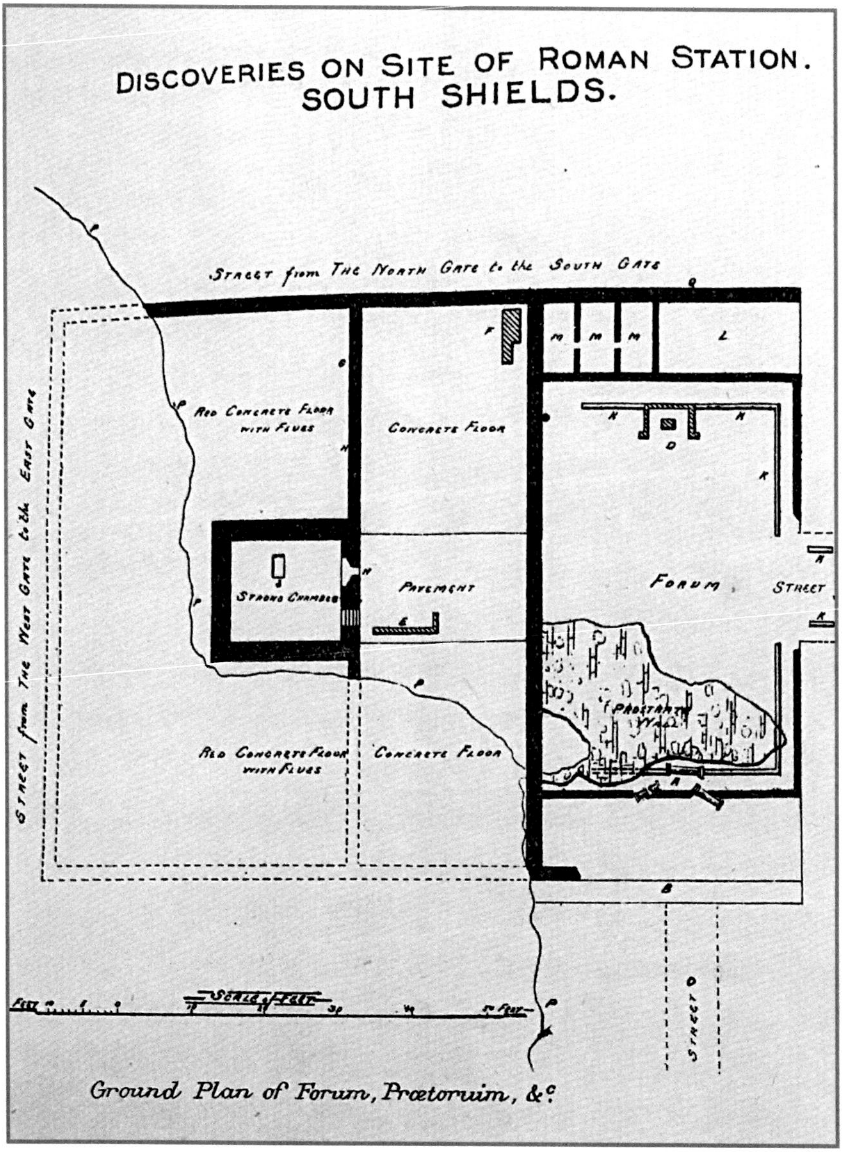

A plan printed in Dr. Hooppell's paper *On the discovery and Exploration of Roman Remains at South Shields in the Years 1875-6.*
Published in Natural History Transactions of Northumberland, Durham & Newcastle upon Tyne, 1879, (Vol VII).
Reproduced by kind permission of the Natural History Society of Northumbria, Great North Museum: Hancock.

Please note:

This plan is of the Fort's Headquarters Building.

Dr. Hooppell called it the forum as it was an open square surrounded by columns which was reminiscent of literary descriptions of the forum in Roman towns.

Its monumental character comes from it being the administrative centre of the fort.

It would be sometime before it was understood that forts did not have a forum.

NOTE.

The dotted portions are conjectural, the earth not having been removed from them.

A. The Columns, as found.

B. Raised flagged footpath.

C. Keystone to arch, with sculptured head of Bos Longipous, as found.

D. Table Altar, of subsequent erection

E.F. Dry Stone Walls, of subsequent erectio

G.H. Breaks in Wall, where windows possibly have been.

I. Stone steps.

J. Cistern or impluvium.

K.K.K.K.K.K. Channelled Stones.

L. Walled Pit.

M.M.M. Supposed shops.

N. Splayed window.

O. This street went from Forum to great building which had portic the portico abutted on the street.

P.P.P. &c. Limit of Exploration of this part of Station.

Q. It was judged probable that a street emerged from the Forum at about this point, but it was not explored.

The portions "hatched" on plan a of a later period.

Rev. Dr. Hooppell in his 1879 paper describes this photograph by Mr. Haggitt as showing the main drains of the Station.

'In the foreground is a portion of the great drains, which ran northward from the centre of the Station out of the North Gate, which was uncovered during the excavations. Beyond are seen the flagstone coverings of the rest. The Northern Gateway of the Station was near the end of the trench. The immense depth of these drains below the present surface of the earth is visible in the Plate. The trench has been filled up, leaving the drains as they were found and before long, it may be presumed, the whole surface shown in this photograph will be covered with houses.'

Reproduced by kind permission of South Tyneside Libraries.

Shields Gazette and Daily Telegraph, Tuesday 30th March 1875

THE EASTER HOLIDAYS

Yesterday afternoon was again observed a holiday in North and South Shields. The weather was favourable for holiday-making, and many pleasure seekers betook themselves to Tynemouth, Marsden, and other favourite resorts. There was a large influx of visitors in South Shields and the site of the Roman remains was again the source of great attraction. The Roman Catholics of North Shields held their annual tea and concert in the Albion Assembly Rooms, and the soiree was attended by a large number of persons. The Theatre Royal, North Shields, was re-opened, and the popular drama, "British Barn" was performed, and at the South Shields Theatre "Uncle Tom's Cabin" was produced to a large audience. There were also social gatherings in North and South Shields.

Shields Gazette and Daily Telegraph, Wednesday 7th April 1875

THE ROMAN REMAINS IN SOUTH SHIELDS.

The excavations at the Lawe have been vigorously pushed on by the Exploration Committee since our last account. Acting on the advice of Dr. Bruce, the committee determined to carry the experimental trench further eastward, until they should reach the eastern rampart. This they succeeded in doing a few days since, and they have subsequently been engaged in uncovering the foundations of southward and northward. They have exposed a length of more than thirty three feet of the wall to the southward, and have discovered the remains of many chambers within the rampart, and of numerous buttresses outside it. Northward of the chambers they have discovered a gateway and many other objects of interest, and they are now engaged following the excavation to the northward, believing they are either on the site of, or very near to, the eastern gateway of the station, they have not space to dwell upon the extremely interesting indications of older important work, and also of occupation in later times, which have been discovered by the committee side by side beyond the rampart itself.

Many coins have been found, ranging between 250 A.D and 350 A.D thus showing that the Romans held possession of South Shields at that time, and numerous interesting articles of daily life or personal adornment.

Photographs of the excavations, 1875.
Reproduced by kind permission of South Tyneside Libraries.

Among these may be mentioned a bronze lamp, quite perfect; several fibula- or clasps, one particularly good; several pins; jar for unguent, and highly ornamental bronze spoon for use with such jars; the bronze handle of a vase; a bronze needle with two eyes; spindle; whorls; etc., etc. Besides the men employed on the eastern rampart and gateway, the committee have also to-day a large force of Moir's men employed on the western rampart and gateway.

Shields Gazette and Daily Telegraph, Saturday 10th April 1875

THE ROMAN REMAINS IN SOUTH SHIELDS.

The workmen employed at the Lawe were engaged yesterday, partly upon the ancient forum or market place, and partly upon the gateway in the western rampart. Those engaged on the forum uncovered a large space more of the paved area, exposing the whole of one side of the forum, fifty three feet in length. The water channel on the inside was originally forty-three feet in length, joining the others running at right angles to it along the other sides. On the floor of the forum the workmen found several pieces of statue, no doubt erected in honour of one of the Emperors, or of some classical divinity. The shoulders and bust are in one piece, and there are some smaller fragments. It hoped that the other parts may be found shortly. Another piece of tile was also found, bearing the same inscription as before, with a portion of an additional letter, thus— OHV C. The contraction mark for N is over the V. We understand that the meaning of these inscriptions is supposed to be the fifth century of the cohort. The only word wanting is the most important one of all, viz., that which would tell the style or title of the particular cohort or body of troops which garrisoned the station. A few days ago an elaborately carved centurial stone was found, which would at once have given the same much desired information, but the inscription, which originally existed upon it, is now so obliterated that only one or two indistinct letters can made out upon it. The workmen employed upon the gateway in the western rampart uncovered yesterday another pier, proving, beyond question, the fact that it is the gateway of the station they are engaged upon. They are excavating to-day the guard chamber, which is on a much lower level than the rest the station, which later generations of occupants had filled up with stones and puddled clay. Under it runs the arched passage, the entrance of which was found a few weeks back with the adjoining narrow chamber, which was one of the first portions of the station excavated.

Above is a photograph of the excavations taken in 1875.
Below are two engravings from the 1870s of the bull key stone and the stone on display in the museum at Arbeia, South Shields Roman Fort.
Reproduced by kind permission of Tyne & Wear Archives & Museums.

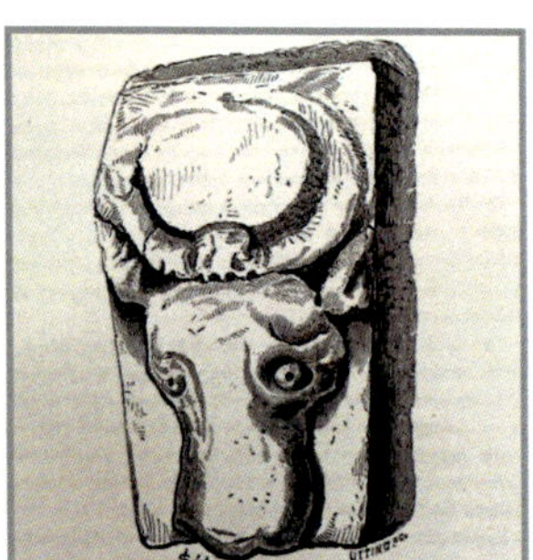

Shields Gazette and Daily Telegraph, Wednesday 14th April 1875

THE ROMAN REMAINS IN SOUTH-SHIELDS.

DISCOVERY OF A HYPOCAUST.

To-day, a portion of the workmen are engaged in opening out a hypocaust, or system of flue passages beneath a floor, used by the Romans for warming their apartments, which has been discovered near the eastern rampart of the station. The floor is supported on numerous pillars of stone, and the heated air from the furnace was allowed to circulate among them before escaping. Many pieces of coal, and many marks of fire, have been come upon by the workmen. In another part of the station several workmen are engaged in excavating an area contiguous to the forum. Nearly the whole of the forum is now uncovered, and its size can be better seen, and the various entrances into it can be traced with some degree of certainty. Yesterday the keystone of an arch, with the head of a bull sculptured upon it, was found. This stone bore evident marks of fire. A singular upright pillar is standing in the forum, upon which there was at one time a flat stone, like a table. This and the pillar are covered with a thin coating of fine plaster. The singular chambers at the westen rampart have been covered over with deals to preserve them. Previous to this being done, some excellent photographs of them were obtained by Mr Charles, who also took several photographs of the fallen wall in the forum. To-day, we understand, he is to photograph the hypocaust.

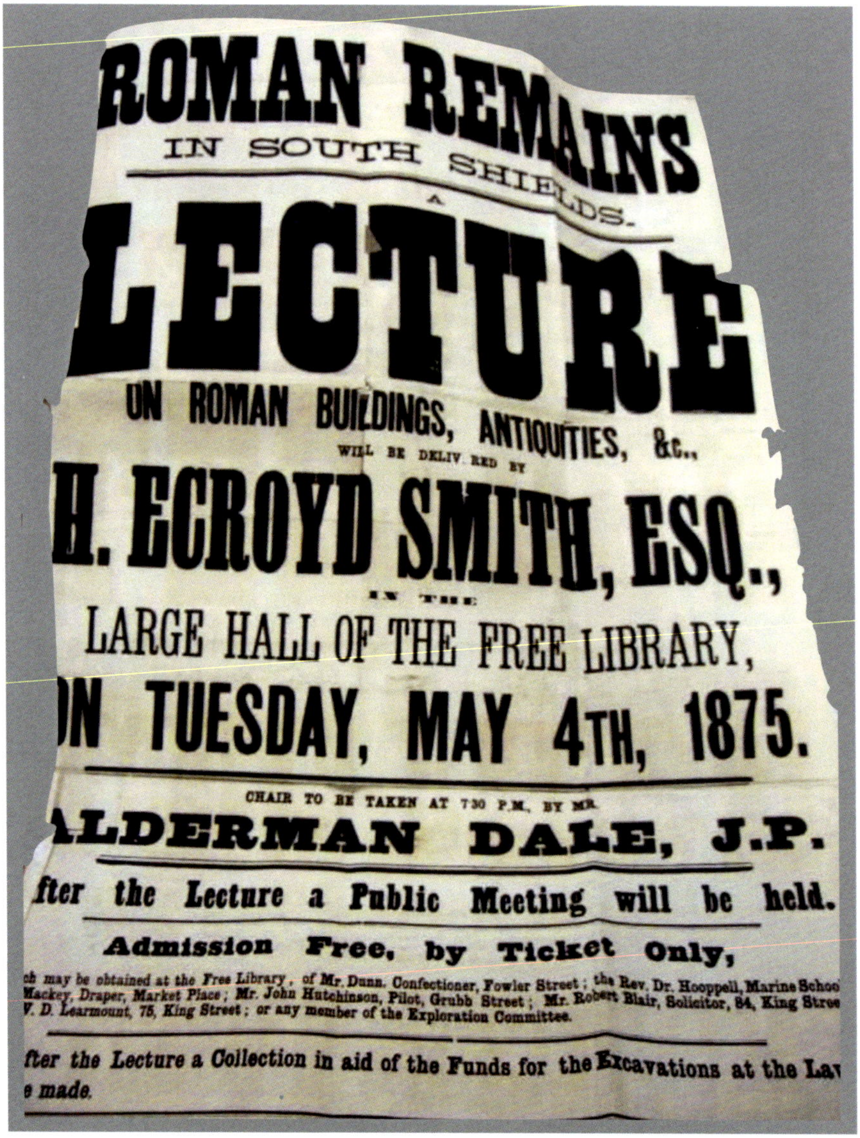

As well as newspaper reports about the finds on the Lawe there were open afternoons when the public could visit and on one Saturday afternoon a policeman had to be called to control the crowds.

There were also frequent public meetings and lectures to inform the local people of the progress of the campaign and the excavations as this bill poster demonstrates.
Blair Scrapbook; courtesy of South Tyneside Libraries.

Shields Gazette and Daily Telegraph, Wednesday 28th April 1875

THE ROMAN REMAINS IN SOUTH SHIELDS.

The work of excavation is still going on in the field between the two wagon ways, and more long walls of public buildings have been uncovered. Yesterday, the two halves of a large millstone were found, fitting exactly together, and half of another small one. Several coins, bone pins and other small articles have also been found recently. The collection of antiquities, in process of formation by the committee for the Free Library and housed at the Marine School, already assuming large proportions. It is singular however, that no altar has yet been come upon. The fact that two altars from South Shields are in existence at Oxford and Durham forbids the supposition that the station at South Shields was altogether denuded before its destruction; at the same time it is remarkable that, during so many weeks, and amid the finding of so many other characteristic remains of Roman occupation, so few symbols of pagan rites have been unearthed. The committee are having the explorations carefully surveyed, with the view of fixing their exact position on the Ordnance Map of South Shields, and also having drawings on an enlarged scale made of them for reference hereafter. This work has been most kindly and liberally undertaken by Mr. Oswald, an architect, of Newcastle, free of cost. Mr. Oswald was on the ground the whole of yesterday, making the necessary surveys and measurements. It affords us great pleasure to record that the person who injured the historic stones of the forum, a few weeks ago, has expressed his great regret to the committee, and has indeed amply apologised. We are glad to observe that less mischief has been done during the past week than before, and we have no doubt that, as popular information respecting the remains and their historic importance is extended, so the cooperation of all classes of persons with the committee in preserving them will increase. We understand that the committee contemplate the delivery of a lecture on an early day next week, on "Roman Buildings and Antiquities," by a well-known antiquary, Mr. Ecroyd Smith, in the Large Hall of the Free Library, granted to them by the Free Library Committee for the purpose, to be followed by an account of the committee's stewardship and an appeal for considerably increased funds to carry on the interesting work to its termination.

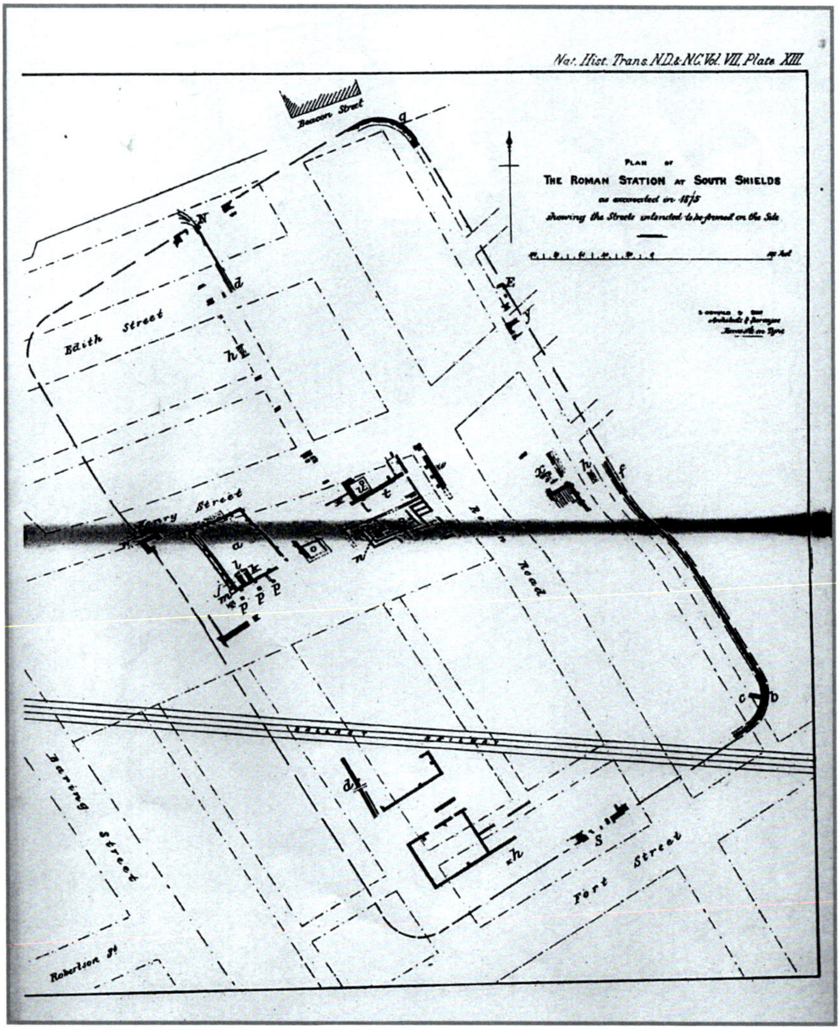

A plan printed in Dr. Hooppell's paper *On the discovery and Exploration of Roman Remains at South Shields in the Years 1875-6.*

Published in Natural History Transactions of Northumberland, Durham & Newcastle upon Tyne, 1879, (Vol VII).
It was printed over two pages, hence the grey blurred line in the centre fold of the book, whereas the repeated drawn line is the position of the ballast railway clearly shown on the 1875 map reproduced on page 2.
Reproduced by kind permission of the Natural History Society of Northumbria, Great North Museum: Hancock.

Shields Gazette and Daily Telegraph, Monday 3rd May 1875

THE ROMAN REMAINS IN SOUTH SHIELDS

Three of the four sides of the Roman Station at the Lawe have now been reached, with almost complete certainty. The western rampart was first found, soon after the excavations commenced; the eastern rampart followed; and now the southern rampart has been found, close to the embankment which was used by the ballast railway before the present low-level wagon way was formed. Indeed, the embankment runs across the south-western corner of the ramparts of the station, so that it would not be possible, without much labour and expense, to expose the whole of it, but the central portion is not interfered with by the embankment, and it is that portion which has been exposed. The workmen have uncovered the gateway, which opened from the station towards the country lying southwards, and are engaged today in following the rampart eastward and westward. A street evidently ran from the gateway, right to the centre of the forum, with branch streets leading from it on the right hand and on the left. Could sufficient funds raised excavate the whole site, it is more than probable that the whole internal arrangements of a fortified town would be brought to light. The field in which this gateway and rampart have been found is exceedingly rich in buildings. A little way beyond the gateway, to the eastward, the present ballast railway crosses the rampart so that in making the railway its contractors must have cut through both the western and southern ramparts, separating a triangular portion of the station from the remainder. During the past few days a band of volunteers has been organised by Mr. Wheatley to work in the evenings after business hours. They have found several objects of interest in particular a flint implement for cutting and a chisel or hatchet. This was found above the level of the Roman town indicating, apparently, that it was owned and used at a period subsequent to the Roman occupation, very likely a member of the tribe or nation that erected the remarkable stone table in the deserted forum, and the rude semicircular edifice, near the western rampart, on the charred ruins of Caer Urfa. There is every prospect of a crowded gathering and a most interesting meeting tomorrow evening, and we would advise those of our readers who wish to be present and have not yet provided themselves with tickets, to do so without delay.

Mr. Storey's engraving and Mr. Haggitt's photograph of the room described in the Gazette account of 13th May, which was quickly realised to be the strong room or treasury chamber of the Fort.

Sources of these images and those on the following page, see page 82.

Shields Gazette and Daily Telegraph, Thursday 13th May 1875

THE ROMAN REMAINS IN SOUTH SHIELDS.

The last few days have been productive with very interesting results at the Lawe, South Shields. The workmen have been engaged this week upon the north side of the forum. They have found the walls of a very important building, apparently of a much older date than any others previously come upon, and belonging probably to one of the very earliest buildings erected by the Romans in South Shields. They are at a great depth below the surface, and form portions of the sides of a chamber, or open square, it is not yet clear which. They are four feet thick, and composed of very massive stones which were originally clamped together with iron or lead. To one of the walls is a staircase and five massive stone steps, as regular and substantial as though they had only been laid yesterday. Several of them are deeply worn with footsteps. The bottom of the chamber, or square, is paved with large flagstones, which are level and perfect. The centre is unpaved. A very gratifying feature in this excavation remains to be noticed. The wall containing the staircase contains also the sill of a window, a circumstance we believe almost, if not quite, unique in Roman excavations in England. The remains of walls found in Roman Stations are seldom high enough to show any traces of the windows. In this instance, however, the sill is there, and more than that, portions of the jambs of the window have been found, thus enabling a very good conception to be formed of the style and character of Roman apertures for the admission of light. The sill is three feet six inches from paved floor, and the stonework of the window appears to have been four feet from side to side. The window is splayed and from holes in the inner sill appears have had iron bars. The wall in which the window and sill are constructed is of considerable length, about fourteen feet, having been fully exposed in this excavation.

Several smaller objects of much interest have been also found in this chamber or square, in particular the skull of a man with some other human bones belonging probably to one of the victims of the last destruction of the fortress. And the capitals of two square pillars of a bold and prominent design. Also a fragment of a tile, with a complete inscription upon it, similar to that of which portions have previously been found but settling beyond doubt the character of the last and most important letter which is plainly G. The whole inscription is COH. V. G., and the identity of the garrison of the station with the Fifth Cohort of the Gauls is now placed beyond doubt. The great point now remaining for

Dr. Hooppell explained this image in !879;

'Large building near the Western Rampart To the left are seen the pedestals, which appear to have once supported the pillars of the portico. There can be little doubt that the entrance was between the piers opposite the two nearest pedestals. Since the photograph was taken, the whole area not represented as excavated in the picture has been uncovered. The building was found to be very large, a rectangular oblong in form, with buttresses outside, and pavement throughout its whole extent, except in the south west corner within. The very singular pier opposite the third pedestal base was, of British, post Roman work. From that pier, along the side wall of the large building, ran one of the curious, paved footpaths, raised on pebbles from the mouth of the River, and manifestly of later date than the Roman occupation of the Station.'

antiquaries to clear up is to discover the name of the place at which that particular cohort was stationed. If that can be discovered from ancient classical records, the Roman name of South Shields will be determined beyond doubt or question.

York Herald, Saturday 29th May 1875

THE ROMAN REMAINS AT SOUTH SHIELDS.
The members of the Tyneside Naturalists' Field Club visited South Shields on Tuesday for the purpose of inspecting the underground fire in Harrison's Court, West Holborn, the collection of Roman antiquities in the Nautical College, Ocean Road and the excavations on the site of the Roman Station at the Lawe. The party, numbering about one hundred ladies and gentlemen, arrived at High Shields Station where they were met by the Rev. Dr. Hooppell, of South Shields, and other ladies and gentlemen. Dr. Hooppell conducted the party from the High Shields Station to the area devastated by the underground fire between Holborn and Commercial Road, and explained the origin and the progress of the fire, as well as the means adopted by the Corporation to prevent the fire from extending. The company next visited the Marine School where the collection of Roman antiquities found at the Lawe were exhibited and explained by Dr. Hooppell, who afterwards conducted the party to the Roman Station at the Lawe, and in a graphic manner described the principal chambers, walls, and other objects of interest brought to light by the excavations, an account of which has appeared in the columns of the Herald from time to time. The party were highly interested in the excavations and spent a considerable time in inspecting the various portions of the remains. In the evening the ladies and gentlemen adjourned to the Golden Lion Hotel, King Street, South Shields, where an excellent tea was served up. The president (Rev. G. B. Hall) presided. After some formal business had been transacted…Dr. Hooppell next gave a brief resume of the excavations for Roman remains. He said that the results of the explorations, so far as the work has proceeded, proved beyond the possibility of doubt the existence of a Roman station at the Lawe. A general desire, he said, existed that the explorations should be continued and with that object it was proposed to raise a fund of £300. If the work was continued there were hopes of finding the entrance to Recken Dyke Lane, as well as further altars and inscriptions. There was also a general feeling that a goodly portion of this station should be.

This is John Dilwyn Llewelyn, a Welsh photographer, with his mobile darkroom used to prepare plates in the field. It is from the 1850s/60s but a similar set up was probably used at the 1875 excavations in South Shields.

Touring photographers had carts but Mr. Haggitt and Mr. Charles who photographed the excavations had shops and so might have used a tent (like the one shown) to take pictures on location where the glass plates had to be prepared on site before pictures could be taken. Pictures of photographers on location are rare because of the equipment needed for photography in the field.

Portrait photography was popular in Victorian South Shields and both Mr. Charles and Mr. Haggit's shops were in Station Road near the Mill Dam.
This photograph is from the Museum of Wales.

preserved and not built over or destroyed. The Rev. Dr. Bruce said that there was no doubt that the Roman Station at South Shields, so much exposed as it was, had been greatly knocked about in ancient times. The variety of changes which the station has undergone rendered it exceedingly perplexing and puzzling to the antiquarians to properly define it and to say to which special period this and that portion of what they found belonged. If the whole of the Lawe were cleared, then they might have a chance of saying which belonged to the early and which to the latest period and which was Roman and which was Saxon. He could not help thinking that the strong chamber they had seen that day belonged to the earliest period of the Roman times, in fact, he could quite fancy that it was built in the time of Hadrian and that the treasure chest of the station was kept there. He had not seen anything like the chamber before. He wished they could find out the name of the station at South Shields, for if they did that it would tend to solve a great number of other knotty questions. Referring to the finding of inscriptions tending to show that the station was occupied by the fifth cohort of the Gauls, he said he was not satisfied with the “G” standing alone, and could not understand the Romans taking pains to use three letters to indicate “cohort " and only using the letter GI to represent "Gallorum." He had always seen it written Gallorum or Gal. However, he could not say but what Dr. Hooppell was right in reading it as Gallorum. At the conclusion votes of thanks, on the motion of Mr. J. M. Moore, were given to Rev. Dr. Hooppell, the Chairman, and to Dr. Bruce, and the interesting meeting separated. [In connection with the Roman remains on Tuesday, Mr. Grey, who superintends the excavations, found two coins in the northern excavation; one was a small bronze and the other was a good sized gold coin. A piece of Samian ware was also found.]

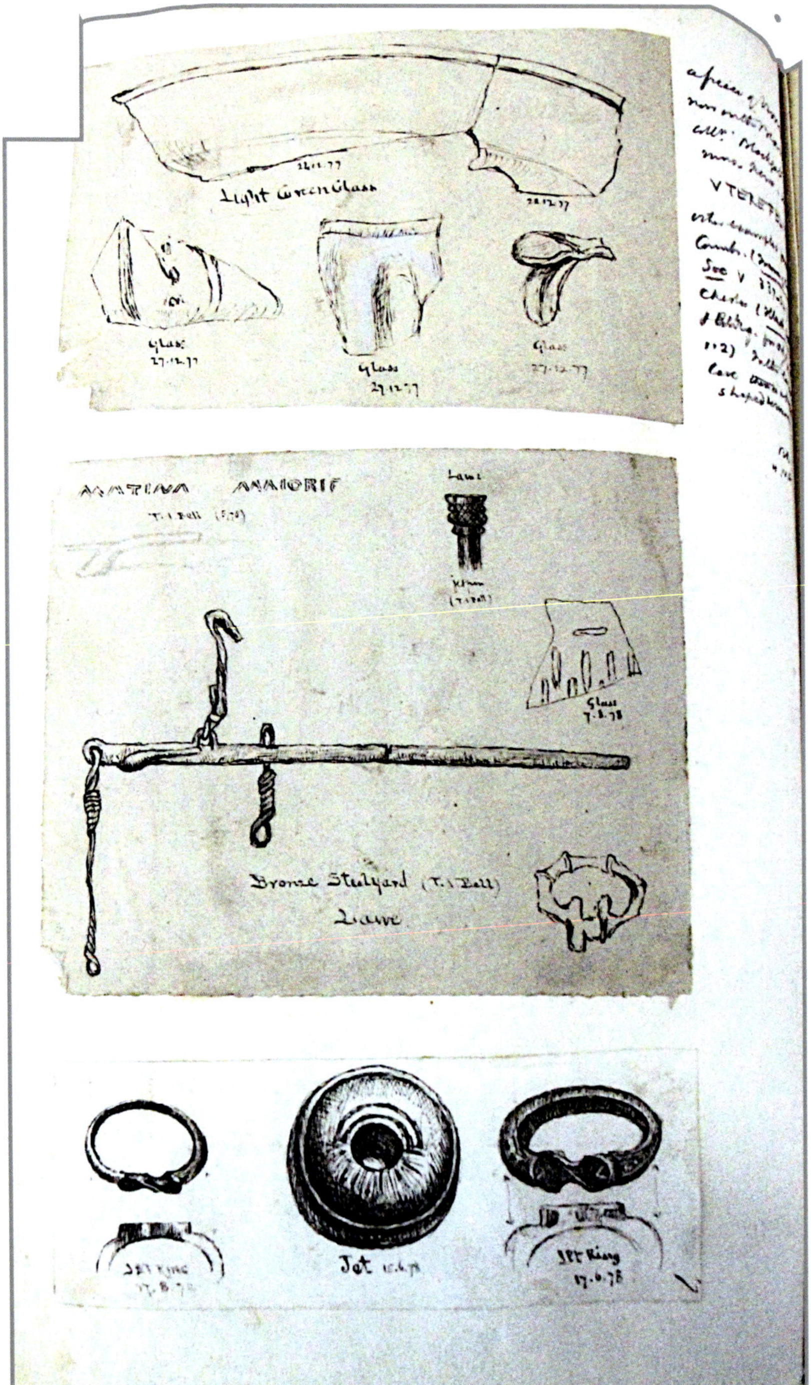

Blair Scrapbook; courtesy of South Tyneside Libraries.

Regina & Victor

A bronze ring-key from the collection of the Arbeia, South Shields Roman Fort.
Photograph courtesy of Tyne & Wear Archives & Museums.

5

This carved cameo of a bear may have once decorated the cloak of a rich and powerful man. It is carved from two contrasting layers of sardonyx, a semi-precious stone that came from India, and probably dates from the third century, perhaps from the Severan period when large numbers of lead sealings of the Imperial Household were found. They were deliberately discarded after use, but this was lost only to be found seventeen centuries later by a man prospecting for treasure on the Lawe who sold it to Robert Blair.

It is now on display at the Great North Museum: Hancock, Newcastle-upon-Tyne and nothing captures, I would suggest, the history of the Roman Fort at South Shields more than this small object.

Photograph courtesy of Tyne & Wear Archives & Museums.

Image taken from Blair Scrapbook; courtesy of South Tyneside Libraries.

In 1906 Edith Nesbit the author of *The Railway Children* published a magical story for children called *The Amulet*. In the book a group of children aided by a strange creature called a Psammead buy a broken amulet in a curiosity shop and have a series of fantastic adventures trying to find the other half. The amulet has the power to open a portal in time to allow the children to travel into the past which they do enthusiastically visiting the ancient civilizations of Babylon and Egypt, boarding a Phoenician ship at Tyre, and travelling to the mythical island of Atlantis on the eve of its destruction. The idea of time travelling seems commonplace now with blockbuster films like *Back to the Future* and the long running BBC TV series *Dr Who* featuring time travel, but in 1906 it was new and exciting catching the popular enthusiasm for H G Wells story *The Time Machine*.

Edith Nesbit rooted her story firmly in reality using her knowledge of the ancient civilizations of Egypt and Babylon to fill her account of them with authentic detail and the book was dedicated to Sir E A Wallis Budge, the keeper of Egyptian antiquities at the British Museum where she was a regular visitor. In the story the children are accompanied by an elderly Egyptologist described as a *learned gentleman* and the book makes gentle fun of the reclusive scholar who has his eyes opened by what he sees on their journeys.

The Amulet was one of the favourite books of my childhood and growing up fascinated by history I often wished I could travel back in time and see what it was really like in Victorian or Roman Britain. Of course, it's not possible but we can get close to the people of the past through their possessions, the things that they used and treasured, and that is the subject of this chapter.

There is a large cameo that was once part of Robert Blair's collection and is now on display at the Great North Museum, Newcastle. Blair documented that he bought the jewel from a prospector who found it on the site of the Roman amphitheatre on the Lawe, but it had come a long way before its owner lost it at South Shields because the semi-precious stone skilfully carved with the image of a bear originally came from India. This seems at first an astonishing fact for an artefact eighteen hundred years old yet it's not unexpected given the extent of the Roman Empire and the cosmopolitan mix of people who made up its population.

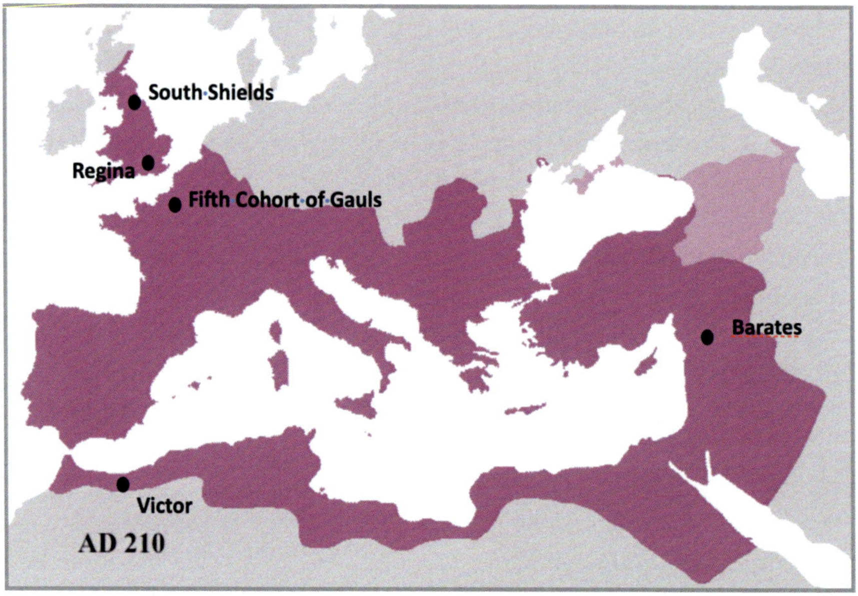

A map of the Roman Empire at its greatest extent under Septimius Severus following his Scottish campaign in 210 (Empire dark pink, dependent territories light pink).

Mohammed Muckble and Rosetta Muckble ,Yemeni seamen's boarding house proprietors, Holborn South Shields.
R*eproduced by kind permission of The Yemeni Project.*

Mohammed Muckble seamen's boarding house at East Holborn South Shields 1930.
Reproduced by kind permission of South Tyneside Libraries.

On Saturday 19th October 1878 workmen digging the foundations for an outhouse at a property in Bath Street (now Coston Drive) on the gentle southern slope of the Lawe found a fantastic example of the cultural diversity of the Empire when they unearthed a broken monument to a Roman lady called Regina, (see page 124) a real person whose presence brings the fort and the debris of its illustrious past to life. Regina, despite her name wasn't a queen; she was a former slave and the seemingly unlikely connection between her and her husband, who erected the stone, excited both antiquarians and the public alike. His name was Barates and he was a merchant from the distant city of Palmyra in Syria, a long way from South Shields. Underneath the ungrammatical Latin inscription, of the type expected in a remote frontier outpost, was his own epitaph in his native language of Aramaic which surprised many people, even in a seaport like South Shields whose ships in 1878 went round the world carrying the commerce of a new global empire.

The discovery of Barates' monument to his beloved wife Regina who died at the age of thirty would have been less surprising a generation after its discovery. By the end of the nineteenth century many Yemeni seamen had settled in South Shields, married local girls, and built a community in the Holborn area on the riverside; so their strange foreign writing, albeit Arabic not Aramaic, was a familiar sight in the town. The opening of the Suez Canal in 1869 and the establishment of coaling stations at Aden for steamships passing up and down the Red Sea brought Arab stokers to Shields where some came ashore, set up business as keepers of boarding houses for Muslim seamen and became part of the identity of the town. Pictures of Yemeni men with their British wives have a strong parallel with the story of Barates and Regina and both make a powerful contribution to the identity of South Shields as a cosmopolitan place with worldwide connections.

The presence of the Syrian merchant Barates at Roman South Shields needs a little more explanation as it would be wrong to assume that just because the Roman Empire was racially and culturally diverse the presence of a Syrian on the North East Coast of England was unremarkable. The fort on the Lawe was built in the middle of the second century some thirty years after the completion of Hadrian's Wall. Its first and to date only definite garrison was the Fifth Cohort of Gauls whose role was probably to police

A drawing by Blair of a lead sealing of the Imperial Household of Septimius Severus and his sons.
Blair Scrapbook; courtesy of South Tyneside Libraries.

A lead sealing of the Imperial Household of Septimius Severus and his sons found on the Lawe.
Photograph courtesy of Tyne & Wear Archives & Museums.

Coins of the Emperors (L to R) Septimius Severus, Geta, and Caracalla found in modern excavations inside the fort, South Shields.
Picture courtesy of Tyne & Wear Archives & Museums.

the coast and the lowlands between the Tyne and the Wear and deal with any incursions. Things changed with the arrival of the Emperor Septimius Severus in AD 208 when the fort was rebuilt and enlarged and took on a new role as a supply base for Severus' invasion of Scotland when it was for a time the focus of a huge military enterprise. Lead sealings of the Imperial household found on the Lawe during the 1875 excavation suggest that the Emperor and his entourage probably passed through South Shields during this high-water mark of the town's Roman history, but the fort's moment in the limelight on the stage of world history didn't last. Severus died at York on 4th February AD 211 after successfully occupying the central lowland and his son Caracalla soon abandoned his father's gains and withdrew to the line of the Wall unable and unwilling to hold the territory in the midst of a deadly power struggle with his brother Geta. The brothers passed through Shields on their way home after their father's death and the first Roman find from the town, an altar dredged up from the river Tyne in the seventeenth century, (see page 78) records the gratitude of the citizens of Lugudunum, the Roman name of the fort on the Lawe at the time, for the safe return of the joint emperors Geta and Caracalla to Rome with the ashes of their father. They might well have returned safely but soon afterwards Caracalla had Geta murdered and ruled alone as a brutal tyrant until AD 217 when he was also assassinated. The Empire reached its maximum extent under Severus and after the retreat from Caledonia the role of the fort on the Lawe changed again, although with the need to defend the new frontier it became an important regional supply base.

South Shields is a long way from Rome but there is evidence of the deadly struggle for power within the Severan family in the finds from the fort. The emperor Septimius Severus was born in what is now Libya while his intelligent and ambitious wife Julia Domna was the younger daughter of the hereditary high priest of the sun god Elagabalus at the cult centre of Emesa. They wanted to establish a lasting dynasty but in the event, the succession following Severus's death in AD 211, was anything but orderly. Caracalla with the help of his mother seized power in a ruthless coup. Julia Domna feared Geta was too weak to secure her husband's legacy and lured him to his death in her chambers where he was murdered by Caracalla's personal bodyguards, the Praetorian Guard. Caracalla ruled with Julia's support as the heir to his father, undertaking a brutal purge of Geta's supporters until AD 217 when he was also assassinated by a member of the guard and

A terra-cotta head vase in the Great North Museum: Hancock, Newcastle which may represent Julia Domna. Found at Chester-le-Street.
Photograph courtesy of Tyne & Wear Archives & Museums.

A large inscribed stone marking the installation of a new water supply at the fort in the year 222 that was discovered in 1893 in three pieces by workmen digging foundations for Baring Street Schools. On display In the Arbeia South Shields Roman Fort.
Photograph courtesy of Tyne & Wear Archives & Museums.

The removal of names from monuments was known as *damnatio memoriae* ***literally condemnation of memory, an official procedure which was intended to erase a person from history.*** ***(See further illustrations on page 192.)***

Julia Domna committed suicide. After a short interlude when Macrinus the prefect of the Praetorian Guard ruled as emperor the Severan dynasty was restored by Julia Domna's sister Julia Maesa, who arranged for her grandson Elagabalus to become emperor with the support of the army. Elagabalus was just thirteen when he was acclaimed emperor by the third legion and rthe power lay with his mother Julia Soaemias and grandmother Julia Maesa who were the real rulers of Rome. Elagabalus was an effeminate young man obsessed with introducing a new religion who inspired little confidence in the legions and he and his mother were murdered after a mutiny by the Praetorian Guard, orchestrated by Julia Maesa in favour of her other grandson Alexander.

Alexander Severus was just fourteen when he was proclaimed emperor by the Praetorian Guard but real power again lay with his mother Julia Mamaea who restored some order to the empire after the chaotic rule of Elagabalus. An inscription found at South Shields during an excavation for a boiler room at Baring Street School marked the accession of Alexander in AD 222 by dedicating a new water supply for the fort to him. (See further illustrations on page 192.) Alexander's name was removed from the inscription following his assassination by soldiers dissatisfied with his leadership during a campaign in Gaul. His mother Julia Mamaea, who was with him in the field, was killed with her son in his tent. The manipulative Julia Maesa, the only one of the Severan women to die of natural causes, had passed away some years earlier in Rome.

The Roman Empire like the British was built on slavery. The role of slavery in Rome was however quite different from the British where one race enslaved another but kept slaves out of sight and out of mind far away from mainstream society. Slavery helped to create the wealth of Britain, but it wasn't visible in British towns. In Roman Britain slavery was everywhere and couldn't be ignored.

Barates' monument to Regina records that she was his freedwoman and wife. We don't know how Regina, a member of the Catuvellaunian tribe from Kent, lost her freedom or came to the remote northern frontier but monuments to former slaves are common throughout the Empire. At first slaves predominantly came through conquest and slavery was a way of assimilating people to Roman rule. Later there was much less opportunity to

A reconstruction of Barates' monument to Regina showing her hair styled with ringlets in a manner which was fashionable in Palmyra at this time.

enslave large numbers of people, and slaves had to be home born, or bought in from abroad. Home born slaves were always preferred and Regina might have been was sold into slavery by her parents. She would have found conditions in the north very different from Kent where the Roman way of life was well established.

Even now Regina remains something of an enigma. Superficially she is represented on her tombstone as a Roman lady but appearances can be deceptive. Her monument has an Aramaic inscription as well as the usual Latin text and the idealised image presented to us on her tombstone was influenced by the culture of a city far away from Britain. Barates came from the ancient city of Palmyra one of the political and cultural centres of the Middle East. He calls her his freedwoman *and* wife in the Latin inscription highlighting the ambiguity of her status in Roman society. Slaves had no control over their own life, could own nothing, and lived with the constant threat of physical and sexual abuse. Freed slaves by economic necessity often maintained a close relationship with their former owner and his family, but it is unlikely that owners and former slaves could ever have been regarded socially as equals let alone man and wife.

Barates clearly had a point to make in the Latin inscription. Slave owners often freed their slaves on their deathbed but Barates went further. In the Aramaic inscription he simply says she is his freedwoman but in his homeland, in Palmyra, the meaning of the image on her monument is clear. She is a housewife with the symbols of her status, a distaff and spindle, in her hand, and an oversized jewel box representing wealth and beauty by her side. If Barates did grant Regina her freedom and declare her to be his wife on her deathbed then her tombstone, surely South Shields greatest Roman treasure, is a monument to a great love story in history. It is a tale that deserves to be told by a Dante or Shakespeare and then Barates and Regina could stand alongside Dante and Beatrice and Romeo and Juliet as one of the most famous couples in history.

Barates' monument to Regina showing the inscription in Latin with the further inscription in Aramaic below. She may been defaced by early Christians who believed her to be a pagan idol, but there is no proof.
Photograph courtesy of Tyne & Wear Archives & Museums.

Shields Gazette and Daily Telegraph, Saturday 7th December 1878

THE ANCIENT TOMBSTONE IN SOUTH SHIELDS

If the antiquaries of the future happen to discover in Kashgar the tomb of a native woman who had been the wife of a Zulu soldier in the English service they would no doubt be impressed by the wide extent of the English Empire. Here they would say, is an African warrior, led by the natives of an island washed by the Atlantic to fight and to marry on the debateable land between China, Russia, and Cashmere. We have not yet moved African troops into these distant regions, though no one can say what we may soon attempt. A precedent for mixture and movement of races at least extraordinary which ventured to imagine has been discovered in a funeral inscription near South Shields. The amazing extent of the Roman Empire is illustrated by a sepulchre which has been puzzling the British Archaeological Association and the learned in general.

Some workmen were digging a few weeks ago in Bath Street, at South Shields, when they lighted on a great carved stone, lying flat on the ground a stone, highly ornamented. A female figure represented seated under a pediment supported by two Corinthian columns. Her face has unluckily been knocked off, but in her hand she holds flowers, and basket of fruit lies at her feet. The whole work, as described, seems rather more ornate than the Greek sepulchral pillars and slabs which are tolerably familiar to anyone who has ever looked in a museum. In these pieces the singular calmness with which the Greeks viewed death is denoted by the composure of attitude and expression the figures represented. A woman takes little article from her maid, and stands like one about to leave the house. A man caresses his dog or man and woman clasp hands in what may be the most tranquil of farewells or the least passionate of recognitions in the next world. The woman whose effigy has been found at South Shields is apparently represented in no significant attitude. The effigy tells nothing of the faith of those who buried her but the inscription, gives a great deal of very mixed and rather dubious information. There are Latin words and words in Oriental writing. The Latin words have been deciphered with more or less success. The husband of Regina (for that was her name), who lies under the sculptured red sandstone, knew about as much of Latin as our Sepoys may know of English.

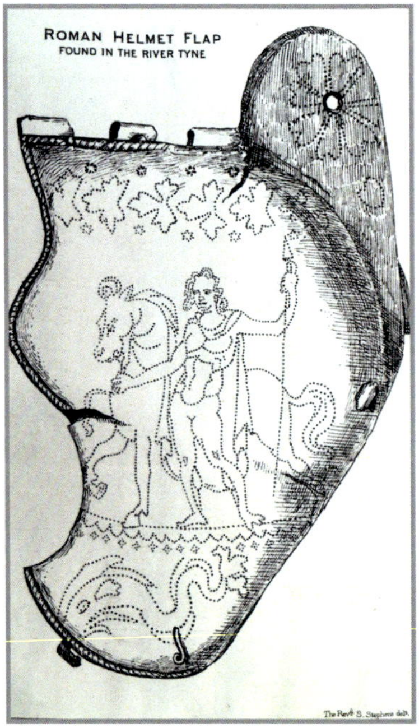

Bronze helmet cheek piece of an auxiliary cavalryman found on Herd Sand South Shields in 1885, possibly from a shipwreck dating from Severus's Scottish campaign.

An engraving from the Blair Scrapbook. The name at the bottom of the image is Rev'd S Stephens.
Courtesy of South Tyneside Libraries.

Below is a photograph of the cheek-piece which is on display at the Great North Museum: Hancock.
Photograph courtesy of Tyne & Wear Archives & Museums.

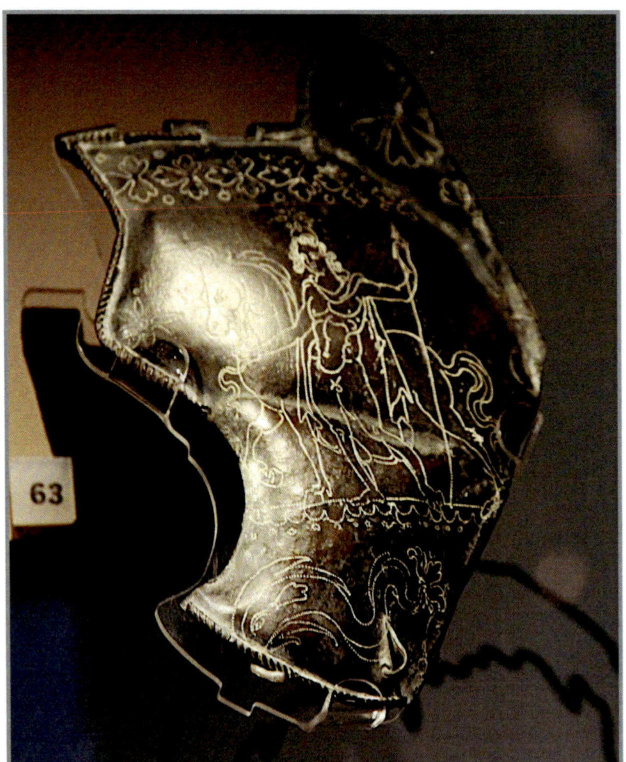

> The monument gives out that it was raised DM.—to the manes of Regina. The next words are exceedingly ungrammatical in that their blunders cannot be described in English at all. The ancient epitaph writer made more mistakes than the words admit "of." Construed as haphazard, they seem to mean that Regina was Catavallaunlan by birth, and that she had been the freed woman and the wife of one Barates, of Palmyra. Palmyra in the Desert was as much one extreme as northern England was at the other end of the Roman Empire. The two points from which Regina and Barates were brought together mark the farthest span of Rome's colossal grasp. The Syrian husband added words of his own Oriental language to the rude Latin which was taught by his Italian masters. A Syrian inscription in northern England is almost as strangely placed as the picture writing of Canadian Redskin would be on a grave in Ceylon. The tomb of this slave is all that remains to speak of the wonderful mixture of the races that Rome hurried from every point of the compass to work her will.

Rome had a professional army. Professional soldiers don't want to die gloriously in battle, they want to survive and collect their pay. Bravery is certainly an essential part of a professional soldier's character but the desire for personal glory isn't, or shouldn't be, because success in the field depends on organisation, training and strategy. The Romans fought tribesmen who believed a glorious and heroic death in battle guaranteed them an eternity of celebration with their comrades in the afterlife. Such tribesmen might have seemed like an invincible force to simple farmers; indeed, intimidation and fear were an important part of their tactics but faced with the disciplined Roman Legions they had little chance of victory without the advantage of overwhelming numerical superiority. Their virtues of strength and courage paradoxically were very much a part of Roman culture and they were celebrated in the games in the same way that we celebrate achievement and determination in sport. Victory in the arena needed few of the qualities that made Rome a military superpower but images of gladiators which were everywhere in Roman society somehow came to symbolise Rome's military might even if, like the blockbuster action films that attracts large audiences now, they bore little resemblance to reality. The Emperor Caracalla himself fought in the games in staged contests that could only have one outcome because he recognised the power of what they stood for, the myth of heroic combat, even if his performances fooled no one.

Ivory clasp knife handle carved in the shape of a gladiator found on the Lawe at South Shields
From Robert Blair's collection.
On display at the Great North Museum: Hancock.
Photograph courtesy of Tyne & Wear Archives & Museums. Engraving from the Blair Scrapbook; courtesy of South Tyneside Libraries.

Lower part of a vase representing the head of a negro gladiator; thought to be one of a series. From Robert Blair's collection but the detailed provenance is unknown.
On display at the Great North Museum: Hancock.
Photograph courtesy of Tyne & Wear Archives & Museums.

A modern gladiator: The heavy weight champion of the world, Muhammed Ali, visits South Shields in 1977.
Photograph by kind permission of Fred Muddittt, Fietscher Fotos Ltd and Family.

Just as in 1875 people in South Shields decorated their houses with mass produced engravings of Biblical scenes by the popular local artist John Martin and collected decorative glass and pottery that cheaply reproduced expensive fashionable pieces hand made for the aristocracy, the Romans had their own mass produced consumer goods. A wealthy Roman lady might have had the beautiful blue vase depicting the head of negro gladiator (illustrated opposite) in her house, while some of the walls would probably have been decorated with murals of dramatic scenes of gladiatorial combat and even the ivory handle of her little household knife could have been carved with the likeness of a gladiator. The survival of the fragile blue glass head, a fragment of a larger vessel is remarkable: it was mass produced in moulded blown glass and was probably one of a set, There are no records of how it came into his possession and it might not even have come from South Shields but the 1875 excavators did find many fragments of mass produced Samian ware pottery decorated with moulded images of gladiators, chariots, birds, and animals and other fashionable motifs. (See pages 152 & 153)

The blue glass vase has a recognisable negro face: in 1977 the heavyweight champion of the world Muhammed Ali came to South Shields and crowds filled the streets to catch a glimpse of him. The face on the vase could almost be of Ali, a modern gladiator if ever there was one, but Roman gladiators weren't celebrities they were slaves. Professional boxing was a route out of poverty for Muhammed Ali but for most gladiators it led nowhere except to an early death. Personal slaves like Regina and Victor the Moor whose monument stands next to hers in the Arbeia Roman Fort Museum were different: they could and did gain the affection of their masters and for them the future could be bright even if the relationship between them was, at the start, at least abusive and exploitative. Gladiators were abstract symbols whose deaths didn't matter as long as they died bravely and entertained the crowd. Regina and Victor were individuals who mattered a lot to their former owners and that's why their memorials still move people with the sadness of their deaths eighteen centuries after they happened.

The Roman Army was at the heart of the Empire: its needs were the main driver of the economy; it was the principal route to advancement for the politically and socially ambitious and it was a way of life for its troops.

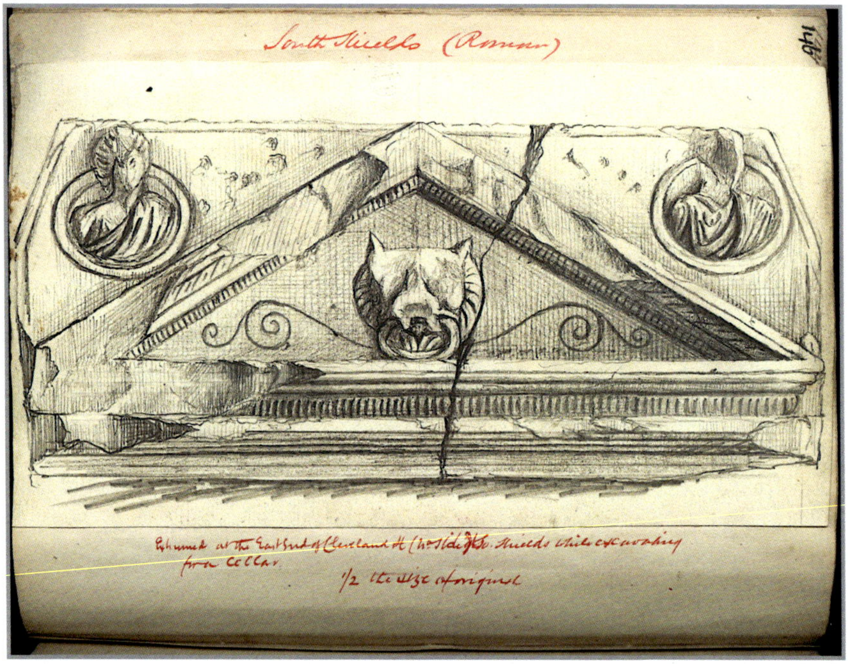

Robert Blair's drawing of the pediment section of Victor's tombstone.
This was discovered in 1881 and four years later was reunited with its base.
Drawing reproduced by kind permission of the Northumberland Archives, Woodhorn.

A reconstruction of the monument erected by Numerianus to his freedman Victor the Moor.

Newspaper reports at the time of its discovery in 1885 described the young man whose face is reconstructed here as an African prince but in fact he was the cavalryman's former slave and the nature of their relationship was ignored in contemporary antiquarian discussions of the find.

A monument to a young slave called Victor found in two parts in Cleveland Street, near Bath Street where Regina's monument was found, gives a unique insight into a soldier's life. The top was found by workmen digging the foundations of a house in Cleveland Street on 25th February 1881. It is a finely carved piece of stone decorated with a lion's head but it was otherwise an unremarkable addition to the large number of stone fragments unearthed on the Lawe during the excavations and it passed into the hands of Robert Blair for safe keeping without any ceremony. The workmen must have missed the lower larger part which was found almost four years later on 8th January 1885 in a pile of rubble being cleared to lay paving stones. Reunited the two parts completed a monument which told the story of a freed slave similar to Regina's but involving the relationship between a Roman cavalryman and his young slave, probably his groom, Victor the Moor.

The monument was erected by Numerianus, a soldier from a cavalry regiment stationed at Condercum (Benwell) about fifteen miles up the Tyne from South Shields. It is likely that he originally brought the young boy from North Africa to be his servant but it is clear from the inscription that their relationship went far beyond that:

To the divine shades of Victor. He was by nation a Moor, he lived twenty years, and was the freed man of Numerianus, a horseman of the first ala of Asturians, who most affectionately followed (his former slave) to the grave. (Translated by Dr. Collingwood Bruce)

Victor's monument records that like Regina he was a former slave although his story is probably less of a love story and more of a lesson about the realities of life in the Roman army. Victor could have been Numerianus' groom, the Moors were famous horsemen, and he would have been the ideal person to look after the cavalryman's horses and their equipment. He would have lived in a barracks with the other slaves and his relationship with his master could have been purely formal but the inscription on his tombstone leaves us in no doubt that Numerianus had a real affection for the young man. Legally before Caracalla's reforms in AD 211 Roman soldiers weren't allowed to marry, although no doubt many would have had unofficial *wives*. Roman men were free to enjoy sex with male partners without legal or moral censure so long as their partners were their political

The monument to Victor the Moor on display at the Arbeia Roman Fort and Museum South Shields The main part was found in a heap of builders rubble 100 yards away from where the top was found by workmen digging the foundations of a house four years later and could easily have been lost after probably being dug up at the same time and dumped.

Photograph courtesy of Tyne & Wear Archives & Museums.

or social inferiors and some, like Numerianus, could have preferred attractive young slaves like Victor who were available and couldn't produce children. Roman soldiers retired at about 45 and were lucky to live much longer so they didn't have a lot of time for family life and there is every reason to believe that Numerianus' feelings for Victor, expressed on his monument, were real and heartfelt, even though the relationship may seem today like abuse and exploitation. Slaves couldn't be freed until they were thirty years old so Victor was probably freed on his death bed as a final token of his master's affection.

Shields Gazette and Daily Telegraph, Thursday 27th January 1881

THE ROMAN REMAINS AT SOUTH SHIELDS

Another addition has been made to the number of Roman relics discovered at South Shields. While digging the foundations of a house at the east end of Cleveland Street, a day or two since, the workmen came upon the top of a Roman tombstone, on which is a pediment of very good workmanship. In each angle above the pediment is a well-carved head, one of them that of a female; the other is so much disfigured that it cannot be ascertained whether it represents a male or female. The centre of the pediment is the front view of a lion's head, with a ring through its mouth. These figures are in high relief. The other parts of the stone are carved a style of workmanship similar to that on the Palmyrene tombstone now at the Public Library, and found some time ago in the vicinity of Cleveland Street. The stone is in the possession of Mr. Blair, solicitor, King Street.

Shields Daily News, Tuesday 20th January 1885

DISCOVERY OF AN ANCIENT BURIAL STONE AT SOUTH SHIELDS

While some workmen were engaged in making excavations on the site of the Roman remains near Livingstone Street, South Shields, they discovered an interesting relic in the form of mural oblong square stone. The stone has a very complete figure upon it, and also a Roman inscription. The top part of the stone was found some time ago. The stone is supposed to have reference to the death and burial of an African Prince who had come over to this country or to the Roman army.

Pages from Blair Scrapbook displaying his drawings or photographs of small finds, all dated post 1875, and the names of the collectors who had bought them.
Blair Scrapbook; courtesy of South Tyneside Libraries.

Roman South Shields was like the modern town a cosmopolitan place. The presence of Numerianus, Victor, Barates and Regina on the Lawe reflects the racial and cultural diversity of the Roman Empire which could be seen even in a population of a rather remote frontier outpost on the edge of the civilized world. It is not surprising that a soldier like Numerianus could be found at a military base. He was a member of the Ala of Asturians stationed at Benwell a little to the west of Newcastle upriver from South Shields. There is no evidence that the Asturians were ever stationed at South Shields but it was not unusual for soldiers to be sent away from their main base for long periods and the presence of the cavalry man and his groom at Shields is not remarkable. Barates occupation is unknown but he came from a distant city at the opposite end of the Empire and probably wasn't a soldier. He may have been a merchant or a trader which could explain his presence at what was an important regional supply base and port on a strategic and defended frontier.

The civilian settlement next to the fort wouldn't have amounted to much at first but it grew into a lively centre for trade and travel, familiar to soldiers from along the line of the wall, home to a variety of merchants and manufacturers, and even visited by Emperors on their way back to Rome. Typically the settlement would be along the road outside the fort, but at Shields it must also have grown up along the riverside on the site which was the core of South Shields and remain undiscovered under the modern town. The windswept heights of the Lawe were unoccupied for more than a thousand years after the fall of Rome but the history of the riverside was very different.

The importance of the east coast shipping route in the later years of the Empire can be inferred by the chain of signal stations along the Yorkshire coast which were built to warn shipping of danger from raiders and act as refuges for the small garrisons in the case of attacks from the sea. The most northerly of the known beacons on the Huntcliff at Saltburn can be seen from the Lawe and it is likely that South Shields was part of this system as well as being the destination for some of the shipping it protected. The range and quality of the finds from the excavations on the Lawe illustrate the importance of trade to the economy of the Roman Empire and the large strong rooms found at the fort are evidence of its value locally.

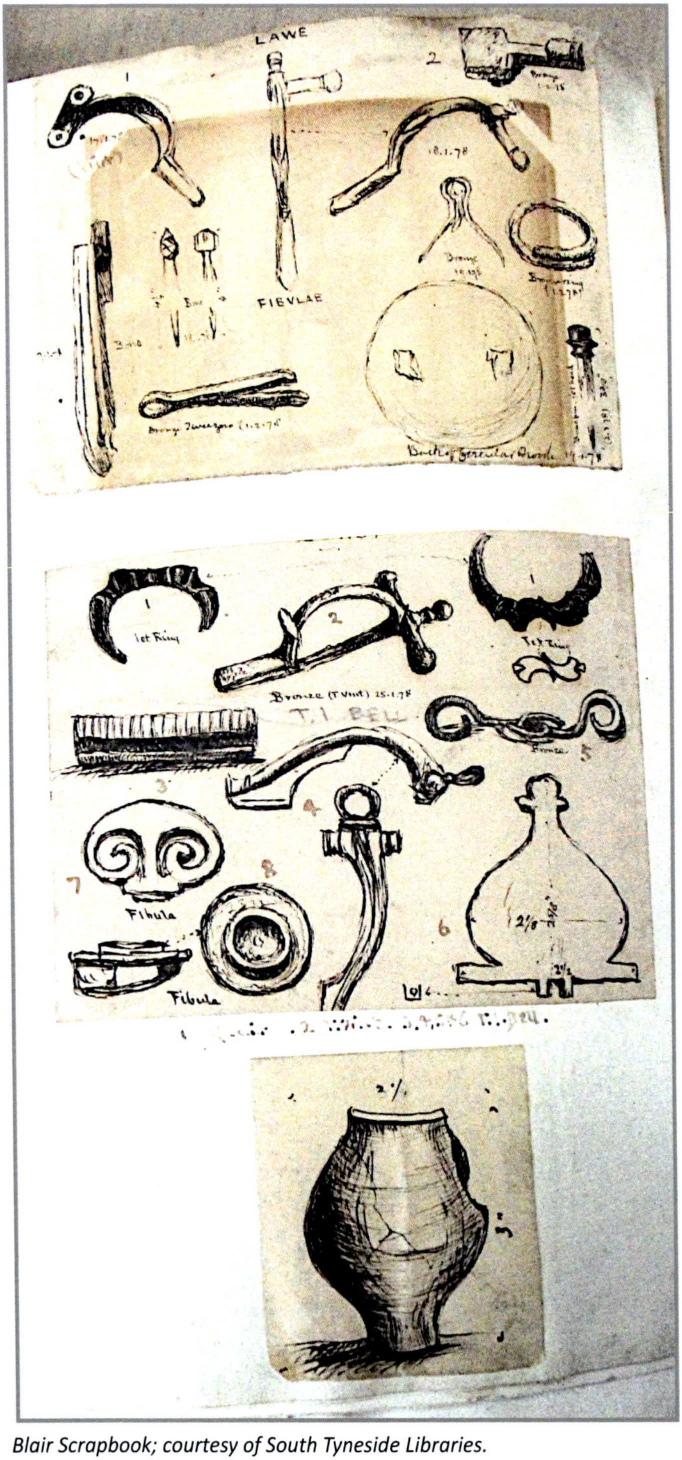

Blair Scrapbook; courtesy of South Tyneside Libraries.

Blair's Scrapbook

A drawing of a small bronze brooch from Robert Blair's Scrapbook.
Picture courtesy of South Tyneside Libraries.

6

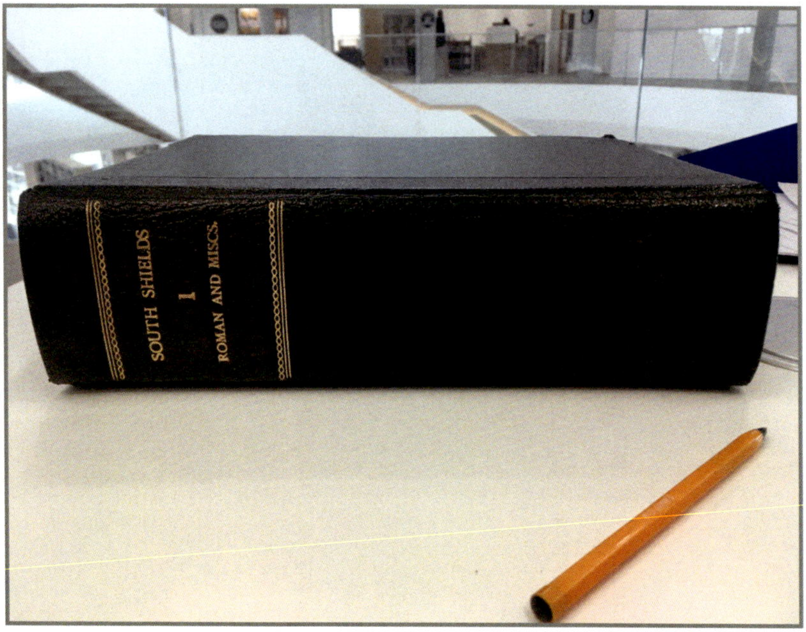

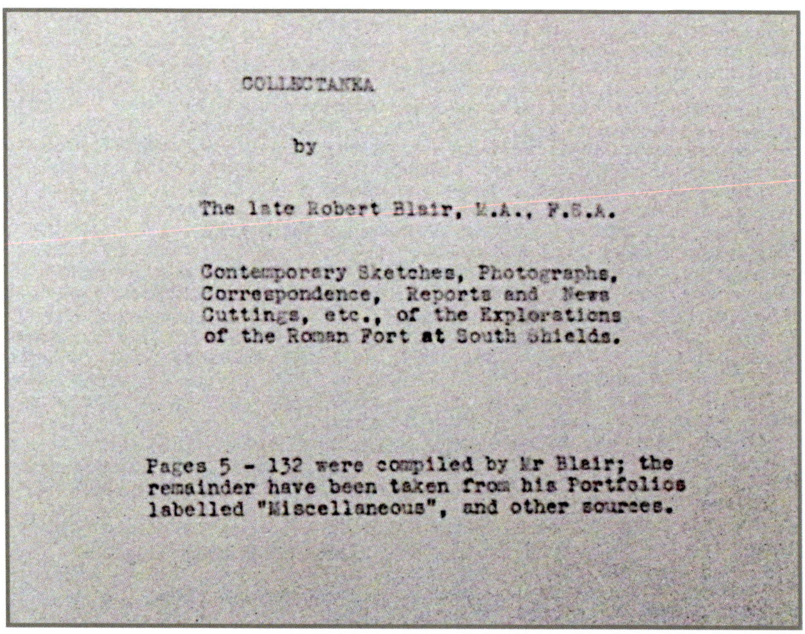

COLLECTANEA

by

The late Robert Blair, M.A., F.S.A.

Contemporary Sketches, Photographs, Correspondence, Reports and News Cuttings, etc., of the Explorations of the Roman Fort at South Shields.

Pages 5 - 132 were compiled by Mr Blair; the remainder have been taken from his Portfolios labelled "Miscellaneous", and other sources.

Robert Blair put part of the scrapbook together himself and then various other items were added after his death by the local historian Amy Flagg, who also added an index and deposited the large scrapbook in the South Shields Library as a resource for the people of the town.
Blair Scrapbook; courtesy of South Tyneside Libraries.

Mr. Blair's scrapbook, photographed opposite, resides in the local history section of The Word containing many of the newspaper articles and drawings of finds already shown in this book and those to be seen later in this chapter.

Robert Blair was born at the Lawe, South Shields, on the 8th June, 1844. In the 1851 census Robert was six years old and his family live at 34 Lawe, South Shields. His mother was Jane Blair and his father James Blair, his brother Edward was four and his sister Elizabeth a year old. Robert was born into a proud family of pilots. Robert's father's occupation was given on the census as *'sea pilot'*. The 1841 census gives information about Robert's grandfather, after whom he is named, and lists his profession as a pilot. Robert's great grandfather, James, was also a pilot.

The following extracts are from Robert Blair's obituary written by Robert Oxberry on the 26th September 1923 and published in *Volume XX of the Third Series of Archaeologia Aeliana*.

> Robert's elementary education began at a dame school, whence after a stay of about twelve months, he graduated to a small private school at the northern termination of Mile End Road overlooking the river Tyne. The instruction he received here included a little Latin, in addition to the ordinary subjects taught at such schools…in the 1850s. He was only thirteen years of age when he left to commence work as an office boy with Thomas Salmon, solicitor, one of the leading men in public life in South Shields at that time.
>
> Robert Blair served his articles with John Salmon, the son and partner of Thomas Salmon, and was admitted a solicitor in the Michaelmas Term of 1874. Shortly after this he commenced practice on his own account at South Shields, devoting himself chiefly to the conveyancing branch of his profession, having a dislike for police court work.
>
> It is not the slightest bit derogatory to his merits as a man, when we say that he was not as prosperous as he might have been if he had devoted his attention to the affairs of the present, and given less time to the study of the things of the days that are past.

Photograph and engraving of Robert Blair. (1844-1923)

The photograph above is of Harton Lodge. It was demolished in 1931 when Marsden Road was widened. It stood at the crossroads of Harton Back Lane (renamed Marsden Road) and Sunderland Road to the south of the Ship Inn in Harton Village. The corner of the Ship Inn can be seen on the left of the photograph.

The area that part of the garden and house occupied is now a small park seating area, behind the bus stop.
Reproduced by kind permission of the Shields Gazette.

His work for Mr. Salmon provided him with valuable training but Robert Blair was set on further educating himself as were many at that time. Throughout the 1860s he attended night classes and lectures at the newly built (1859) South Shields Mechanics' Institute on Ocean Road, (later to become the Library and Museum). He took courses in Latin, French and other subjects, attended historical and scientific lectures and taught himself to draw.

It would seem safe to assume that many of the evening lectures Blair attended were given by Rev. Hooppell, the Headmaster of The Winterbottom Marine School. Maybe it was at this point that their friendship and mutual interest in the study of antiquities was realised.

Robert Blair's practice was in the Exchange Buildings on the corner of King Street and Russell Street in South Shields, next to the town's post office and beside the police station and courts in Keppel Street.

According to the 1861 census Robert Blair's family had moved from 34 Lawe to 3 Beacon Street. In 1866 Robert married Elizabeth Eleanor Watt, daughter of James Watt, a South Shields shipowner. On his marriage in 1866 to Elizabeth the newly weds may have moved directly to Harton Village, certainly in the 1871 census they are living at Harton Lodge. Robert is now 25 years old, Elizabeth 23 years old and they have three young sons James who is three, Herbert two and Ernest one month old. At that time they have a live in servant, Hannah Boyd, who was eighteen years of age.

It would appear that Harton Lodge remained the home of Blair and his family until his death in 1923 at the age of seventy-seven. They had a family of thirteen children, two of whom died in infancy. Elizabeth Blair died in 1905 and Blair married his second wife, Mary, in 1907, and she died in 1945. They are buried in St Peter's Churchyard directly opposite the family home, Harton Lodge, Harton Village.

Blair became a member of the Society of Antiquaries of Newcastle-upon-Tyne on 7th January 1874 a few months before he completed his articles and prior to the commencement of the campaign to save the Roman fort on the Lawe. He was 29 years old. John Clayton presided at the meeting when he was unanimously elected.

Above are images of the front and reverse of a medal which the Society of Antiquaries in Newcastle-upon-Tyne struck to commemorate Robert Blair's distinguished service to the Society.
The medal is now in the possession of the Museum in South Shields.
Reproduced by kind permission of Tyne & Wear Archives & Museums.

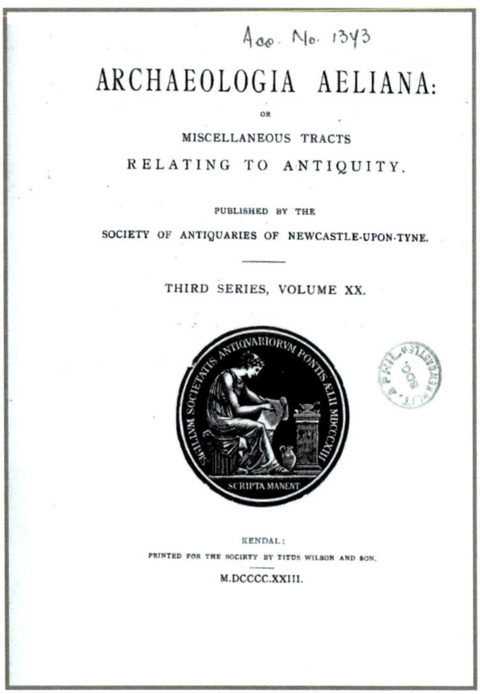

ARCHAEOLOGIA AELIANA:

OR

MISCELLANEOUS TRACTS

RELATING TO ANTIQUITY.

PUBLISHED BY THE

SOCIETY OF ANTIQUARIES OF NEWCASTLE-UPON-TYNE.

THIRD SERIES, VOLUME XX.

SIGILLUM SOCIETATIS ANTIQVARIORVM PONTIS AELII MDCCCXIII

SCRIPTA MANENT

KENDAL:

PRINTED FOR THE SOCIETY BY TITUS WILSON AND SON.

M.DCCCC.XXIII.

The** Archaeologia Aeliana **is the journal of the Society of Antiquaries of Newcastle-upon-Tyne, which Blair edited for forty years of his life. The Society of Antiquaries of Newcastle-upon-Tyne, the oldest provincial antiquarian society in England, was founded in 1813.
The Society's library and meetings are currently held in the Great North Museum: Hancock, Newcastle-upon-Tyne.
Reproduced by kind permission of the Literary and Philosophical Society, Newcastle.

Mr. Blair was not appointed secretary until 31st January 1883 but from October 1881 the minutes are in his hand. He introduced a much needed change. For some past time the minute book had been kept in a very perfunctory fashion. A line or two recording that a meeting had been held and that a paper had been read was deemed sufficient.........The two or three lines grew, under Mr. Blair's control, to as many pages. All vital matters were chronicled... He was keen and willing and at the end of his first year of office Dr. Hodgkin, who had been appointed editor at the same meeting as Mr. Blair had been elected secretary, moved that Mr. Blair take his place as editor because, as he frankly confessed, though he nominally occupied the position the whole of the editorial work had been done by his colleague... ... and our late senior secretary and editor was accordingly on 30th January 1884, installed in the dual office which he held without intermission until the day of his death.

For the most part it was quiet, unseen work, but none the less work that was absolutely essential to the maintenance of the Society as a useful and effective institution. Only an enthusiast could have done what Mr. Blair did as joint secretary and editor.

A seventeenth century bell or a sixteenth century chalice was as attractive to him, from an antiquarian standpoint, as a coin of Hadrian. As he was first and chiefly a Roman student he did not scorn the mediaevalist on the one hand or the stone-age investigator on the other.

There is probably not a town or village in the two northern counties, where an object of historical or archaeological interest is to be found that he did not visit....His diary is full of references to these excursions, many of them taken on foot - for in his younger days he was a vigorous walker...Then there were the cheap excursion trains that the railway company ran at that time. These were a boon that he relished and regularly utilised... ...a few examples from his diaries will show how far he was willing to travel and what trouble he was willing to take in his search for first hand information.

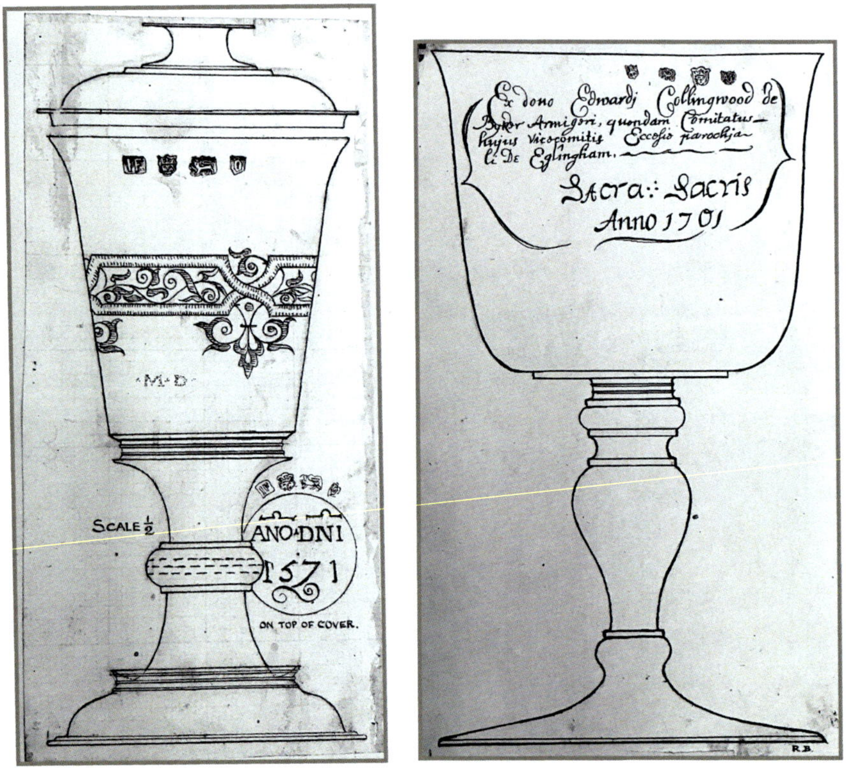

Drawings of silver chalices which Robert Blair made for his article on the Communion Plate and Bells of the Diocese of Newcastle.
Reproduced by kind permission of the Natural History Society of Northumbria, Great North Museum: Hancock.

Reproduced by kind permission of Northumberland Archives, Woodhorn.

On Monday 24th September 1877 Blair had arranged to meet Dr Bruce at Falstone and we read this account in his diary:

> "Rose at 5-40 & left Otterburn at 6 with the view of catching 1st train at Bellingm. Ar. a stiff climb of the fells betn. the Rede & No. Tyne, found when abt. 3 m. from Bellm. that I had only then abt. half an hour: immediately diverged by road to Tarset, at wh. pl. had mortifn. to see train departing, then by way of fell road to N. of N. Tyne to Falstone, where kept prisoner for abt. 3 hrs. until my shoe repaired, then to the rectory to see coll. of the coins of the late vicar. Bot. sevl. late English ones. Left with Dr. Bruce per last train."

On Whit Sunday 16th May 1880, Robert Blair recorded in his diary, using his unique abbreviations:

> "Left S.S. per 9-35 a.m. train for N'Castle. Walked thence via Scotswood, Lemington, Newburn (fine old ch. & pleasant ch.yd., from wh. fine view of Ryton, &c) & Throckley to Heddon-on-the-Wall. Very unpretentious lookg. ch. (with bell turret), exterior; but fine interior with Norman arch, zig-zag ornt. in chancel & origl. groined roof. Spent an hour in ch. yd. & walked thence to N'Castle, by mily. way catchg. the 7-10 train to S.S. Heard cuckoo for first time this season."

While taking every opportunity to travel the length and breadth of the local counties and beyond to record whatever antiquities there were in the days before easy photography Robert honed his drawing skills to record his finds. Filling small sketchbooks with what quickly became exquisite drawings.

> Blair was elected a member of the Surtees Society on 4th December 1877 and on 21st April 1879 he received an intimation that the German Archaeological Institute had appointed him a corresponding member, and forty one years afterwards, on 6th June 1920, he was elected a corresponding member of the Academic Royale D' Archaolgie de Belgique. In June 1884 just when he reached his thirty nineth birthday, he was elected a Fellow of the London Society of Antiquaries, and a few years later he was appointed its local secretary for Northumberland... ...the University of Durham, on 27th June 1922, conferred upon him the honorary degree of Master of Arts. This distinction was merited because he had, 'devoted the energy and enthusiasm of a lifetime to antiquarian research'.

Following Blair's death in 1923 his huge amount of research was arranged by Miss Flagg of Westoe Village. Those related to County Durham were presented to the University of Durham and those to Northumberland can now be viewed at the Northumberland County Archives at Woodhorn Museum.

Northumberland Archives has 27 sketch books of Robert Blair's work, but these are not small as on each page of these archived books there is generally three or four of Robert's smaller sketchbook pages assembled together, as can be seen in the example above.
Reproduced by kind permission of Northumberland Archives, Woodhorn.

Blair's obituary points out how useful his methodical, determined approach to research linked with his considerable drawing skills proved to be.

In 1884 when Dr. Collingwood Bruce read his paper on the Roman Camp on the Lawe at South Shields, as an appendix to this paper (Arhaeologia Aeliana, 2 s., x, p.275) Robert Blair gave an account of the coins he had discovered in and near the Roman Camp on the Lawe, that had passed through his hands from 1874 to 1884. The list extends to 36 pages, and exemplifies the careful and thorough manner in which he performed his duties as secretary of the Lawe Excavation Committee and, at the same time, exhibits such a mastery of his subject that we are not surprised at the praises he won from such keen and accomplished students of the Roman period as Collingwood Bruce and John Clayton.

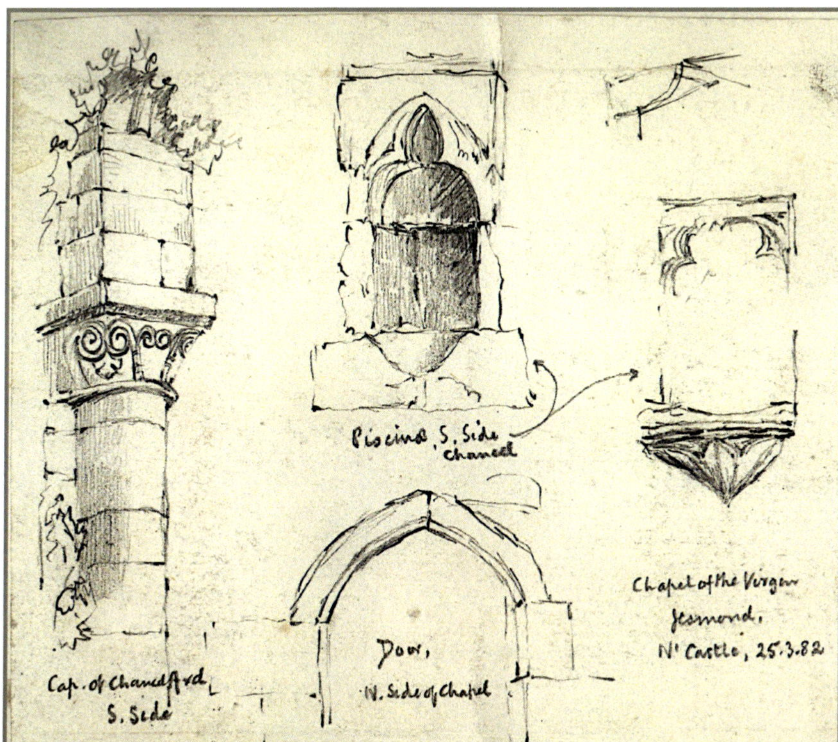

Architectural details of the Chapel of the Virgin, Jesmond dated 25th March 1882.
Reproduced by kind permission of Northumberland Archives, Woodhorn.

Final worked up drawing by Robert Blair, the original note can be seen opposite on the diary page; Wednesday's entry.
Blair Scrapbook; courtesy of South Tyneside Libraries.

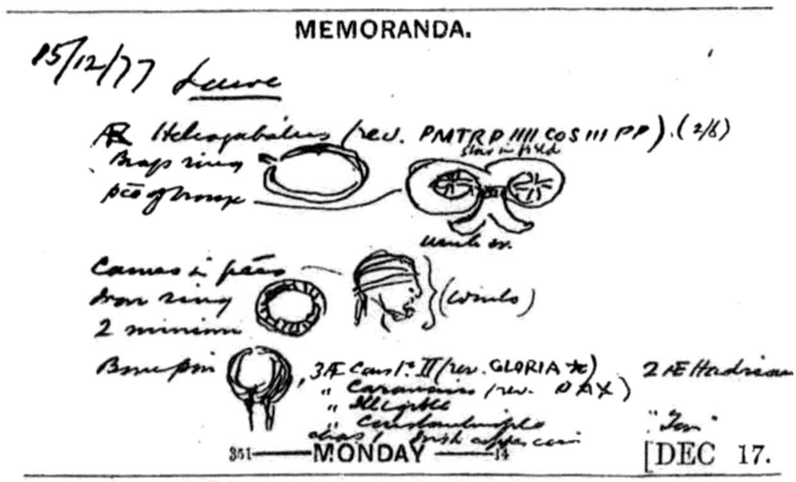

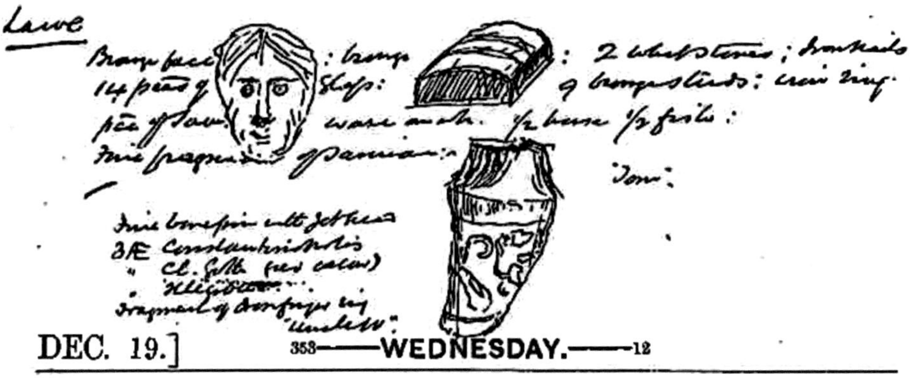

While attending the site Robert Blair would make impromptu sketches of some of the finds in his diary or on any scrap of paper he had to hand. The above image is taken from Robert Blair's 1877 diary, over two years after the official excavations had ended. The above diary extracts were printed in Blair's obituary in *Aleana Archaeologia*, sadly the original diary or diaries have been lost.

Wednesday 19th 1877 records discoveries from that day at the Lawe; a bronze face, two whetstones, a fine bone pin with jet and a large fragment of pottery together with simple sketches of three of the items. On the opposite page is Blair's final worked up drawing of the fragment of Samian Ware, recording the date of its find.

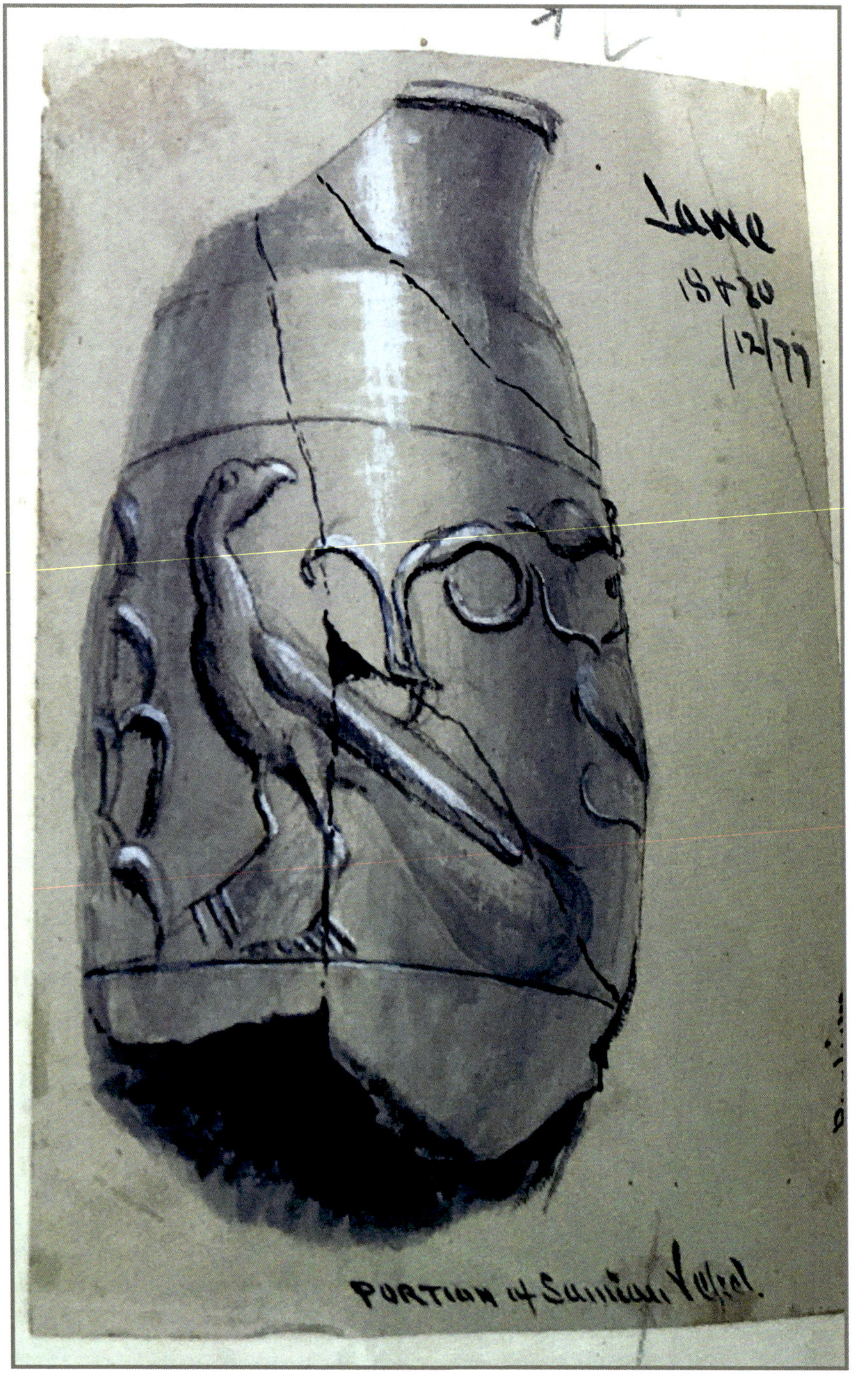

Dates tell us this was found in two separate pieces, two days apart. Drawing by Robert Blair.

Blair Scrapbook; courtesy of South Tyneside Libraries.

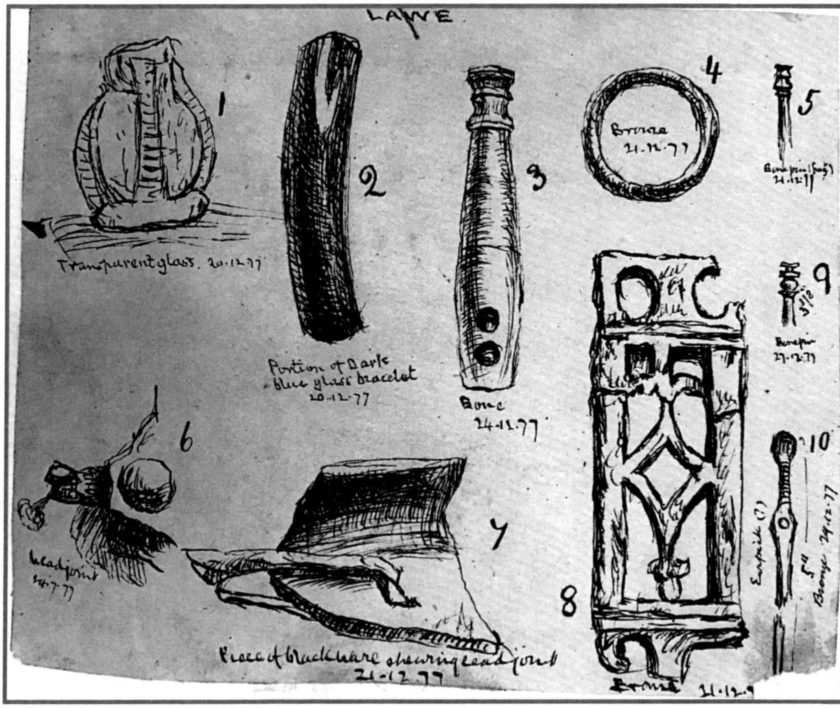

Sketches by Robert Blair.
Blair Scrapbook; courtesy of South Tyneside Libraries.

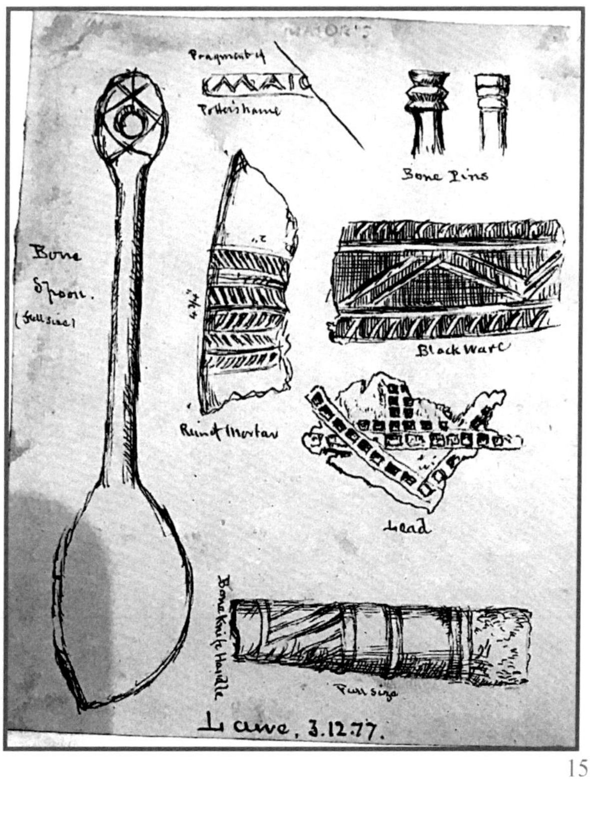

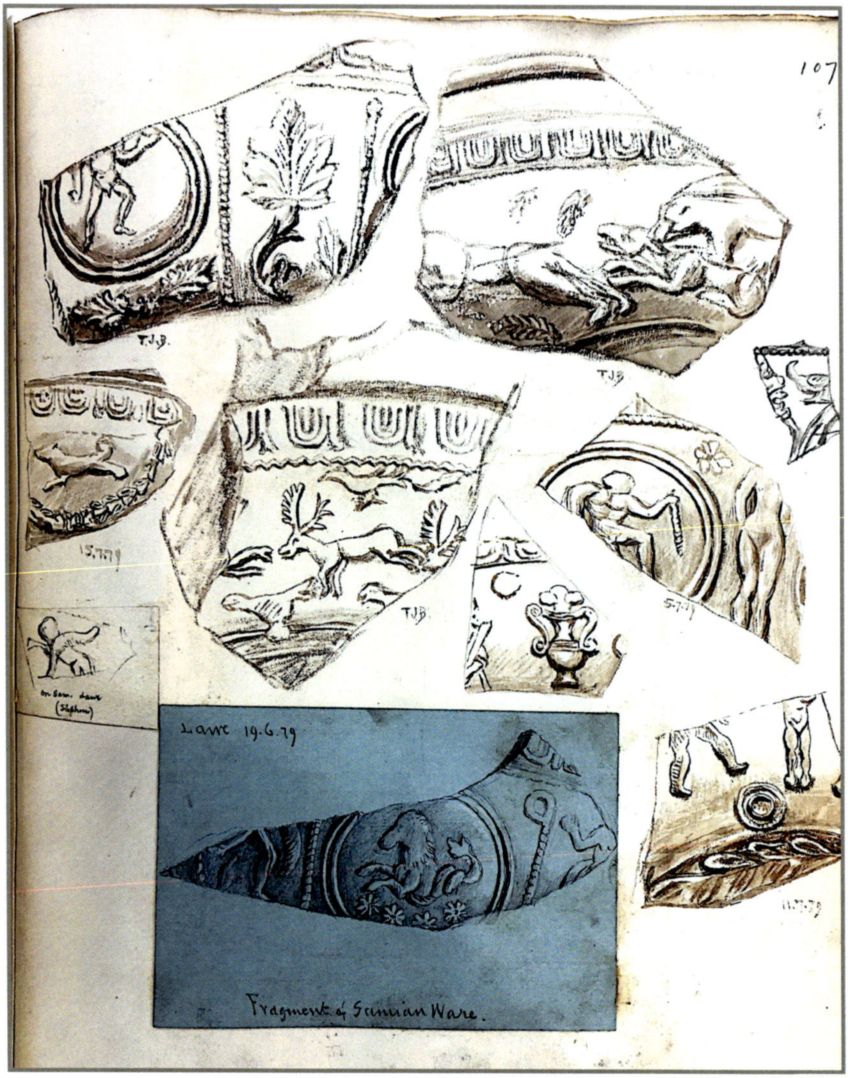

Drawings by Robert Blair. Most of the Samian pottery fragments on this page were found in 1879, long after the formal excavations had been completed.
Note the initials TJB after quite a few of the pieces so maybe they were now owned by Mr T J Bell, who is mentioned on the subscription list on page 52 and newspaper article on page 57. Mr Bell was the Secretary of the South Shields Geological Club, established on 9th October 1862.
Blair Scrapbook; courtesy of South Tyneside Libraries.

Dr. Hooppell in his paper *On the Discovery and Exploration of Roman Remains at South Shields in the Years 1875-6.* ***explained that****, 'Beside the Collection of Roman Antiquities, from the Station at South Shields, deposited in the Museum of the Free Library, a very fine collection has been made by Robert Blair, fine ones by Mr T Vint and Mr T J Bell, and a large number of articles have been dispersed among the inhabitants generally of South Shields and its vicinity.'*

Here are some examples of pieces of Samian ware currently in the store at Arbeia South Shields Roman Fort. Neither of the above pieces exactly match the drawing Blair did of the deer and the birds section in his scrapbook (see centre illustration on the opposite page).. It would appear that the pieces he drew were in the possession of another person (Mr. T J Bell) and their whereabouts are no longer known.

Photographs courtesy of Tyne & Wear Archives & Museums.

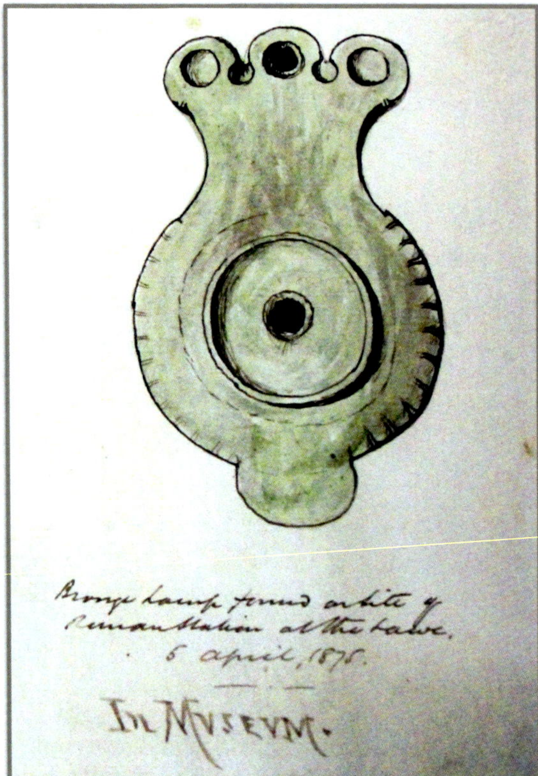

Watercolour and ink drawing by Robert Blair. *Blair Scrapbook; courtesy of South Tyneside Libraries.*

Bronze oil lamp at Arbeia, South Shields Roman Fort. *Photograph courtesy of Tyne & Wear Archives & Museums.*

In another spot, not far from the eastern rampart, the remains of a large and wealthy house were found. Here was a very perfect hypocaust, with sooty flue, coal, and many rooms. A portion of the wall of one room was within a few inches of the surface of the earth, though the concrete floor adjoining was five feet below the surface. Here was found a bronze lamp, not a common find in the Stations "per lineam valli,"* (Woodcut, No. 6,)

No. 6.

a writing stilus, of which the following Woodcut (No. 7) is an exact representation, of the precise size of the original, a bronze

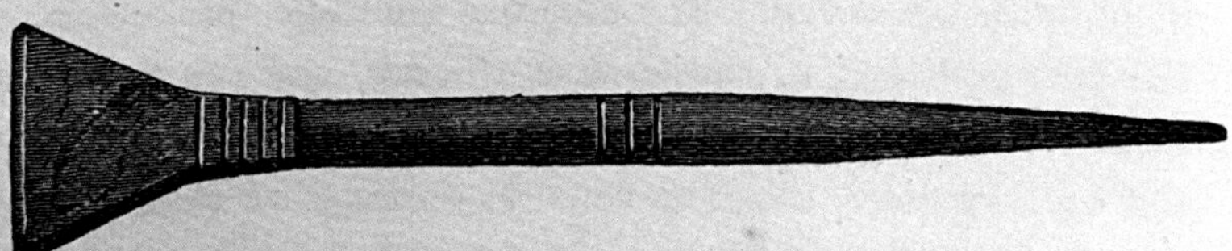

No. 7.

* Since writing the above two more lamps have been found, one of bronze, and the other of earthenware. The latter is very curious, of a design somewhat resembling a scallop shell, pierced for *five* wicks.

Part of a page from the published paper by Dr. Hooppell;
On the Discovery and Exploration of Roman Remains at South Shields in the Years 1875-6.
By the Rev R.E. Hooppell. Ma LLD, FRAS
Published in the Natural History Transactions ND & NC 1879, (Vol Vii).

The central engraving is of the oil lamp shown opposite, which as Dr. Hooppell said, *'was not a common find in the Stations,'* ***(though two more were found later).***

This is certainly an ostentatious item, using more oil with its three wicks than the usual one wick oil lamp, although a five wick earthenware lamp was also found on the Lawe ***(see page 218).***

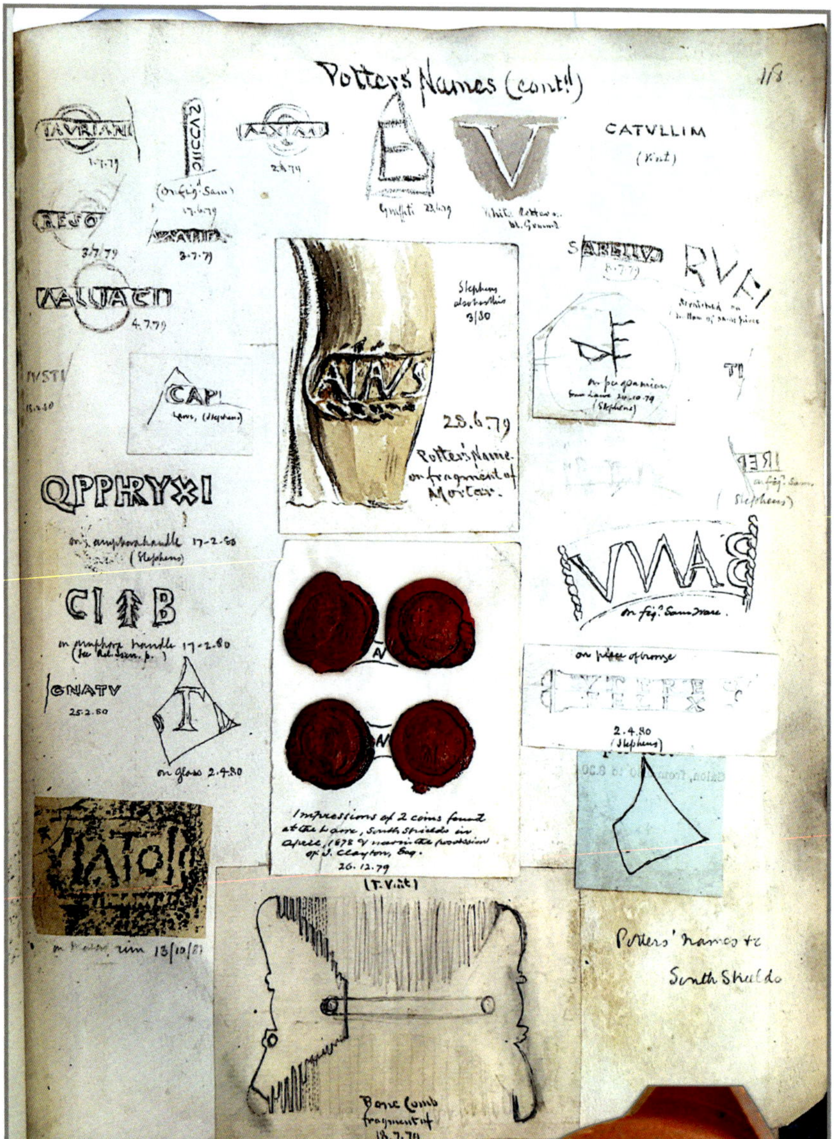

A page of drawings by Robert Blair primarily showing Roman potters' names found on ware discovered at South Shields. Many on this page are dated 1880.
Blair Scrapbook; courtesy of South Tyneside Libraries.

The base of a piece of Samian Ware displaying the name of the potter.
Photograph courtesy of Tyne & Wear Archives & Museums.

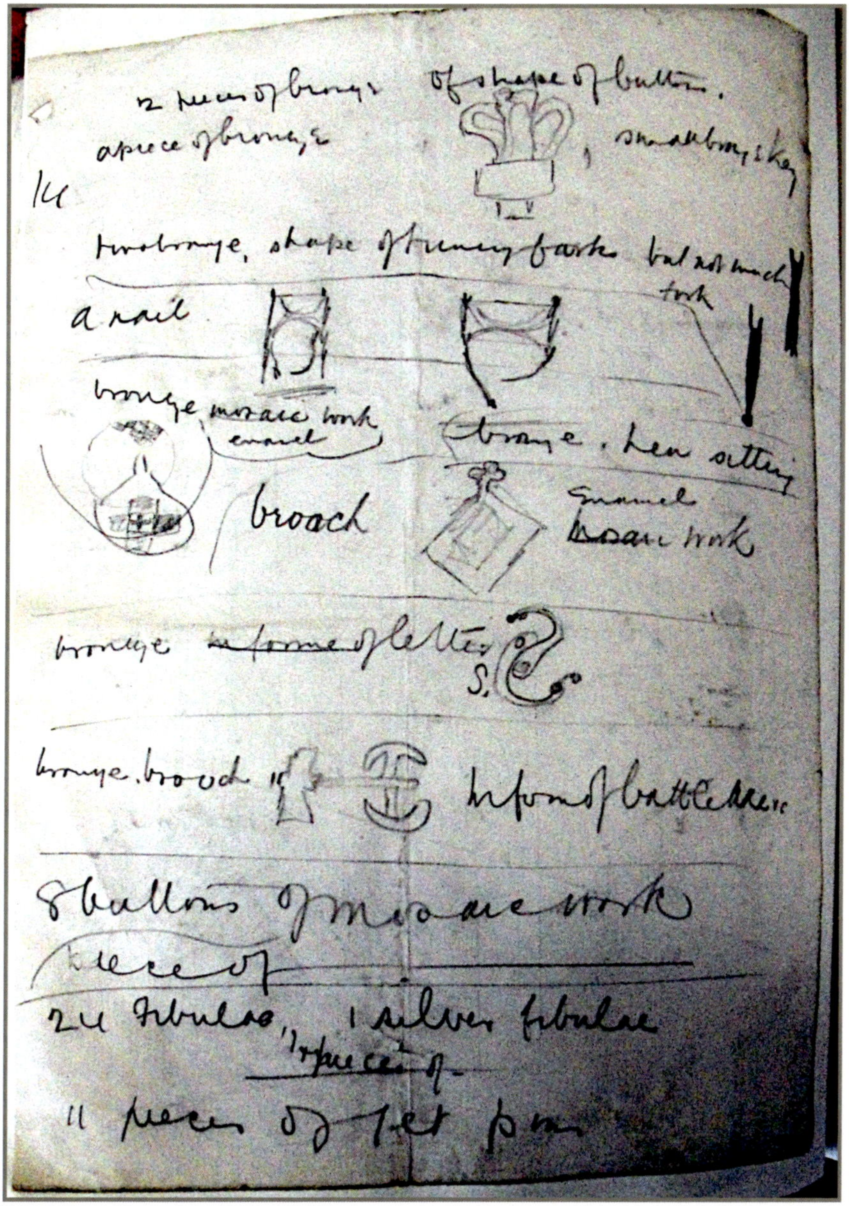

The scrapbook in The Word is full of Blair's rough sketches, worked up drawings, letters and collected newspaper articles. Note the image top right which can be seen worked up into a final drawing overleaf as well as a photograph of the original item which is in the store at Arbeia, South Shields Roman Fort.

Also note the rough drawing mid page of the dragonesque brooch, the final watercolour of which is reproduced on the title page of this chapter p137.
Blair Scrapbook; courtesy of South Tyneside Libraries.

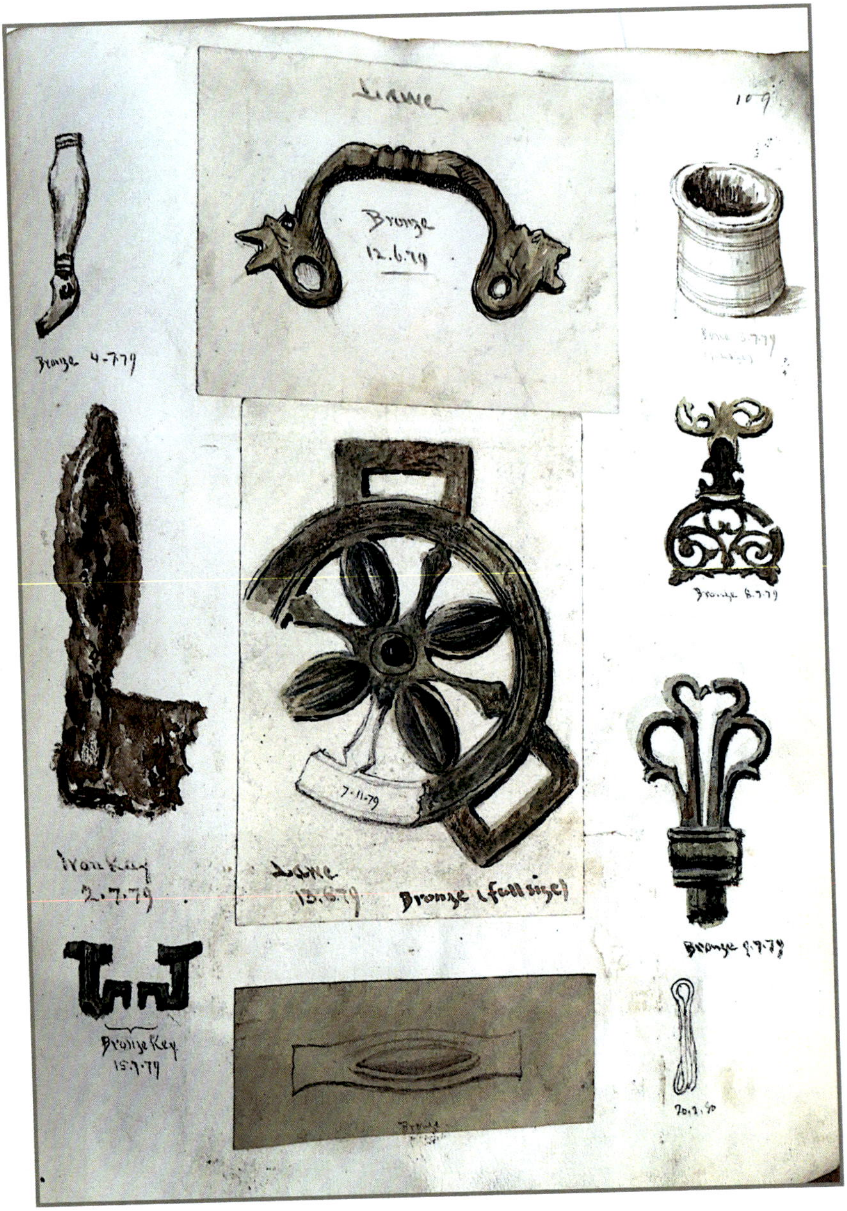

Above is a page of drawings by Robert Blair.
Blair Scrapbook; courtesy of South Tyneside Libraries.

Opposite are photographs of some of these items.
The horse harness fragment (top) and the key handle (lower right) are in the collections of the Great North Museum: Hancock; while the ring-key (middle left) is in the collection of Arbeia, South Shields Roman Fort.
Photographs courtesy of Tyne & Wear Archives & Museums.

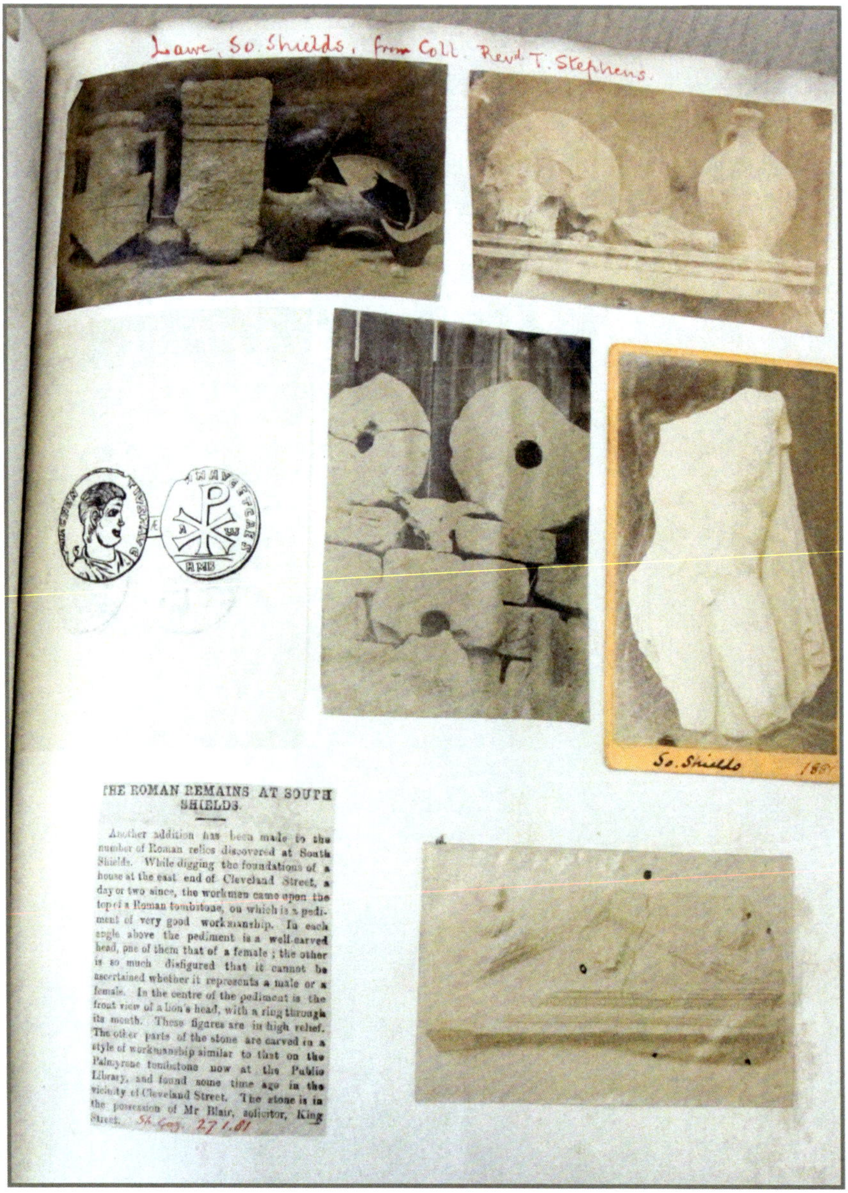

Photographs of items on a page in the Scrapbook.

Note top two photographs appear to be items in the collection of Rev. T Stephens.

The 1881 photograph of a male torso relates to the sculpture opposite with the accompanying drawing by Robert Blair recording that it was discovered on the Lawe in January 1881.

Blair Scrapbook; courtesy of South Tyneside Libraries.

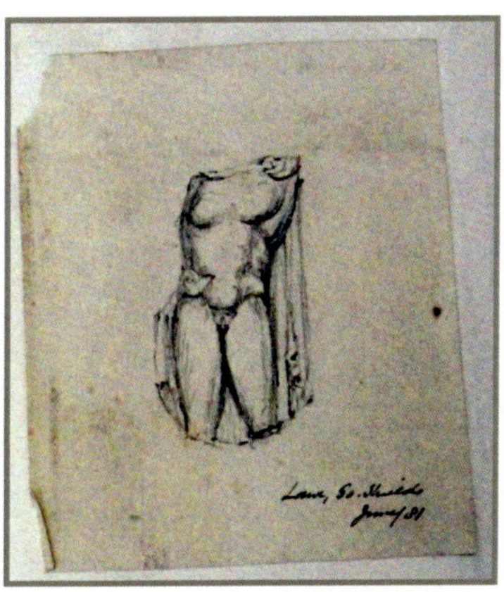

Sculpture in Arbeia Museum.
Photograph courtesy of Tyne & Wear Archives & Museums.

Robert Blair drawing.
Blair Scrapbook; courtesy of South Tyneside Libraries.

Another interesting discovery shows that the Romans resident in Britain were not neglectful of the fine arts. The wood-

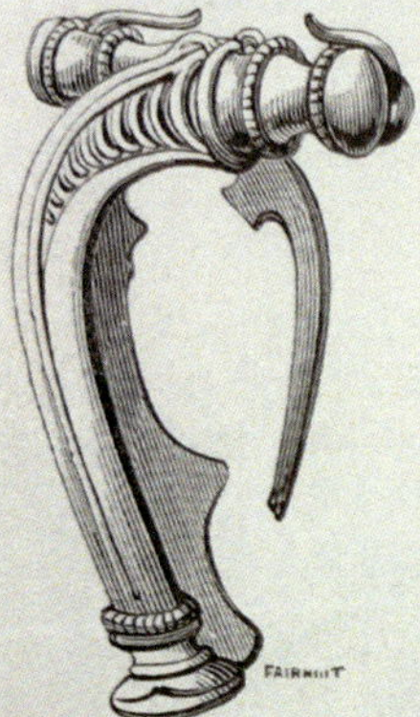

Fig. 1.

Fig. 2.

cut above (fig. 2) represents a cameo, found at South Shields, and now in the possession of Mr. Blair, of that town. The stone is Indian sardonyx of two layers, the upper opaque white, the lower a rich translucent brown. The subject is a bear. The

Part of page 268 in the Sixth Edition of *The Handbook to the Roman Wall* ***by the late J Collingwood Bruce, preface by R Blair.***
Reproduced by kind permission of the Natural History Society of Northumbria, Great North Museum: Hancock.

Photograph of the cameo on display at the Great North Museum: Hancock.
Photograph courtesy of Tyne & Wear Archives & Museums.

C W King MA began a two page article about this *Antique Cameo found at South Shields Durham* published in the *Archaeological Journal Volume XXV* pages 103-107 by saying:

> The discovery of an antique cameo in this island is so uncommon an event that every well-authenticated instance of the kind deserves to be brought under the notice of the Institute, and therefore I have much pleasure in communicating the following particulars respecting the most important one that has ever come to my knowledge.
>
> In March, 1878, a poor man, whilst engaged in "prospecting" upon the site of the Roman castrum at South Shields, picked up a large gem, which shortly afterwards came into the possession of Robert Blair, Esq., of that town, who kindly forwarded it to me for examination.
>
> It is an elliptical Indian sardonyx, 2 by 1½ in. in its greatest and least diameters, of two layers; the upper, opaque white; the lower, a rich translucent brown.

Photograph of the cameo in Blair's Scrapbook.
Blair Scrapbook; courtesy of South Tyneside Libraries.

ROMAN CAMEO FOUND AT SOUTH SHIELDS IN 1878.

The above is the representation of an Indian Sardonyx Cameo 2 ins. by 1½ ins., of two layers,—the upper, opaque white, the lower a rich translucent brown,—of the early part of the third century, discovered on the site of the Roman Castrum at South Shields, on the 20th March, 1878. It is now in the possession of Mr. Blair of that town. Such a find is a very uncommon event in the United Kingdom. In the white stratum is cut in rather high relief the figure of a black bear (the colour of the animal on the Cameo being due to mere accident), at his feet lies the skull of some animal, his recent prey, whether goat or calf cannot now be determined the gem being damaged in that part. Camei of this character were mounted in gold and silver—as we learn from ancient authors—and served for fastening the great military cloak upon the shoulder in the manner of the modern solitaire. Heliodorus makes his hero Theagenes fasten his *chlamys* with a bust of Pallas carved out of amber: in imperatorial statues, like the Spada Pompey, a great gem is seen carved with the Gorgon's head; and in the magnificent Cameo of the family of Severus, the Ægis on the breast of Caracalla is secured by a large oval gem. This Cameo, of 'Ursus,' was, in all probability, a decoration of the same nature as the large one in blue paste with the bust of Antonia Augusta (see below) found some years ago at Stanwix, near Carlisle. (From the Rev. C. W. King's description of the object in the Journal of the Brit. Arch. Inst., Vol. p.).

Only 20 Copies Printed.

Blair Scrapbook; courtesy of South Tyneside Libraries.

The eternal problem of lack of funds was a huge issue for the excavations committee. We see them appealing at every opportunity for further subscriptions. Blair's scrapbook informs us that attempts were made in May and July 1875 and again in January 1876 to collect more funds but these were not met with any great enthusiasm. The following transcribed section taken from the *Shields Gazette and Daily Telegraph*, May 1875 explains that with the aim of securing more funds for the excavations, Dr. Hooppell took to the floor after the lecture given by the antiquarian, H Ecroyd Smith to propose a motion to raise a further £300.

If they could raise sufficient funds to fully carry out the excavations and to trace out the whole arrangement of the fortified station, they would doubtless find a great many more objects of interest and come upon inscriptions which would give them more information than they yet had about the people who garrisoned the place and of the original name of it. The committee thought that the least sum of money that they could ask was £300. They had had many suggestions as to preserving the ground for the town. Nothing would more delight the committee than to know of such a scheme being set on foot and possessed of ground, either by gift or purchase, it would have to be enclosed and properly kept. Money would, however, be required, and it was for the public to say whether it wished the site to become its property. He moved (Dr. Hooppell) 'That the excavations having become so interesting and important, and the sum already subscribed having been nearly expended, a further sum of £300 be raised to continue the excavations; and that a subscription list for that amount be immediately opened'. (Applause.)

Mr. G. Lyall seconded the motion, and remarked that he thought the excavations fully warranted them in prosecuting the work to a complete success. He thought what they had already found had been deeply interesting, so much so as to warrant them in expecting the public to assist in the completion of the work. They had expended the £100 already subscribed in the most economical manner possible and conducted their operations in such a way as to achieve the desired; without spending money at a loss. The result of their labours was open to public inspection and criticism, and now the committee thought what they had discovered warranted them again in appealing to the public in order to obtain means for prosecuting the work and making further discoveries.

The original Golden Lion Inn dating from the 1790s was rebuilt in 1875, so presumably it was to this, the newest venue in town, that Dr. Hooppell brought his party to wine and dine them before asking for donations.

Inset is a photograph of the original building and the lower photograph was taken in the mid-twentieth century.
Both photographs by kind permission of South Tyneside Libraries.

On the 25th May 1875 Dr. Hooppell brought the Naturalists Club, of which he was a member, to South Shields on their first field meeting. After initially gathering at the new Golden Lion Hotel in King Street he took them to the new Nautical College on Ocean Road to see the finds that were being preserved there and then on up to the Lawe to view the amazing work that had been achieved in the previous two and half months.

They then returned to the Golden Lion for tea and various speeches were made. Hooppell finished his address by asking them to contribute to the subscription fund.

> Before concluding I would say that it is the conviction of gentlemen residing in South Shields that the excavations should be pursued. It was Dr. Bruce and Mr. Clayton's advice to us, at starting with the work, that we should endeavour to raise a fund of £100......That sum has been raised and expended and you have seen the results of that expenditure. It has been deemed advisable to carry on the work, and we now wish to raise the sum of £300 for that purpose.
>
> It is desirable that more information should, if possible, be obtained... We wish if possible to obtain the entrance of the Wrecken Dyke to the station. If we pursue the work we may hope to find more inscriptions. Many years ago some altars were found at this place.
>
> A fund of £300 has been started and we shall be glad if any gentlemen present will aid us. Mr Archibald Stevenson has sent us a cheque for ten guineas and we hope that many other gentlemen will follow his example.
>
> I may also say that the committee are very anxious that the best part, at any rate, of the station should be preserved I think that no antiquarian can visit the ground, and look for instance on that remarkable chamber which we uncovered not long ago near the forum, without feeling that at all costs, that relic should be preserved...

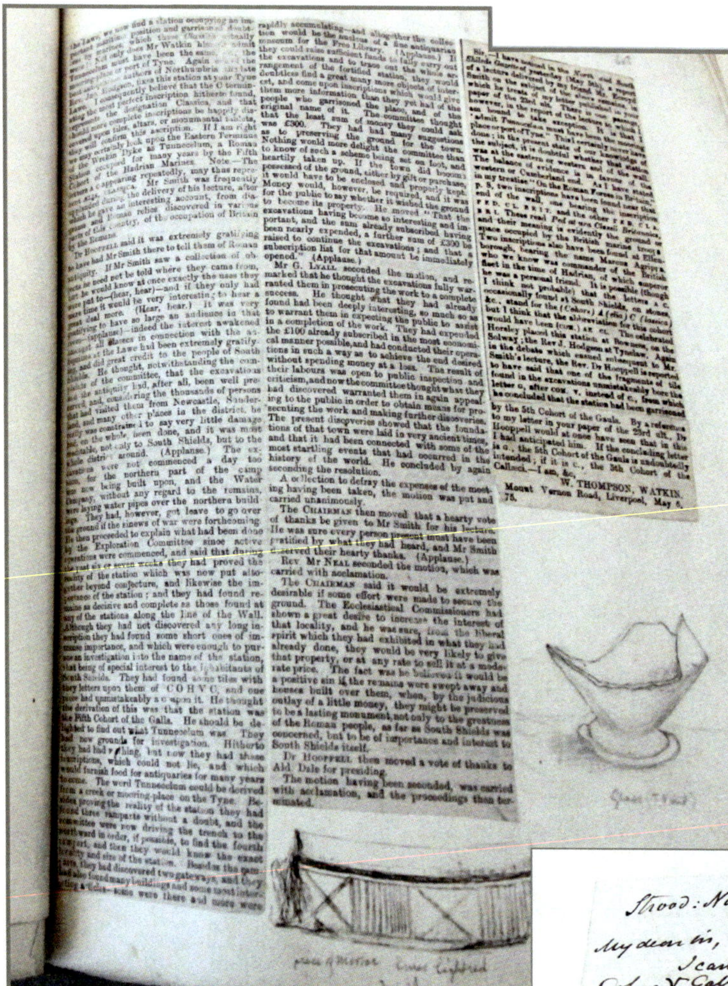

...the Lawe, we now find a station occupying an important maritime position and garrisoned doubtless by marines, which these Classis actually were. Not only does Mr Watkin himself admit Tunnocelum must have been the same, [illegible] the mooring-place or port of Tyne. Again [illegible] the best authors of Northumbria [illegible] late Rev. Jno. Hodgson, fixes this station at your Tyne Lawe. I consequently believe that the C terminating the most perfect inscription hitherto found, represents the designation Classica, and that should more complete inscriptions be happily discovered upon tiles, altars, or monumental tablets, they will confirm this ascription. If I am right we may certainly look upon the Eastern Terminus of the Wrekin Dyke as Tunnocelum, a Roman Station occupied for many years by the Fifth Cohort of the Hadrian Marines. Note.—The letters A C appearing repeatedly, may thus represent [illegible] Classica. Mr Smith was frequently applauded during the delivery of his lecture, after which he gave an interesting account, from diagrams and Roman relics discovered in various parts of this country, of the occupation of Britain by the Romans.

Dr Hooppell said it was extremely gratifying to have had Mr Smith there to tell them of Roman antiquity. If Mr Smith saw a collection of objects he need not be told where they came from, for he would know at once exactly the uses they were put to—(hear, hear)—and if they only had more time it would be very interesting to hear a great deal more. (Hear, hear.) It was very gratifying to have so large an audience in that town—(applause)—indeed the interest awakened amongst all classes in connection with the antiquities at the Lawe had been extremely gratifying, and did great credit to the people of South Shields. He thought, notwithstanding the complaints of the committee, that the excavations and the antiquity had, after all, been well preserved, and, considering the thousands of persons that had visited them from Newcastle, Sunderland, and many other places in the district, he really was constrained to say very little damage had, on the whole, been done, and it was most creditable, not only to South Shields, but to the whole district around. (Applause.) The excavations were not commenced a day too soon, for the northern part of the camp was now being built upon, and the Water Company, without any regard to the remains, were laying water pipes over the northern buildings. They had, however, got leave to go over the ground if the sinews of war were forthcoming. He then proceeded to explain what had been done by the Exploration Committee since active operations were commenced, and said that during the past six or seven weeks they had proved the reality of the station which was now put altogether beyond conjecture, and likewise the importance of the station; and they had found remains as decisive and complete as those found at any of the stations along the line of the Wall. Although they had not discovered any long inscription they had found some short ones of immense importance, and which were enough to pursue an investigation into the name of the station, that being of special interest to the inhabitants of South Shields. They had found some tiles with the letters upon them of C O H V C, and one piece had unmistakeably a G upon it. He thought the derivation of this was that the station was the Fifth Cohort of the Galls. He should be delighted to find out what Tunnocelum was. They had new grounds for investigation. Hitherto they had had nothing, but now they had these inscriptions, which could not lie, and which would furnish food for antiquaries for many years to come. The word Tunnocelum could be derived from a creek or mooring-place on the Tyne. Besides proving the reality of the station they had found three ramparts without a doubt, and the committee were now driving the trench to the southward in order, if possible, to find the fourth rampart, and then they would know the exact locality and size of the station. Besides the ramparts, they had discovered two gateways, and they had also found many buildings and some most interesting [illegible]—some were there and more were rapidly accumulating—and altogether the collection would be the nucleus of a fine antiquarian museum for the Free Library. (Applause.) If they could raise sufficient funds to fully carry out the excavations and to trace out the whole arrangement of the fortified station, they would doubtless find a great many more objects of interest, and come upon inscriptions which would give them more information than they yet had of the people who garrisoned the place, and of the original name of it. The committee thought that the least sum of money they could ask was £300. They had had many suggestions as to preserving the ground for the town. Nothing would more delight the committee than to know of such a scheme being set on foot, and heartily taken up. If the town did become possessed of the ground, either by gift or purchase, it would have to be enclosed and properly kept. Money would, however, be required, and it was for the public to say whether it wished the ground to become its property. He moved "That the excavations having become so interesting and important, and the sum already subscribed having been nearly expended, a further sum of £300 be raised to continue the excavations; and that a subscription list for that amount be immediately opened." (Applause.)

Mr G. Lyall seconded the motion, and remarked that he thought the excavations fully warranted them in prosecuting the work to a complete success. He thought what they had already found had been deeply interesting, so much so as to warrant them in expecting the public to assist in a completion of the work. They had expended the £100 already subscribed in the most economical manner possible, and had conducted their operations in such a way as to achieve the end desired without spending money at a loss. The result of their labours was open to public inspection and criticism, and now the committee thought what they had discovered warranted them in again appealing to the public in order to obtain means for prosecuting the work and making further discoveries. The present discoveries showed that the foundations of that town were laid in very ancient times, and that it had been connected with some of the most startling events that had occurred in the history of the world. He concluded by again seconding the resolution.

A collection to defray the expenses of the meeting having been taken, the motion was put and carried unanimously.

The Chairman then moved that a hearty vote of thanks be given to Mr Smith for his lecture. He was sure every person present must have been gratified by what they had heard, and Mr Smith deserved their hearty thanks. (Applause.)

Rev Mr Neal seconded the motion, which was carried with acclamation.

The Chairman said it would be extremely desirable if some effort were made to secure the ground. The Ecclesiastical Commissioners had shown a great desire to increase the interest of that locality, and he was sure, from the liberal spirit which they had exhibited in what they had already done, they would be very likely to give that property, or at any rate to sell it at a moderate price. The fact was he believed it would be a positive sin if the remains were swept away and houses built over them, when, by the judicious outlay of a little money, they might be preserved to be a lasting monument, not only to the greatness of the Roman people, as far as South Shields was concerned, but to be of importance and interest to South Shields itself.

Dr Hooppell then moved a vote of thanks to Ald. Dale for presiding.

The motion having been seconded, was carried with acclamation, and the proceedings then terminated.

Sir,—I have noticed in the North and South Shields Gazette of yesterday (May 5th), a report of a lecture delivered by my friend Mr. Ecroyd Smith on the subject of [illegible] which he treats of my letter [illegible] paper of the 23rd ult. There [illegible] however, in the report of the lecture [illegible] am bound to take exception. It is that I "admit Tunnocelum must have been the mooring-place or port of Tyne." This I certainly never have done; in the present state of our knowledge of the subject, it is doubtful whether that station was at the eastern or western end of the wall. The balance of evidence is in favour of the western or Cumberland end. As I have stated in my treatise "On the Roman Forces in Britain," p. 8, two inscriptions have been found near that end of the wall, one bearing the inscription PRÆF. CL. BRIT. and the other PRÆ. CL. [illegible] These read *Præfectura Classis Britannica*, and their meaning is evidently the ground or space occupied by the British marine troops. Two inscriptions also have been found at Ellenborough, bearing the name Marcus Agrippa, who we know was commander of the British fleet in the time of Hadrian, of which emperor he was a personal friend. It is possible (though I think not probable) that the letters A C, &c., occasionally found at South Shields, on stones, stand for the (*Cohors*) A (*elia*) C (*lassica*), but I think that the abbreviation for this cohort would have been (COH.) AE CL. Horsley placed this station at Bowness, on the Solway; the Rev J. Hodgson at Tynelaw. Again in the debate which ensued subsequent to Mr Smith's lecture, the Rev. Dr Hooppell is reported to have said that one of the fragments of tile found in the excavations unmistakeably bore the letter G, after COH. V. instead of C., from which he concluded that the station had been garrisoned by the 5th Cohort of the Gauls. By a reference to my letter in your paper of the 23rd ult. Dr Hooppell would at once have seen that in this I had anticipated him. If the concluding letter is G., the 5th Cohort of the Gauls is undoubtedly intended; if it is C., the 5th Cohort of the Callaeci.—I am, &c.,

W. THOMPSON WATKIN.

Mount Vernon Road, Liverpool, May 6, 75.

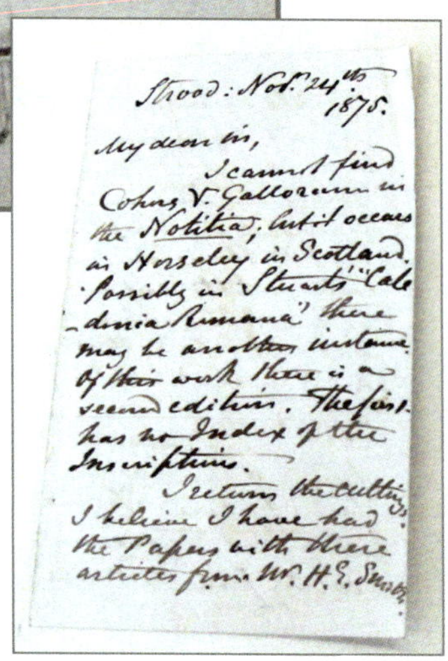

Strood: Nov. 24th 1875.

My dear Sir,

I cannot find Cohors V. Gallorum in the Notitia, but it occurs in Horsley in Scotland. Possibly in Stuart's "Caledonia Romana" there may be another instance. Of this work there is a second edition. The first has no Index of the Inscriptions.

I return the cutting. I believe I have had the Papers with these articles from Mr. H. E. Smith

One of the pages in the Blair scrapbook, showing the newspaper cuttings of the record of Mr.H Ecroyd Smith's speech; it was reported in full and covers two consecutive pages of the scrapbook, followed by Dr. Hooppell's motion to raise £300 and a letter from H Ecroyd Smith dated May 1875. The poster advertising his lecture is shown on page 102.
Blair Scrapbook; courtesy of South Tyneside Libraries.

Mr. J. M. Moore moved a vote of thanks as the president of the club to Dr. Bruce and to Dr. Hooppell, and in doing so remakes that he thought, as Dr. Hooppell was about to leave South Shields, it was a fitting time to express the thanks of the town, for the great interest which he had taken in the Roman remains.

The motion was carried with applause and the company separated.

Dr. Hooppell in his 1878 description, does state that in total the sum of £279 16s 8d had been raised and expended for the explorations with the account finally being closed on August 16th 1877. One assumes this amount consists of the original £100, plus further donations totally far from the hoped for £300 extra. For despite another contribution from the Duke of Northumberland at the end of January 1876 it seems the project could no longer be sustainable.

On 3rd February Blair wrote a letter to one of the Newcastle papers commenting on the report of the AGM of the Society of Antiquaries of Newcastle-upon-Tyne, which stated the Society's regret at the suspension of the excavations at South Shields. The following week a meeting of the exploration committee resolved to make a fresh appeal for subscribers but it appears that organised excavation was effectively at an end from this point. Finds continued to be discovered at the Lawe between 1875-1885, while building work in the area continued, however much to the sadness of the committee not all of this was completed under their jurisdiction.

It is difficult to discover the exact date when formal excavations ceased, but it was most likely early in 1876, so possibly after less than a year. Items continued to be unearthed by the workmen building houses in the area or by another group of individuals whom Blair called prospectors. Blair writes of these prospectors unearthing objects which were then sold to the highest bidder. He was reduced to buying as many of these as he could to secure them from being sold on the open market for antiquities.

Hooppell, Collingwood Bruce and Blair still continued to champion the importance of the finds being made and pursued a determined effort to keep the site at South Shields in the specialists' and public's attention.

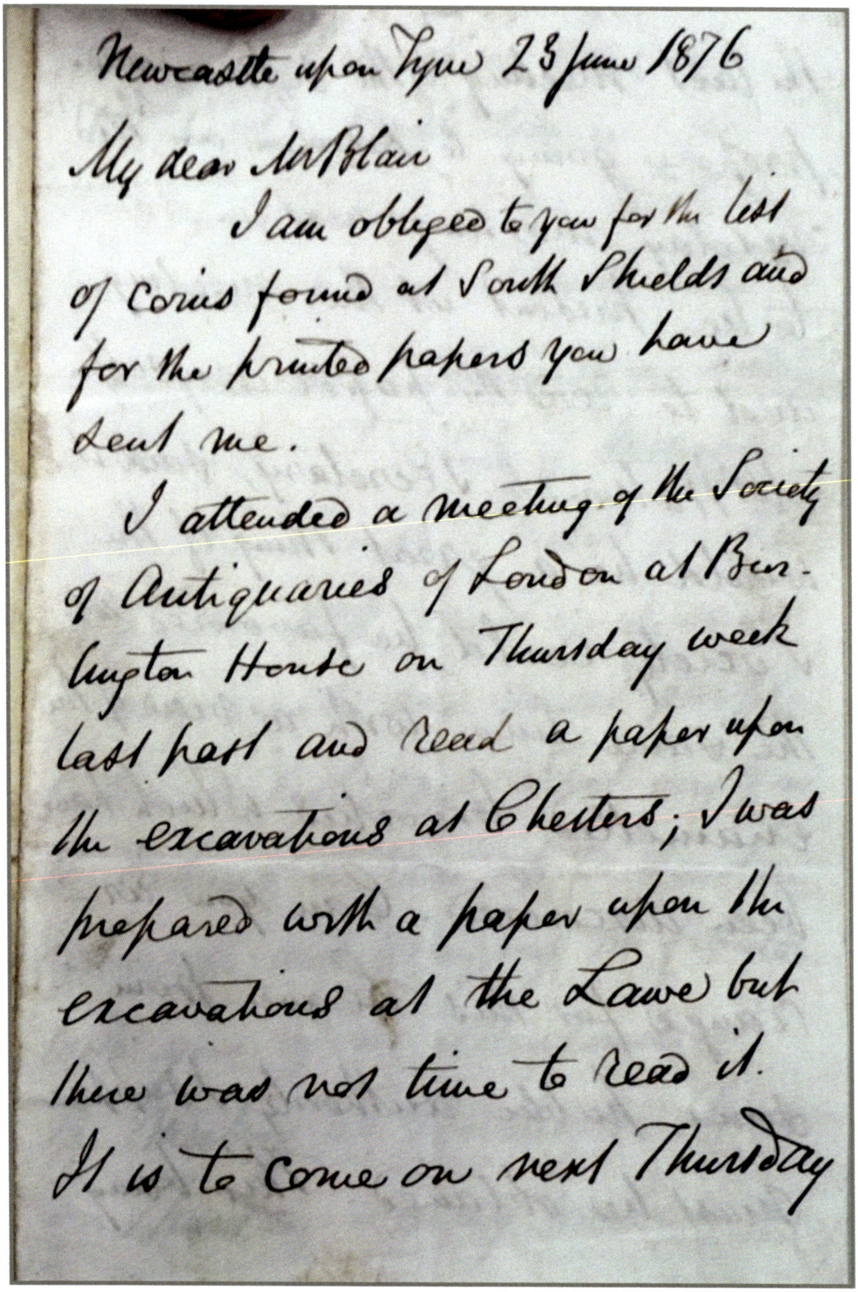
Newcastle upon Tyne 23 June 1876

My dear Mr Blair

I am obliged to you for the list of coins found at South Shields and for the printed papers you have sent me.

I attended a meeting of the Society of Antiquaries of London at Burlington House on Thursday week last past and read a paper upon the excavations at Chesters; I was prepared with a paper upon the excavations at the Lawe but there was not time to read it. It is to come on next Thursday

Blair Scrapbook; courtesy of South Tyneside Libraries.

This four page letter from Dr. Collingwood Bruce to Robert Blair concerns a presentation he was to make at the Society of Antiquaries of London at Burlington House on 29th June 1876. The final page asks Blair to accompany him. The Journey will be via the steamer, from the Tyne to the Thames, staying over in London.

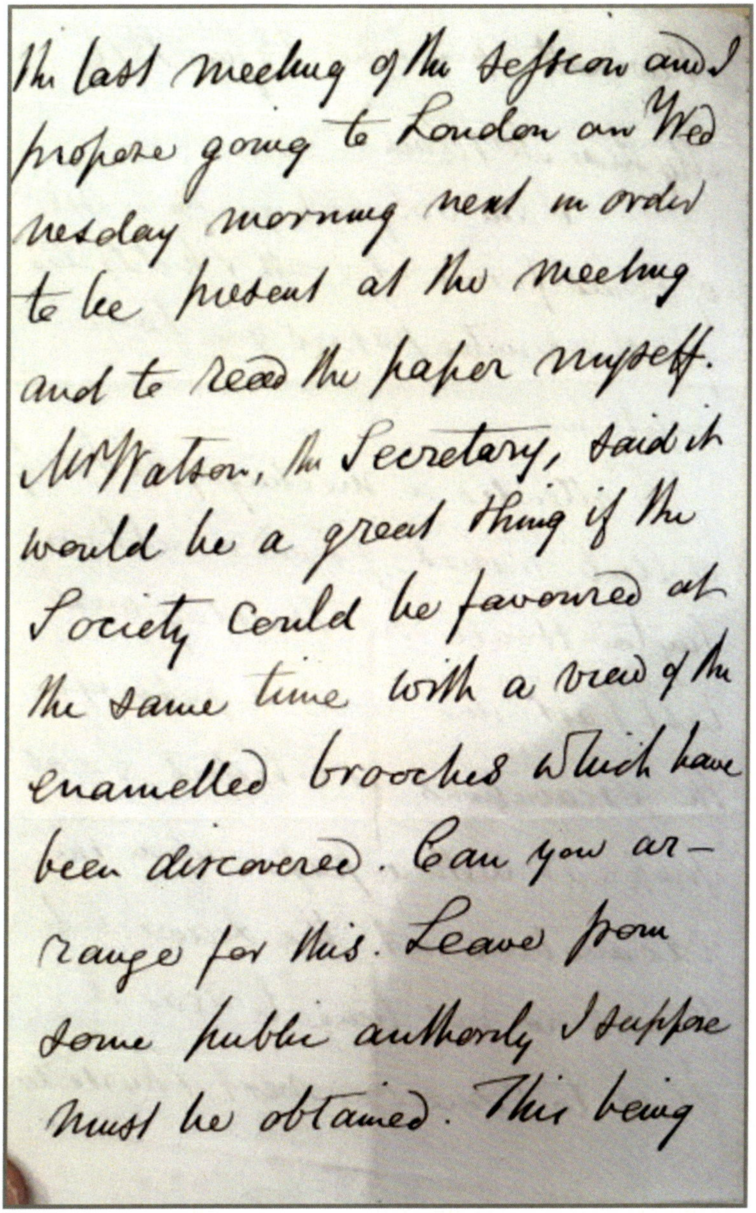

the last meeting of the Session and I
propose going to London on Wed
nesday morning next in order
to be present at the meeting
and to read the paper myself.
Mr Watson, the Secretary, said it
would be a great thing if the
Society could be favoured at
the same time with a view of the
enamelled brooches which have
been discovered. Can you ar-
range for this. Leave from
some public authority I suppose
must be obtained. This being

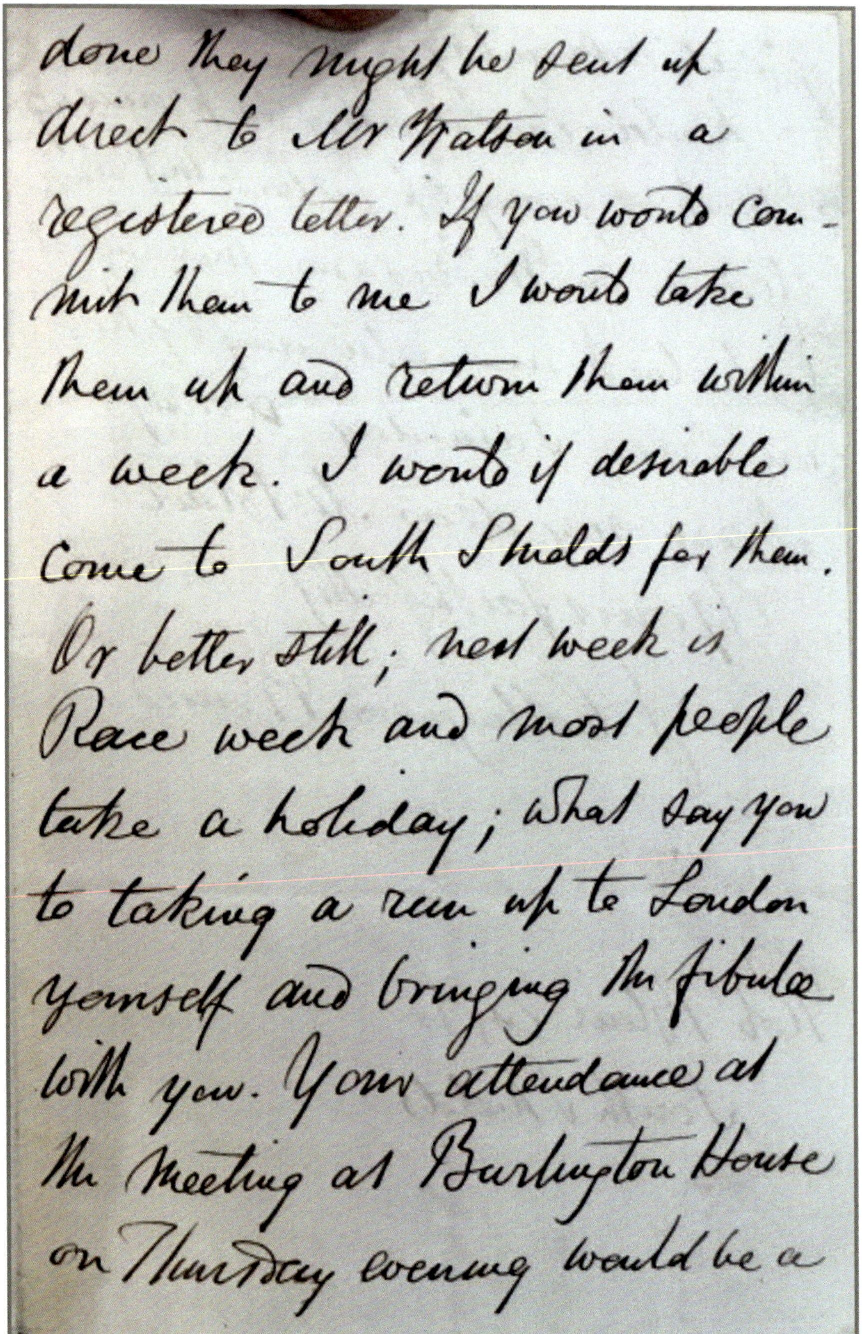
done they might be sent up
direct to Mr Watson in a
registered letter. If you would com-
mit them to me I would take
them up and return them within
a week. I would if desirable
come to South Shields for them.
Or better still; next week is
Race week and most people
take a holiday; what say you
to taking a run up to London
yourself and bringing the fibulae
with you. Your attendance at
the meeting at Burlington House
on Thursday evening would be a

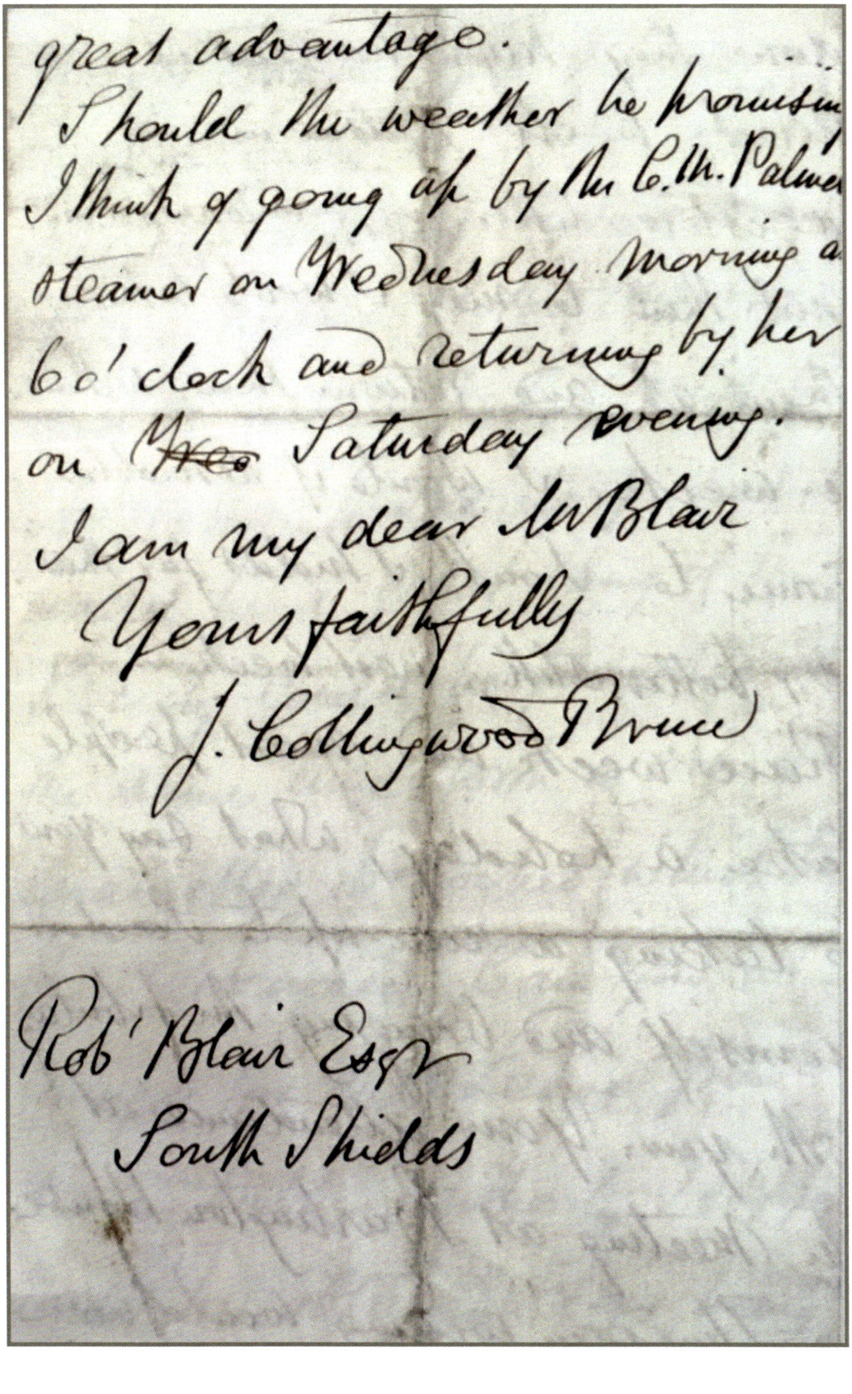
great advantage.
Should the weather be promisin
I think of going up by the C. M. Palmer
steamer on Wednesday morning a
6 o'clock and returning by her
on ~~Wed~~ Saturday evening.
I am my dear Mr Blair
Yours faithfully
J. Collingwood Bruce

Robt Blair Esqr
South Shields

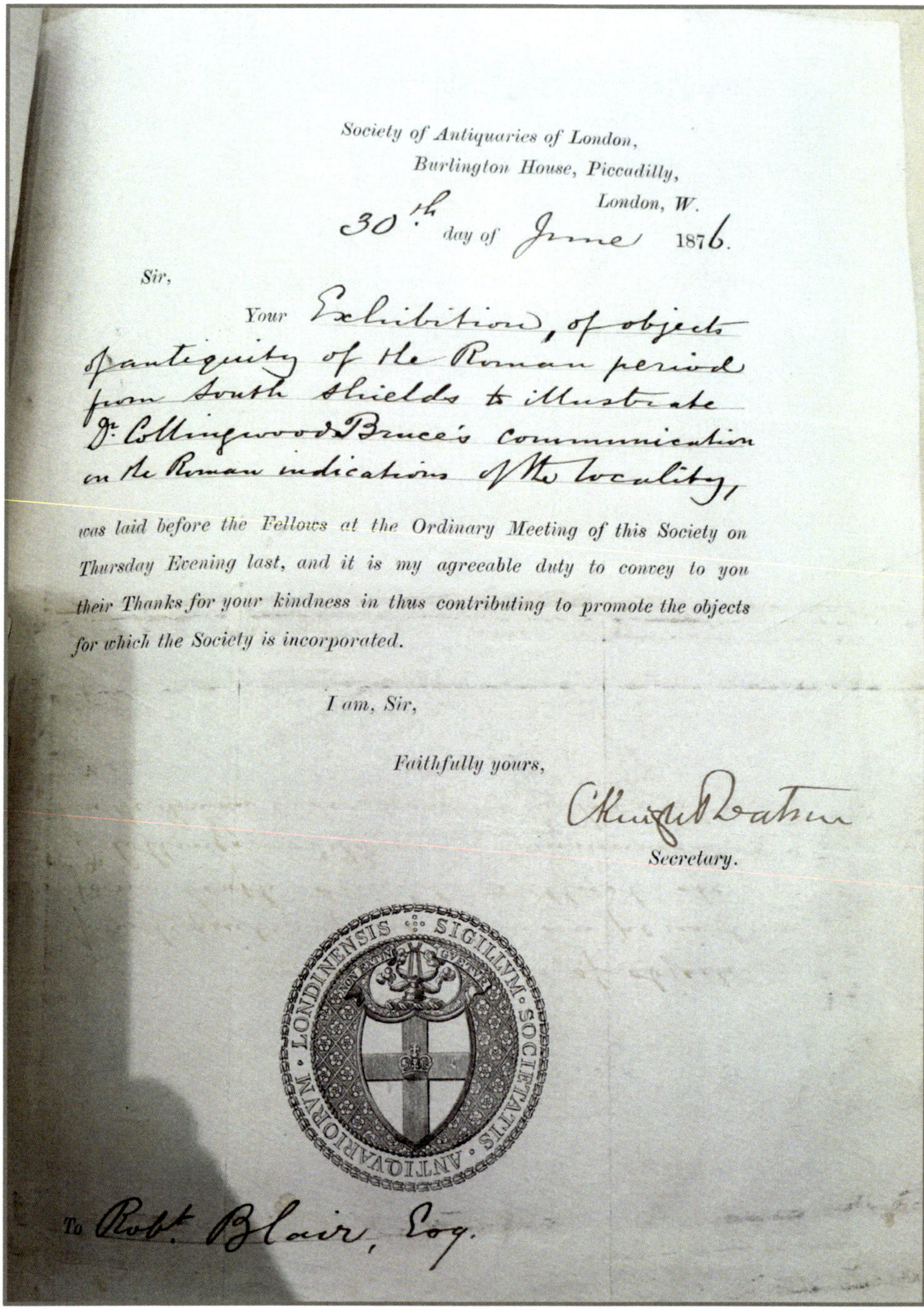

Society of Antiquaries of London,
Burlington House, Piccadilly,
London, W.

30th day of June 1876.

Sir,

Your Exhibition, of objects of antiquity of the Roman period from South Shields to illustrate Dr. Collingwood Bruce's communication on the Roman indications of the locality, was laid before the Fellows at the Ordinary Meeting of this Society on Thursday Evening last, and it is my agreeable duty to convey to you their Thanks for your kindness in thus contributing to promote the objects for which the Society is incorporated.

I am, Sir,

Faithfully yours,

C. Knight Watson

Secretary.

SIGILLVM · SOCIETATIS · ANTIQVARIORVM · LONDINENSIS

To Robt. Blair, Esq.

Both this letter and the minute page opposite are preserved in the Scrapbook.
Blair Scrapbook; courtesy of South Tyneside Libraries.

Opposite is the letter Blair received thanking him for bringing items from the Lawe, such as the buckle shown on the next page, to the Society of Antiquaries of London. Below is a page from the minute book of the Society of Antiquaries of London recording a communication from Robert Blair dated 4th May 1876 and subsequently the talk by Dr. Collingwood Bruce on the *'interesting excavations at the South Shields.'*

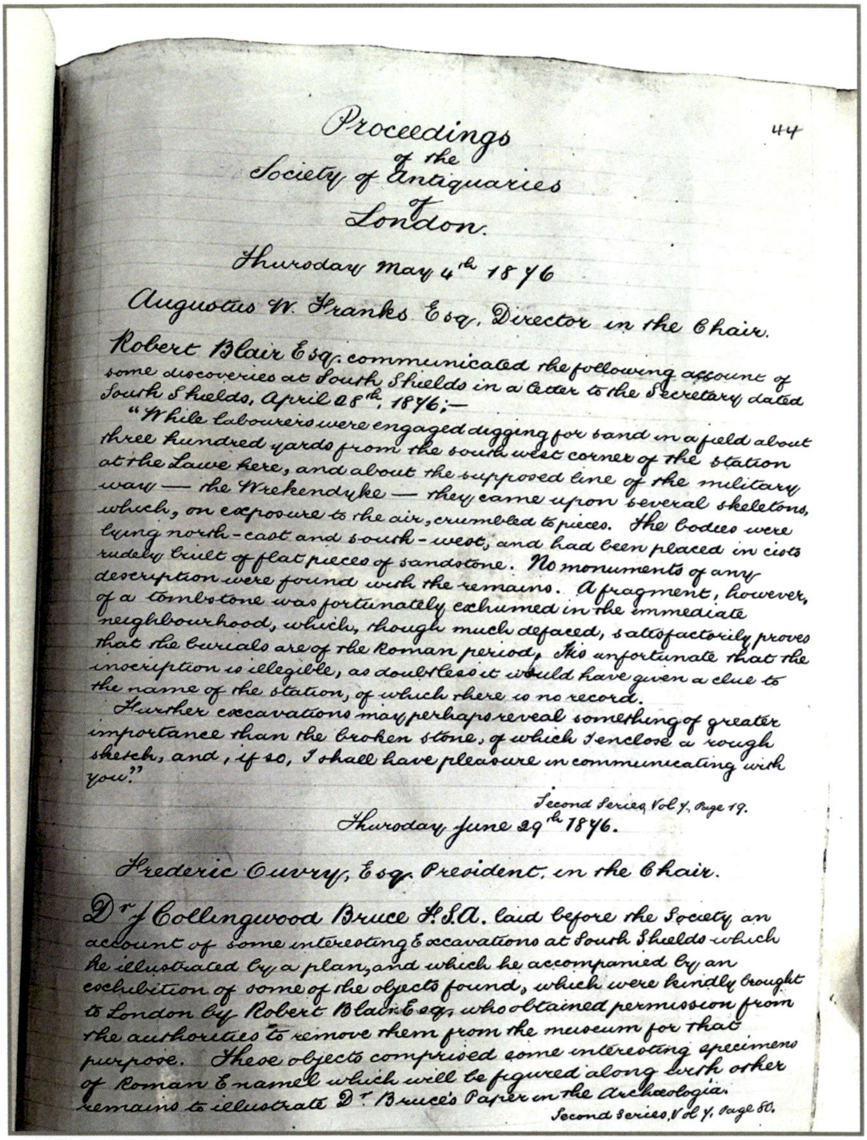

Proceedings
of the
Society of Antiquaries
of
London.

44

Thursday May 4th 1876

Augustus W. Franks Esq. Director in the Chair.

Robert Blair Esq. communicated the following account of some discoveries at South Shields in a letter to the Secretary dated South Shields, April 28th, 1876:—

"While labourers were engaged digging for sand in a field about three hundred yards from the south west corner of the station at the Lawe here, and about the supposed line of the military way — the Wrekendyke — they came upon several skeletons, which, on exposure to the air, crumbled to pieces. The bodies were lying north-east and south-west, and had been placed in cists rudely built of flat pieces of sandstone. No monuments of any description were found with the remains. A fragment, however, of a tombstone was fortunately exhumed in the immediate neighbourhood, which, though much defaced, satisfactorily proves that the burials are of the Roman period. It is unfortunate that the inscription is illegible, as doubtless it would have given a clue to the name of the station, of which there is no record.

Further excavations may perhaps reveal something of greater importance than the broken stone, of which I enclose a rough sketch, and, if so, I shall have pleasure in communicating with you."

Second Series Vol 7, Page 19.

Thursday June 29th 1876.

Frederic Ouvry, Esq. President, in the Chair.

Dr J Collingwood Bruce F.S.A. laid before the Society an account of some interesting Excavations at South Shields which he illustrated by a plan, and which he accompanied by an exhibition of some of the objects found, which were kindly brought to London by Robert Blair Esq., who obtained permission from the authorities to remove them from the museum for that purpose. These objects comprised some interesting specimens of Roman Enamel which will be figured along with other remains to illustrate Dr. Bruce's Paper in the Archaeologia.

Second Series, Vol 7, Page 80.

Above is Robert Blair's sketch with a photograph below of the original, of what was thought at the time to be an enamel brooch.

This is one of the items Blair took to show the members of the London Society of Antiquaries.

It is now recognised to be a belt plate, one of a group of four which were part of a complete belt found together with a hoard of swords near the SE rampart of the fort during the excavation.

Currently on display in Arbeia, South Shields Roman Fort.
Blair Scrapbook; courtesy of South Tyneside Libraries.
Photograph courtesy of Tyne & Wear Archives & Museums.

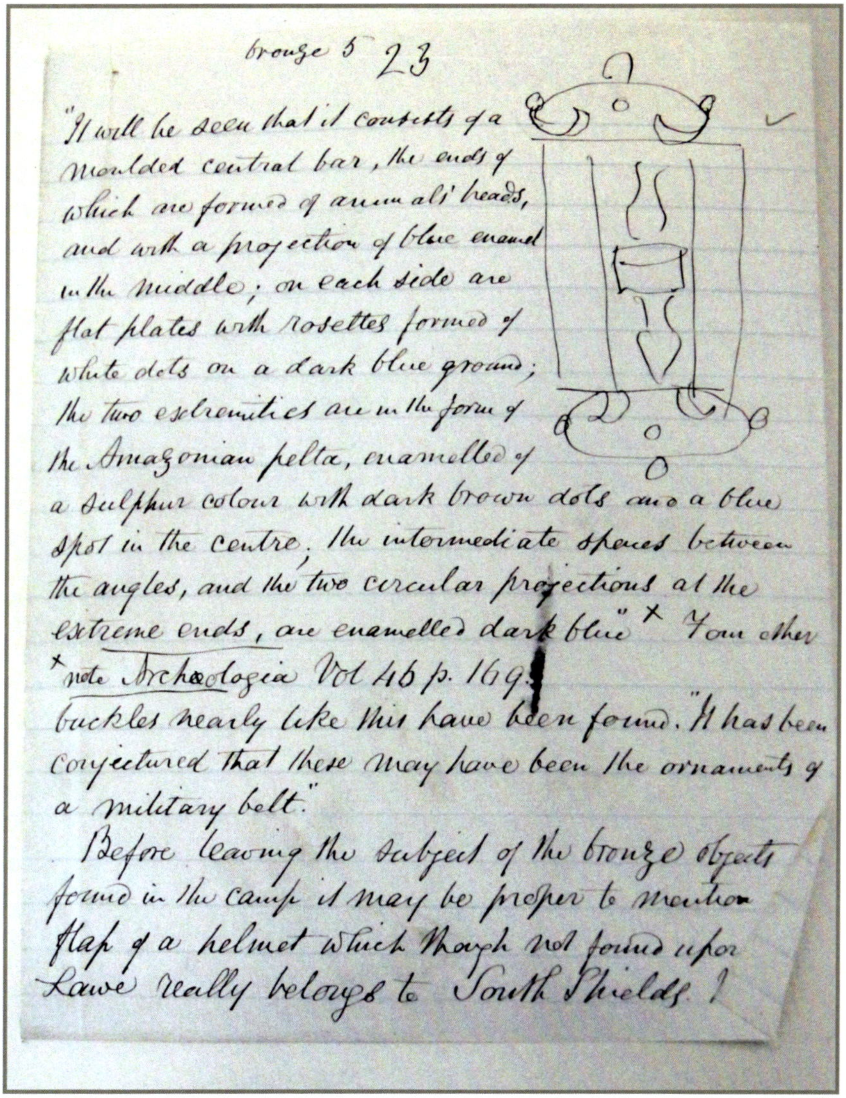

bronze 5 23

"It will be seen that it consists of a
moulded central bar, the ends of
which are formed of animals' heads,
and with a projection of blue enamel
in the middle; on each side are
flat plates with rosettes formed of
white dots on a dark blue ground;
the two extremities are in the form of
the Amazonian pelta, enamelled of
a sulphur colour with dark brown dots and a blue
spot in the centre; the intermediate spaces between
the angles, and the two circular projections at the
extreme ends, are enamelled dark blue" x Four other
x note Archaeologia Vol 46 p. 169.
buckles nearly like this have been found. "It has been
conjectured that these may have been the ornaments of
a military belt."

Before leaving the subject of the bronze objects
found in the camp it may be proper to mention
flap of a helmet which though not found upon
Lawe really belongs to South Shields. |

Page 23 of Dr. Collingwood Bruce's hand written notes, plus his amendments, for the speech he gave at the Society of Antiquaries of London in June 1878. Another page is displayed overleaf.

The notes for the entire speech are pasted into the Scrapbook.
Blair Scrapbook; courtesy of South Tyneside Libraries.

12 ON ROMAN REMAINS AT SOUTH SHIELDS,

cup, (Woodcut No. 8,) with foot and stem of beautiful design, though much decayed, and many minor articles.

Near the south-east corner of the rampart were found some choice enamelled ornaments, more perfect than anything of the same kind in the British Museum. A Woodcut, (No. 9,) is given of the most perfect one, the exact size of the original. The rest,

No. 8.

No. 9.

there were four in all, were very similar, though not identically the same. I would direct particular attention to the boars' heads, included in the design. The boar was the badge, or emblem, of the twentieth legion, stationed at Chester, and the finding of these ornaments, taken in conjunction with other circumstances and considerations, seems to point to a somewhat close connection, or at any rate frequent intercourse, between Deva and the Lawe.

A page from the published paper by Dr. Hooppell;
On the Discovery and Exploration of Roman Remains at South Shields in the Years 1875-6. By the Rev. R.E. Hooppell. Ma LLD, FRAS.'
Published in the Natural History Transactions of Northumberland, Durham & Newcastle upon Tyne, 1879, (Vol VII).
Reproduced by kind permission of the Natural History Society of Northumbria, Great North Museum: Hancock.

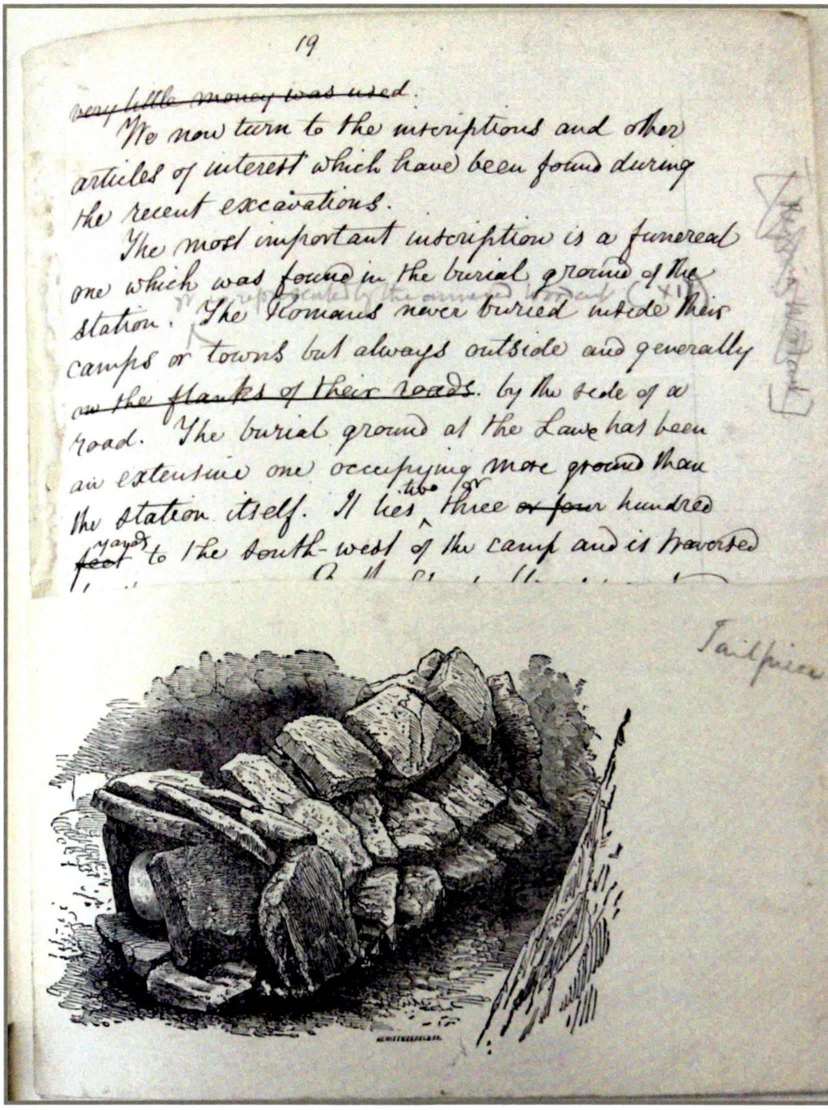

19

~~very little money was used.~~

We now turn to the inscriptions and other articles of interest which have been found during the recent excavations.

The most important inscription is a funereal one which was found in the burial ground of the station. The Romans never buried inside their camps or towns but always outside and generally ~~on the flanks of their roads~~. by the side of a road. The burial ground at the Lawe has been an extensive one occupying more ground than the station itself. It lies two or three ~~or four~~ hundred ~~feet~~ yards to the south-west of the camp and is traversed

Tailpiece

Page 19 of Dr Collingwood Bruce's hand written notes, plus his amendments for the speech he gave at the Society of Antiquaries of London in June 1878.

The notes for the entire speech are pasted into the Scrapbook.
Blair Scrapbook; courtesy of South Tyneside Libraries.

Photograph from 1876 of one of the graves found near the fort site.
Blair Scrapbook; courtesy of South Tyneside Libraries.

Shields Gazette and Daily Telegraph, Friday 18th February 1876

ROMAN REMAINS
This morning, the workmen engaged in excavating the foundations for a house on ground the property of Mr. Pollard, came upon a Roman grave roughly flagged, and containing the almost perfect remains of a human skeleton. This, we may say is the third grave that has been discovered, and will doubtless awaken fresh interest on the subject. The remains have been removed to the museum in the Free Library which will be opened shortly.

Sunderland Daily Echo, Saturday 10th June 1876

DISCOVERY OF A ROMAN GRAVE AT SOUTH SHIELDS
Mr. John Hinde, South Shields, who has taken a great interest in the explorations at the Roman remains, Lawe, South Shields, yesterday morning, while examining the sand pits behind Bath-street, came upon a Roman grave containing the skeleton of a body in an excellent state of preservation. This is the seventh coffin found in the locality, and is the best specimen that has yet been found. The body was lying with its head to the north-east, the usual direction being south-east. The remains were carefully exhumed, and conveyed the Roman Remains Museum, Free Library, South Shields.

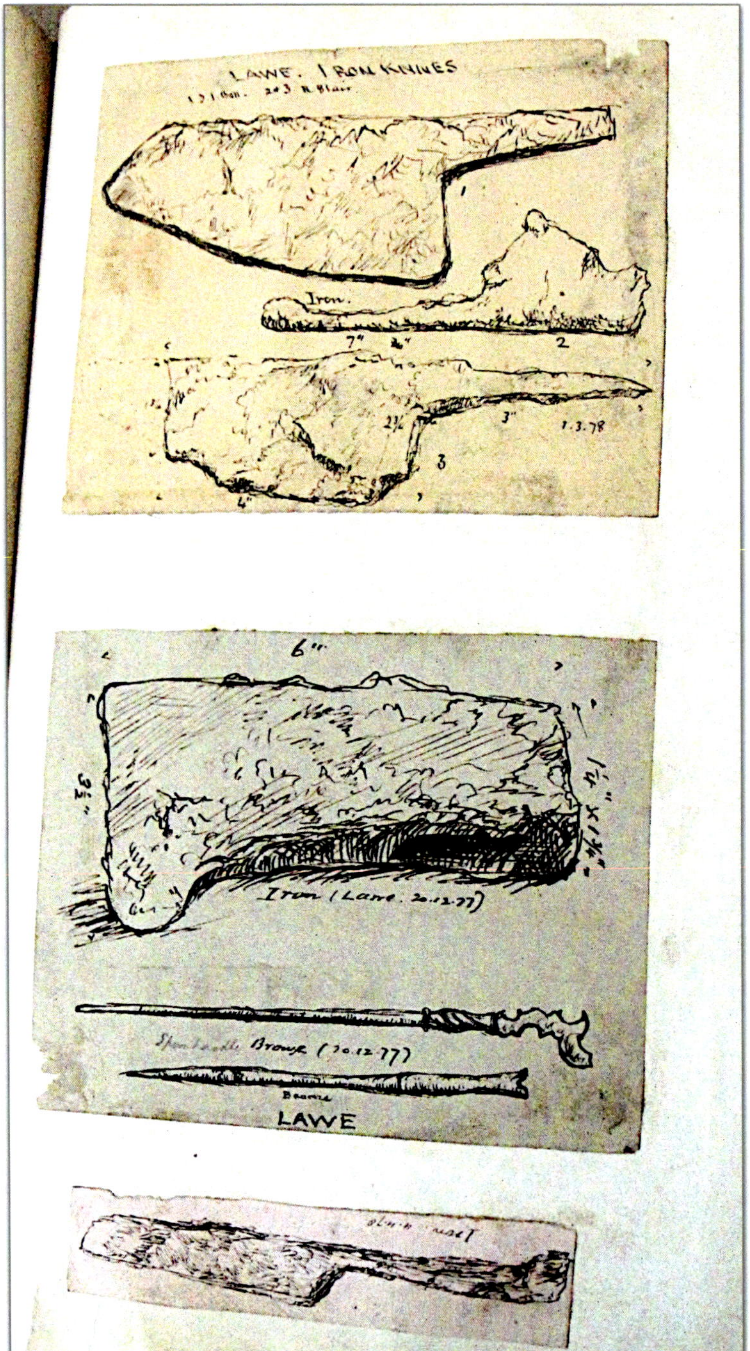

Robert Blair's drawings of finds from the Lawe.
Blair Scrapbook; courtesy of South Tyneside Libraries.

The People's Roman Remains Park

The Victorians identified this as a metal goblet but modern research indicates it was a candlestick (the base should be a mirror image of the top) in the collection of Arbeia South Shields Roman Fort.
Photograph courtesy of Tyne & Wear Archives & Museums.

7

The Library and Museum, Ocean Road in the 1930s before the removal of the Roman remains to the new purpose built museum at the fort in 1953.
Photographs reproduced by kind permission of South Tyneside Libraries.

No one could ever accuse the Victorian South Shields Town Council of a lack of ambition. Moving into the monumental new Town Hall in 1910, a building that reinforced the Corporation's powerful sense of its own importance, councillors could congratulate themselves on having transformed the town in just a few decades.

The Corporation's own electric trams ran along Ocean Road to the North and South Marine Parks, reclaimed from the old ballast heaps, and terminated at the lifeboat memorial on Ocean Road, a confident statement of the town's identity symbolised by its coat of arms featuring the lifeboat and the motto *'always ready'*. Who remembers now that the clock tower was built to celebrate Queen Victoria's Golden Jubilee? With its Customs House, Marine School and the largest coal dock in the world in South Shields anything seemed possible. Most of what the councillors did was a credit to both the Corporation and the town but in 1875 securing the legacy of the excavations on the Lawe, after the success of the summer excavations, brought no credit to anyone. Perhaps the businessmen on the council were suspicious of the antiquarians and couldn't see a profit in expenditure on ancient relics or maybe they were just too absorbed in their own concerns to appreciate the value of the Roman Fort to the town.

The unfortunate story of the arrival of the tramway to South Shields illustrates the Corporation at its worst and shows councillors were quite willing to spoil the ship for a *'ha'porth of tar'*. The Corporation was empowered to construct a standard gauge (4ft 8.5ins) tramway (an essential amenity for any up and coming town) by an act of Parliament in 1881. They built it themselves with the intention of leasing it to the operator, seen as a profitable arrangement, but unfortunately changed the specification in the planning process to a narrow gauge (3ft 6ins) line to save money. So when an inspection took place with full ceremonial honours the inspector refused to allow the tramway to open because it was not built as authorised. It was an unpleasant reminder to the Corporation that there were limits to their power. The tramway cost more than £15,000, a saving of £2,000 on the original proposal but the delay cost more than was originally saved. It may have been the result of some councillors willingness to pursue petty local rivalries as it was suggested at a council meeting that one of the benefits of the narrow gauge was that it would keep other operators (Jarrow, who had sought running powers over the system) out of the town.

Two early twentieth century postcards from the collection of E Lewthwaite.
Above the New Town Hall.
Belowthe tram terminus which was shown as the Pier Head on the destination board.

In the 1930s trams from the Ridgeway to Mile End Road were named after Roman Emperors and one was named *Caer Urfa* ***which was then thought to be the Roman name of South Shields.***

The trams to the Pier Head were replaced by trolley buses on 4th April 1937. Trams disappeared from the town centre in 1938 but continued to run along King George Road to the Ridgeway until 1946.

Rebuilding was not an option, so the corporation had no choice but to go back to Parliament for an amendment to the original act to authorise the narrow gauge. In 1905 the tramway was eventually rebuilt to the original standard gauge.

The 1875 excavation was a private project funded by public subscription but the spectacular finds and the substantial remains of the fort itself presented the town council with a problem they didn't expect when the Ecclesiastical Commissioners gave permission for the archaeological exploration of the site on the Lawe (see page 63). It was a condition of the agreement that any finds should be handed over to the Corporation and put on public display, but the number and quality of finds was a problem which threatened to overwhelm the Free Library.

South Shields had a museum in 1875, the '*curiosity shop*' as it was lovingly nicknamed, but it was an embarrassment to the town – a neglected and run-down collection of oddments in rotten cabinets and mouldy examples of the taxidermists art displayed in an inaccessible room at the back of the free library. Joint curators for a new museum were appointed on the 23rd October 1875, a geologist (Mr. Lyall) and a naturalist with an interest in taxidermy (Mr. Yellowly), but it wasn't until the 9th February 1876, just two weeks before the planned opening that the excavation committee agreed to hand over its finds to the Corporation and as a result the Roman artefacts were hardly displayed to their best advantage at the opening. Roman finds continued to be made even though the formal excavation ended in the autumn of 1875 and in the weeks before the opening of the museum. In February 1876 a stone flagged grave complete with (unusually for the area) an almost perfect skeleton (see page 180) was discovered by builders on the south side of the Lawe towards Ocean Road just in time for it to be shown at the opening ceremony and further spectacular finds would follow from the Roman cemetery in the area.

It took an outsider to tell South Shields that the Roman Fort was a key part of its new identity. There is no doubt that the Reverend Dr. Collingwood Bruce was the star at the opening of the museum on Thursday 24th February 1876. He arrived late at the end of the Mayor, Mr. Broughton's opening speech and made a grand entrance to warm applause before making an impromptu address of his own, flattering his hosts by placing Shields ahead

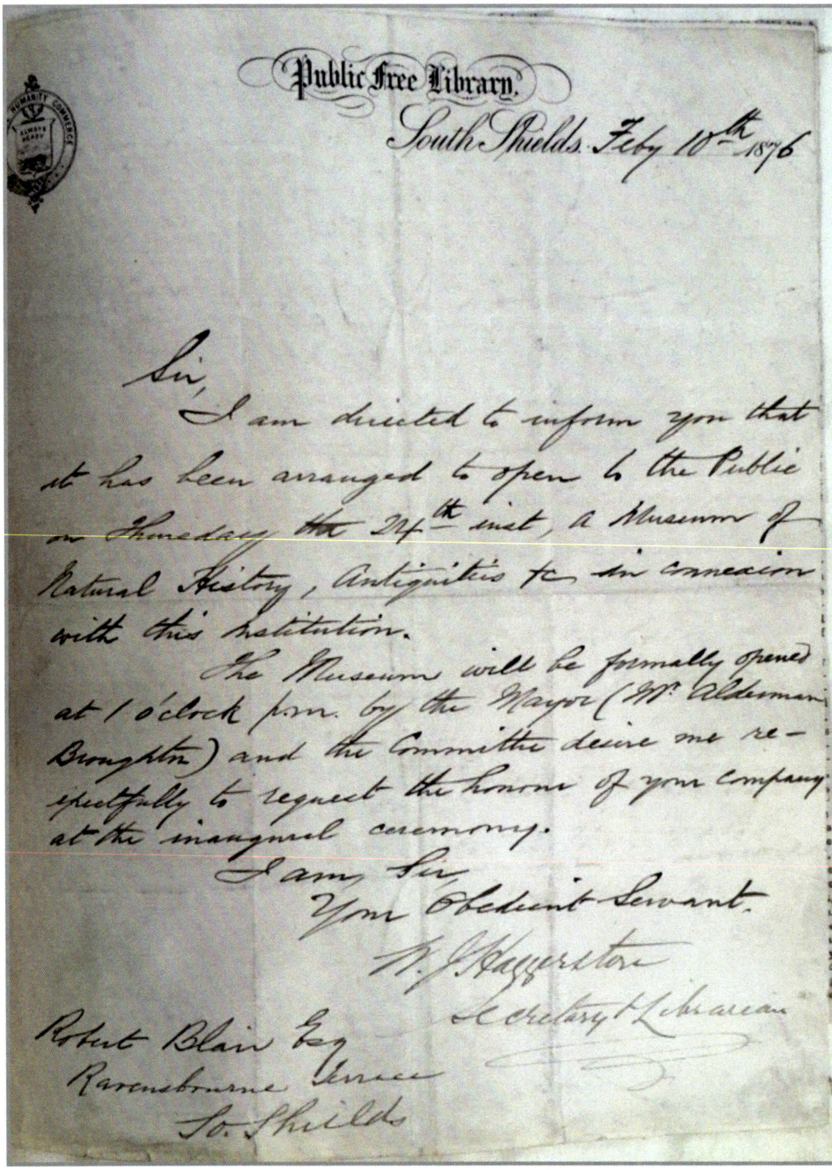

Public Free Library.
South Shields. Feby 10th 1876

Sir,

I am directed to inform you that it has been arranged to open to the Public on Thursday the 24th inst, a Museum of Natural History, Antiquities &c in connexion with this Institution.

The Museum will be formally opened at 1 o'clock p.m. by the Mayor (Mr Alderman Broughton) and the Committee desire me respectfully to request the honour of your company at the inaugural ceremony.

I am, Sir,
Your Obedient Servant.
W. J. Haggerstone
Secretary & Librarian

Robert Blair Esq
Ravensbourne Terrace
So. Shields

Robert Blair's invitation to the opening of the new museum preserved in his scrapbook. The letter is transcribed on the opposite page.
Blair Scrapbook; courtesy of South Tyneside Libraries.

of Newcastle in establishing a public museum and leading the way so others might follow. Toasting the success of the new venture Dr Collingwood Bruce declared that South Shields had a general museum which demonstrated the common humanity of mankind in contrast to the private museums of Newcastle which were limited to the district. Referring to the Roman remains he said that Great Britain and, by implication, South Shields now stood in the place of Rome at the centre of the world and should learn from its history.

> *Public Free Library*
>
> *South Shields Feb 10th 1876*
>
> *Sir,*
> *I am directed to inform you that it has been arranged to open to the Public on Thursday 24th inst., a museum of Natural History, Antiquities etc., in connection with this institution.*
> *The Museum will be formally opened at 1 o' clock by the Mayor (Mr Alderman Broughton) and the Committee desire me respectfully to request the honour of your company at the inaugural ceremony.*
> *I am Sir,*
> *Your Obedient Servant,*
> *N J Haggerston*
> *Secretary to Librarian*

It was a bold claim for a museum that occupied a single room of a modest library in an obscure northern industrial town, but Dr. Collingwood Bruce was an experienced speaker and he caught the feelings of the moment perfectly - Shields' folk then were not noted for modesty about themselves or their town. Surprisingly, given the circumstances as he declared the museum open, the mayor was less enthusiastic about the project than the Reverend Doctor. Mr. Broughton commented that he was '*rather surprised that a museum had not been formed before for he had himself seen specimens of each curiosities, brought home from afar by travellers, and had long since come to the conclusion that very few of the inhabitants of South Shields took an interest in anything of the kind, but on the contrary gave their minds up to the best freights and the highest repayments; in fact, to pounds, shillings, and pence*'.

Discovered at South Shields.

THE MONUMENTAL STONE FOUND AT THE ROMAN REMAINS, SOUTH SHIELDS.—It will be recollected that on the 19th of October of last year some workmen in digging out the foundation for a building at the back of some premises in Bath Street, South Shields, discovered a gravestone, on which was carved the figure of a woman sitting on a chair or throne with flowers in her lap, and a basket of fruit at her left side. At the base of the stone was a well executed Latin inscription, and below this is a line of writing conjectured to be in Syriac characters. These characters have been variously interpreted. Professor Wright, L.L.D, in a paper which he has published on the subject, says in reference to the characters:—More than one person has surmised that the last word might be read in the sense either of a sailor, or of a ropemaker, but an examination of other inscriptions in which it occurs, shows that this is out of the question. Much more plausible is another suggestion, first made by the Rev. P. Philippstein, of North Shields, namely, that the last letters may be a contraction of some eulogistic, or other formula in common use when speaking of the dead. If so, Dr Schiller-Szinesy thinks that it might be read, "May his (or her) portion be in the life everlasting." Be this as it may, such contractions were certainly in use at a very remote period, for example, in the Phenician inscription commonly called the "M lt Quifuta," the difficult phrase at the beginning of line 4, is really to be read "in the time of one most worthy magistrate."

The discovery of the Regina stone: a newspaper cutting from Robert Blair's Scrapbook
Blair Scrapbook; courtesy of South TynesideLibraries.

The administration of the museum by the Council's Free Library Committee had more of the spirit of Mr. Broughton in it than that of Dr. Collingwood Bruce and it would be fair to say that it was starved of funds throughout its early life which had a lasting effect on its later development. The acquisition of the fantastic monument to Regina, freedwoman and wife of Barates, which was accidentally discovered in the Bath Street area of the Lawe in 1878 (see pages 121 - 127) and presented to it by the finder, should have been a massive boost to its prestige but despite the efforts of its curators lack of space and focus was a continuing problem. When another large stone commemorating the installation of a new water supply at the fort was found at Baring Street School (see illustrations page 192) the school board were initially reluctant to donate it to the museum because of fears that it wouldn't be properly displayed as the large stones were then laid under the tables in the museum and impossible to study properly.

The name of Robert Blair doesn't appear on the list of distinguished guests at the opening ceremony for the new museum in 1876 although he was almost certainly present (see invite page 189). Is it just that the newly qualified solicitor who was secretary of the excavation committee wasn't considered important enough to merit a mention in the local newspapers? Dr. Hooppell, the former headmaster of the Marine School who played such an important part in the campaign, was invited but having moved to Binchester he sent his apologies. So it was left to Mr. Ralph Carr Ellison, the third of the original campaigners who wrote to the Gazette in 1875, to remind the gathering that despite the success of last summer's excavations much remained to be done and *'they must first find their Roman antiquities, and then place them in a museum more worthy of South Shields'* if they wished to complete the work started in the summer.

Robert Blair kept his scrapbook partially because of his concerns about the future of the site on the Lawe and the preservation of the growing collection of finds which could not be properly displayed in the museum. He built up his own collection of artefacts from South Shields usually bought from prospectors who scoured the site after the formal excavations ended and who, despite the Dr. Collingwood Bruce's entreaties in his speech at the opening of the museum, declined to donate them to the Corporation which did not have the funds to purchase them. Unlike Dr. Hooppell and Dr. Collingwood Bruce Robert Blair was a Shields-man born and bred, the son of

A photograph of the waterstone on display in the Arbeia, South Shields Roman Fort.
Photograph courtesy of Tyne & Wear Archives & Museums.

An engraving of the waterstone.
Blair Scrapbook; courtesy of South Tyneside Libraries.

a Tyne pilot from the Lawe, he lived in the town, and his office in King Street was the first port of call for anyone with an interesting artefact to sell. Perhaps he shared their suspicion of the Corporation and all its works due to his frustration with their failure to build on his work and secure the preservation of the Roman fort at the end of the 1875 excavations. He was co-opted onto the management committee of the museum in 1881 and did play a crucial role in securing (for the museum) the waterstone and the monument to Victor the Moor. During the 1875 excavations he was accused of attempting to exclude the public from the dig but he was at heart an enthusiastic antiquarian, a collector who wanted to secure the future of objects that might otherwise have been lost in the chaotic circumstances after the end of the excavation, when the site was effectively abandoned and open to all comers seeking treasure.

An Editorial from the Shields Gazette and Daily Telegraph, Tuesday 11th June 1878

THE ROMAN REMAINS MUST BE PRESERVED

The Roman Station at South Shields has not late months occupied much of public attention in the town or neighbourhood, but its importance has not been lost sight of at a distance for those who are more particularly interested in such antiquities. Within the last few weeks the desirability of preserving a portion of the Remains from the destruction which threatens them by the progress of building operations at the Lawe has been considered by the Council of the British Archaeological Association in London, as well as by the local Exploration Committee, and the Committee of the Public Library. The result of this combined movement has been the opening of communications with the Municipal Corporation, which, last Wednesday, sanctioned the preparation of a memorial for presentation to Ecclesiastical Commissioners, asking for a gift of a portion of the land in which the discoveries had been made. The Church of England so largely indebted to South Shields in respect of its temporalities, that the request preferred by the Town Council ought on that ground alone meet with a favourable reception at the hands of the Commissioners. Apart, however, from a claim of this

To the Editor of the Shields Gazette Daily & Telegraph.

SIR,—Kindly permit me to trouble you again. The Roman Remains at the Lawe; are they worth preserving? That depends upon how we look at them. Some people see with their eyes only; others with their hearts also. The former regard these remains merely as old walls, broken and dispoiled—better may be seen any day. The latter see in the ruins a whole page of ancient history. They see the Island Hill, now called the "Lawe," sixteen or seventeen centuries ago, crowned with its Roman fort, a parallelogram 618 feet long, by 375 feet wide, enclosed by a rampart wall 6 feet thick, having four gateways, east, west, north, and south, garrisoned probably for a period extending over three hundred years, with its Cohort of Roman Soldiers (COH. V. G.), these soldiers marching up the Reken Dyke, across the Mill Dam, by the Barns, over where Tyne Dock houses now are, and on to Lanchester, thence to head-quarters at York. They see them "in piping times of peace," assembled at their Forum, seated in their guard rooms, or gossiping at their gates; and at other times stoutly defending their Castrum from the incursions of fierce Caledonian hordes. How much more may be learnt from their pottery, their personal ornaments, their domestic animals, &c., time and space forbid me to say. The annals of their history, unrecorded elsewhere, are written in the soil, and are readable to-day. Archæology is History. Old, old Shields presents itself vividly to our minds in the walls, chambers, hypocausts, and pavements, which cover more than five acres of ground at the Lawe. Then surely they are worth preserving!

Yours truly,

T. LINCOLN.

Mr. Lincoln's letter to the Shields Gazette and Daily Telegraph, Tuesday 21st September 1875, cutting from Robert Blair's Scrapbook.
Blair Scrapbook; courtesy of South Tyneside Libraries.

> **character, a body such as that about to be approached by the Corporation may be expected to recognise the national importance of preserving all such relics as those in question.**
>
> **This is not a hobby or a fad, but a project for retaining to the town, and to England itself, a remarkably distinct record of a period of profoundest interest to every reflective man and woman in the island. When the reply of the Ecclesiastical Commissioners is received it will be time enough to deliberate on the nature and extent of the Council's contributions to the preservation of the Station; but that it would be warranted in regarding any such expenditure contributing to the common good in every sense of the term, and therefore perfectly legal, would scarcely be questioned by the most pronounced of economists.**

The absence of some of the most striking artefacts from the fort at South Shields remains however an unfortunate gap in both the history of the excavation and the public record of the remains. Robert Blair made his reputation as an antiquarian as secretary of the excavation committee at South Shields, but he now is better known for his forty years' service to the Society of Antiquaries of Newcastle-upon-Tyne as secretary and editor of its journal *Archaeologia Aeliana*, a role he took over from his mentor Dr. Collingwood Bruce, whose *Handbook to the Roman Wall* he also edited. Robert Blair received a unique honour from the Society, a medal in recognition of his outstanding contribution to their work, and his collection passed to them on his death. It is now part of the Roman collection of the Great North Museum: Hancock, Newcastle.

If the condition of the museum at South Shields was sometimes an embarrassment to the Corporation the state of the Roman Remains excavated in 1875, against the background of popular enthusiasm, was by 1876 a disgrace that became a national scandal which forced the Corporation somewhat reluctantly to spend money preserving them. The preservation of the remains was first suggested by Mr. Lincoln, a member of the excavation committee, in a letter to the Gazette on 21st September 1875 when the future of the site was being openly discussed in the town although it wasn't part of the original agreement with the Ecclesiastical Commissioners or one of the objectives of the excavation committee. It was assumed that the site

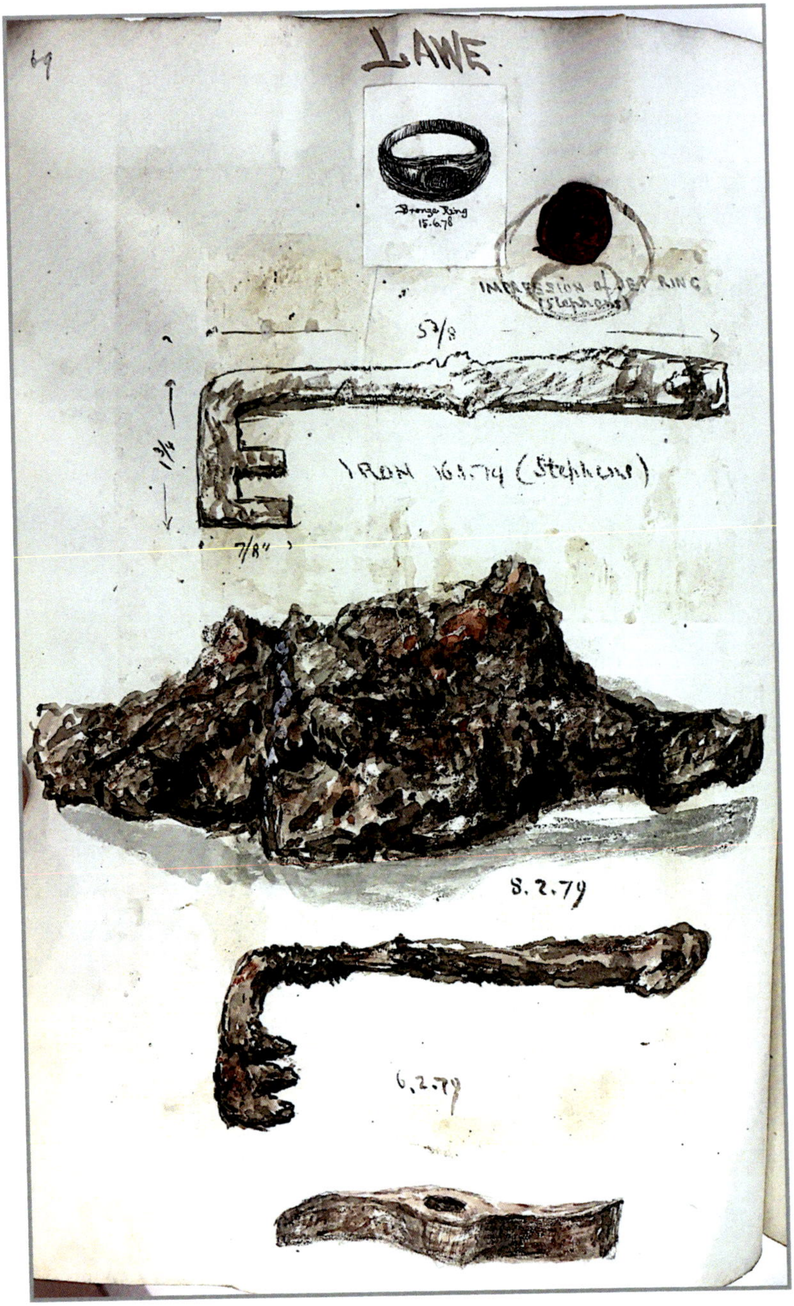

Page 6 from Robert Blair's Scrapbook: Small finds from the Lawe include many items which illuminated the everyday life of the population of Roman South Shields. Most were deposited in the museum but they weren't well displayed and the legacy of the excavation was at first very disappointing.
Blair Scrapbook; courtesy of South Tyneside Libraries.

would eventually be let for building after the excavation, especially since the houses built all around it had greatly increased its value, but the town council seems to have been reluctant to take any decision regarding its future which might have re-opened the 1875 campaign. By the time the Museum was opened, in the Free Library, in 1876, the archaeological site was effectively abandoned due to lack of funds to continue the work, as it depended upon paid workmen to do the excavation. The Roman remains at South Shields certainly weren't abandoned by Dr. Hooppell, who had built a reputation for himself by his lectures and papers on the excavations and who was now beginning to build another with the excavation of the Roman fort at Binchester.

Speaking to a meeting of the Tyneside Naturalist's Field Club at Newcastle on the 23rd January 1877, in the presence of Dr. Collingwood Bruce and John Clayton, Dr. Hooppell described the neglected condition of the remains, robbed by builder's labourers and turned over by children, and called for their preservation. In another lecture to the St Hilda's Church Young Men's Institute he called the state of the remains lamentable, but his complaints came to nothing as councillors had no desire to spend money on the site. That is until matters came to a head when the land was about to be let for building and the Corporation received a letter from the British Archaeological Association calling for the preservation of the remains.

The exact circumstances that led to the letter from the Association informing the Corporation of a resolution passed on the 11th May 1878 calling for the Corporation to purchase and preserve the surviving portion of the site is unknown. It seems likely that Dr. Hooppell, who was a member, was the instigator. The resolution, like the letters that launched the campaign to save the fort in 1875, was certainly part of an organised campaign supported by a timely editorial in the *Shields Gazette,* prior to a meeting of the Town Council on the 4th June. Councillors faced with the resolution from the British Archaeological Association, a supporting memorandum from the Free Library Committee and a letter from the Excavation Committee signed by Robert Blair had no idea they were about to make history by approving the creation of the first public archaeological park in the country when they agreed in principle to let the matter proceed.

Even with the support of the British Archaeological Association the preservation of the remains was by no means assured although the

An Edwardian postcard sent from South Shields in 1906, depicting the People's Roman Remains Park, with the Baring Street Schools in the background.

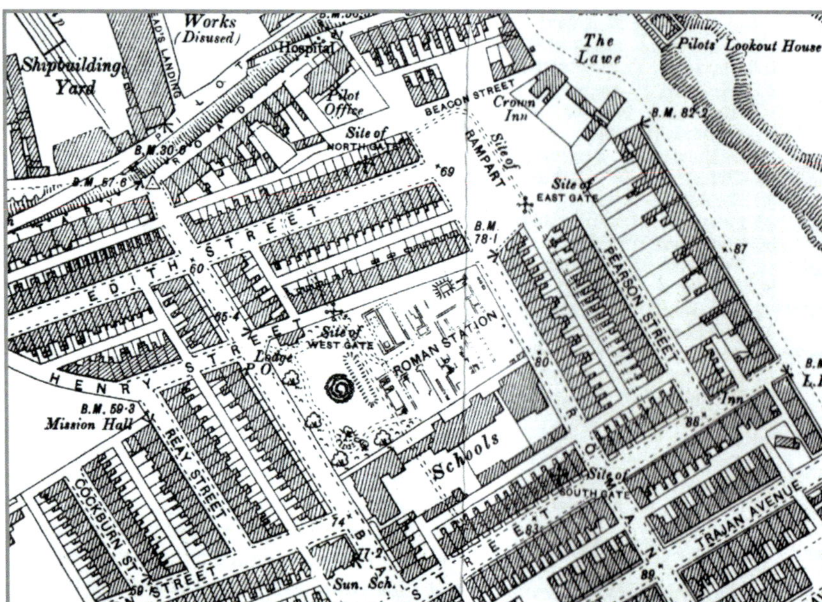

The area which became** The People's Roman Remains Park **was a much smaller area than the current large site given over to the Fort on the Lawe. At the end of the nineteenth century many terraced houses, with running water and individual outside toilets, were constructed in the area as well as schools.
1895 Godfrey Map of the Mouth of the Tyne.

Ecclesiastical Commissioners did smooth the path by gifting the land to the Corporation. There was still some opposition within the council to the cost of building a caretaker's house and erecting a wall around the site but with the story now being covered in national newspapers the reputation of the town was at stake, so the Corporation really had no option but to proceed with the scheme. The People's Roman Remains Park, the first of its type in Britain, a publicly owned archaeological park, was complete in 1881 though the Corporation was at best a reluctant parent to what has become a beloved child. We are fortunate to have a full description of the Park from the Newcastle Courant of November 1881 and later reprinted with approval like a Victorian *trip advisor* review in the *Shields Gazette*. The writer who calls himself an antiquary is probably Dr. Hooppell who regularly wrote a column for the newspaper. He included helpful suggestions for the future development of the park such as roofing the treasure chamber in the forum to form a museum, recreating the ditch to provide an appropriate entry to the park and expanding the site by taking possession of adjacent waste land.

Dr. Hooppell, were he to return to the place now, would be impressed that his vision has been realised with the expansion of the park to cover most of the area of the fort following the demolition of the surrounding houses in the 1960s and improved by the presence of a museum on the site. He would undoubtedly be amazed by the reconstructed west gate, courtyard house and barrack block which bring the fort to life without the imagination demanded in Mr. Lincoln's letter which started it all.

Reprinted by the Shields Daily Gazette from the Newcastle Courant, 29 November 1881

AN ANTIQUARY SOUTH SHIELDS.

A writer, signing himself " H ," has the following in the Newcastle Courant :— Upon visiting Shields recently I was glad to see the progress made by the authorities of the town, in enclosing, preserving, and laying out the portion of the site of the old Roman station which was presented to the Corporation a year or two back by the Ecclesiastical Commissioners. The Roman station at South Shields was a very fine, and a very important one. It was extensively explored by committee 1875-6, aided by liberal subscriptions from

The photograph shows the Roman fort excavations in 1967 by members of the South Shields Archaeology and History Society. They are digging a trench from north to south across Edith Street, which had been recently demolished. In the background can be seen Baring Street Secondary School which was subsequently demolished in November 1980.
Baring Street Primary School still stands now providing display areas and offices related to Arbeia, South Shields Roman Fort.
Photograph by kind permission of South Tyneside Libraries.

many residents of the town and friends at a distance and, ever since that time, it has been diligently searched by pilots and others living in the neighbourhood, for any relics of the Roman period which they might be fortunate enough to light upon.

The antiquarian treasure it has yielded has been very great. Many of the "finds" have been deposited in the Museum of the Public Free Library, Ocean Road. Many have been acquired by Robert Blair, solicitor. Many more have, doubtless, been dispersed in all directions. The Fortress was situated on "the Lawe," a lofty promontory at the junction the Tyne with the sea. It covered more than five acres. Part of this is now built upon Part of it included the portion of land given the town by the Ecclesiastical Commissioners. About four acres of it still remain waste. This remaining portion, I was to hear, the Town Council have just requested the Commissioners add to their former grant. If the prayer of their memorial is complied with it will be a great boon to the town It will enhance the value of the rest of the Commissioner's property, which surrounds it on all sides, and has been, and will doubtless, hereafter continue to be, very extensively built upon. And it will be an important gain to archaeology. In fact some of the finest remains stand upon it. There is the eastern rampart, running for many scores of yards perfect, its lower courses, as when it was erected the Romans. If the Corporation secured the land, and expose, and preserve, this remarkable wall, I believe they will possess historical monument of the early existence and importance of their borough such as no other populous town in England can exhibit. In the case of the two already acquired, the Corporation have acted with much judgment. They have enclosed the whole with a dwarf wall, surmounted with iron railings of good design. They have erected a caretaker's cottage near to the principal entrance and have laid out the portion of the ground adjoining the modern street and extending between it and the western rampart the station as a lawn and shrubbery.

The rest of the ground, which filled with the foundations of Roman buildings, the pavement the Roman forum or market place, the walls of temples and chambers, they have cleared off the superincumbent earth, and intend I suppose, to plant, wherever they can find room to, with hardy perennial flowers and shrubs. They cannot of course do anything in the way of breaking the level, or they would destroy the

A purpose built Museum to house the finds was not built until 1953. The new building is shown in the above photograph, but note how close the houses were on the north (left) side of the building.

The lower photograph shows the back view of the museum with the reconstructed west gate now standing on this area cleared when the Victorian housing was demolished in the 1960s.

Photographs reproduced by kind permission of South Tyneside Libraries.

very objects, for the purpose of preserving which they have acquired the ground. Nor will it do to plant large shrubs, or trees, for these, when they grow, would displace the stones of the old Roman town, and interfere besides with the visitor's view of its arrangements. The only thing to be done is keep the area of the Roman city clear of accumulations of earth and dust, and to occupy any favourable nook with a flower or plant. There is one spot, however, where a diversity of surface might be effected. All round the ramparts, outside the fortress, there ran a deep fosse or ditch. This, in the course of ages, became choked with earth. But it is there, plainly discoverable by the clay slope on each side. This, the western side, between the Modern street and the ancient rampart, could be cleared out. The earth which was removed could be used for an artificial mound or mounds on the spot which is now devoted to a level lawn. Thus, the aspect of the ornamental ground next to the street would be improved; and, by the clearing cut of the fosse, the ancient appearance the approach to the Roman buildings from the west would be restored. Another very desirable work, which might be accomplished, is the roofing over the most important chamber existing on the ground. Besides being one of the best-preserved portions of the remains in South Shields, this chamber is, in itself, peculiarly interesting. It is probably unique in this country. A flight of steps, worn by the passage up and down of innumerable feet, in Roman times, leads into it from the great building which stood immediately north of the Forum. The walls are composed of enormous blocks of stone. The. floor is paved, and the floor at one spot there is a sunken cistern. When found, the sill of a window and portions of the jambs were in position. These, probably, could still be recovered and replaced, and if a dwarf wall were raised upon the massive Roman Walls, and a roof, lighted with slabs rough plate inserted in it, placed upon them, the chamber would be effectually preserved, the rain kept out of it, which now, from time to time, stands in it as in a reservoir; and a museum would be provided for such fragments of the columnar work, and other sculptured and massive stones, as cannot well find a home in the limited space of the Public Free Library available for heavy objects. That the Corporation may succeed in their application, the Ecclesiastical Commissioners grant them the rest of the site of the Roman Town still remaining in their hands, for similar careful treatment and preservation, is a result every antiquary and lover of his country's monumental history cannot fail most earnestly to desire.

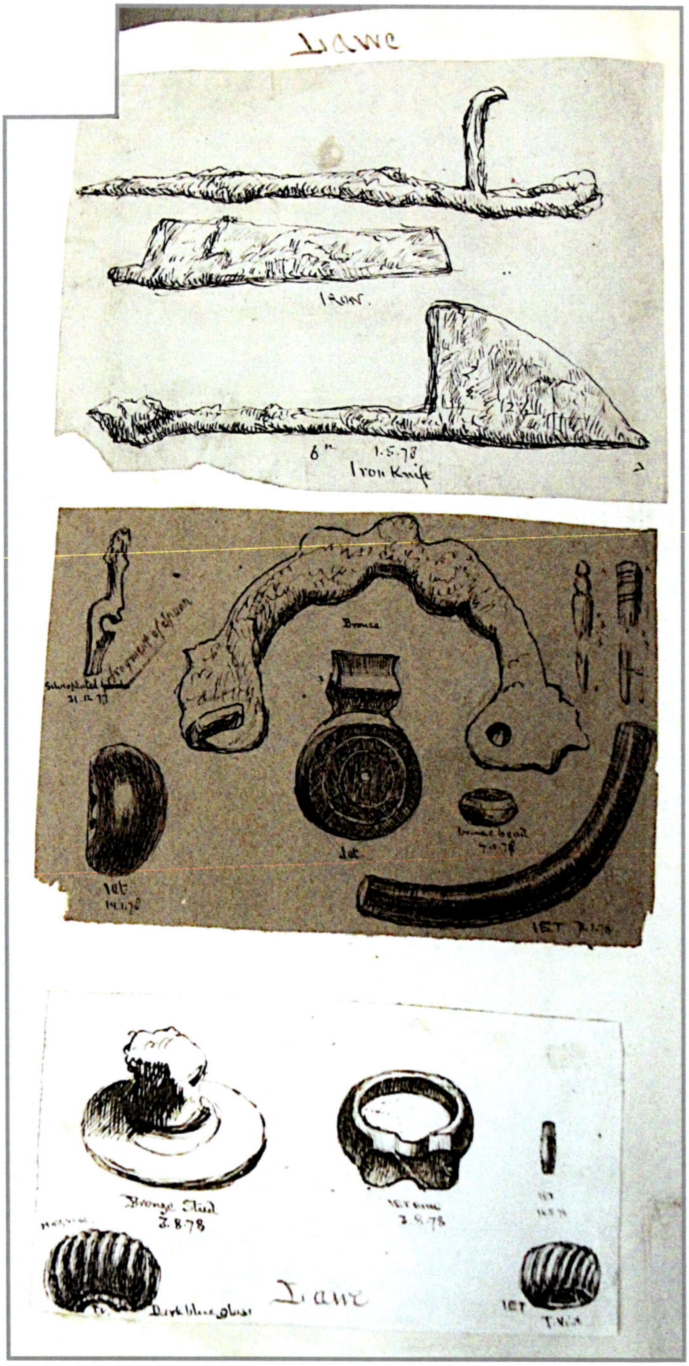

A page of drawings by Robert Blair of finds at the Lawe dated 1878.
Blair Scrapbook; courtesy of South Tyneside Libraries.

Heritage & History

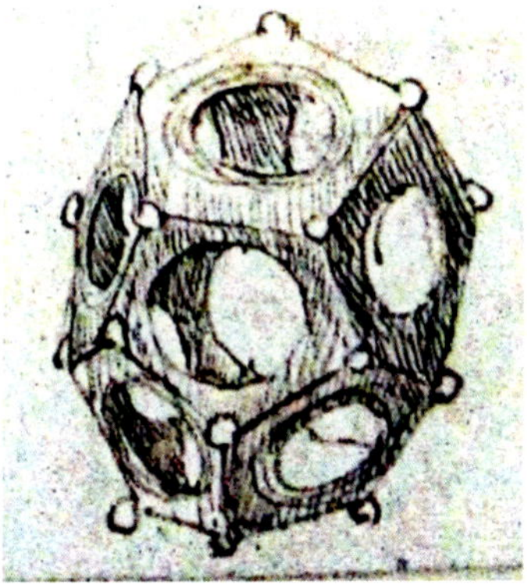

Drawing by Robert Blair of a bronze dodecahedron thought to be a puzzle or toy. The object is in the collection of the Great North Museum:Hancock, Newcastle.
Blair Scrapbook; courtesy of South Tyneside Libraries.

8

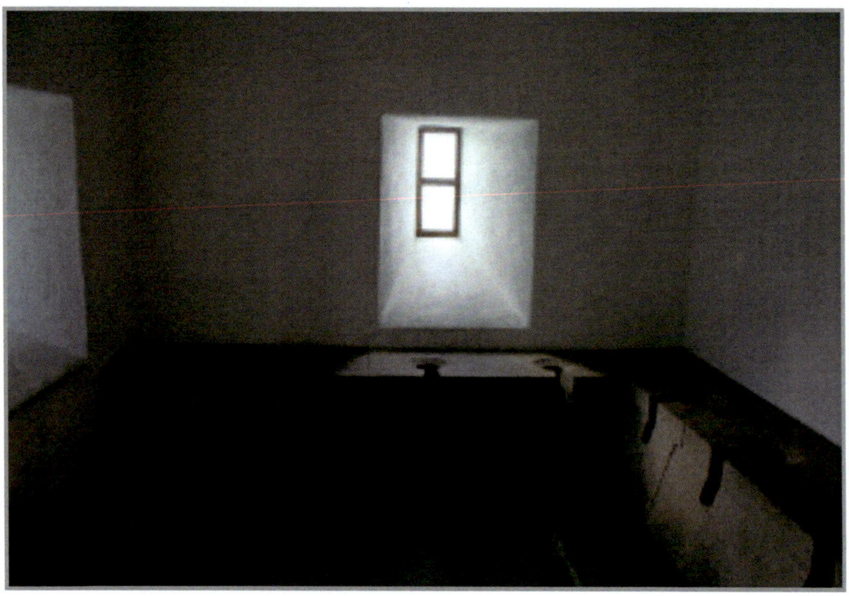

The reconstructed bath house at Segedunum Roman Fort, Wallsend which includes the communal Roman toilets, shown in the lower photograph.
Photographs courtesy of Tyne & Wear Archives & Museums.

Travellers new to the Tyne and Wear Metro might be surprised arriving at Wallsend to find the name of the station and other notices written in Latin. The makeover was part of a campaign to promote the nearby newly excavated Roman Fort of Segedunum which was opened to the public in the year 2000 following the demolition of terraced housing and the closure of the Swan Hunter Shipyard that covered the site. Segedunum is the neighbour of the fort at South Shields, the second on Tyneside to be opened as a public museum 125 years after the first and, like North Tyneside Council, at the turn of the new millennium South Shields Corporation promoted their Roman heritage though public transport by naming trams after Roman emperors, something which was unique in Britain.

In 1922 South Shields Corporation opened the final section of its electric tramway system, a light railway down King George Road serving the new housing estates at Cleadon on the Borough boundary. Despite the disasters that overtook the town following the end of the Victorian era, a world war followed by an economic depression that hit the local coal industry hard, the Corporation was as ever optimistic about the future. The new estate at Cleadon was just the start of a slum clearance scheme that changed the shape of the town and moved its focus inland away from the riverside and supported the Corporation's municipal bus services until the privatisations of the Thatcher era. When luxurious new tramcars were introduced on the route between Mile End Road and the Ridgeway, a route described by the managers as a gold mine in 1928, they were named after Roman Emperors: Vespasian, Julian and Hadrian. The names, like the Roman streets around the fort on the Lawe were an expression of pride in South Shields' Roman heritage, and an example of the confidence that linked the town's future to its Roman past. If *The People's Roman Remains Park* with its low walls and grassy banks still needed Mr. Lincoln's imagination to come alive, it was now part of the town's identity and part of the story of what it meant to be a Shields-man or Shields-woman. Other tram cars in an uninhibited outpouring of local patriotism were named after local heroes like Henry Greathead, James Mather and Willie Wouldhave, or ships built on the Tyne like *Mauretania, Monarch of Bermuda* and *HMS Nelson*. One above all the others was the flagship: it was called *Caer Urfa*, long thought to be the Roman name of South Shields by the 1875 excavators and now passed from obscure antiquarian journals into popular consciousness.

The South Shields Corporation Tramcar *Caer Urfa.* ***It is painted crimson lake and cream with gold lettering.***
Photograph reproduced by kind permission of South Tyneside Libraries.

The South Shields Corporation Tramcar *Julian* ***at the Pier Head; Julian never came to the Lawe but the Emperors Severus, Geta and Caracalla are believed to have passed through South Shields.***
Photograph reproduced by kind permission of South Tyneside Libraries.

The Corporation liked to name streets in South Shields to mark local history or to honour prominent figures in the town's history so we still have Trajan Avenue, Vespasian Avenue, Julian Avenue, Fairles Street, Salmon Street and Urfa Terrace recalling the events of 1875 on the Lawe. The origins of Marshall Wallis Road off Dean Road, near what used to be the Corporation tram sheds, are now almost forgotten but the Reverend William Marshall Wallis, whose name it commemorates, was a member of a famous Shields family whose story reflects the rise of Shields itself from obscurity and deserves to be remembered. Marshall Wallis had left the town by 1875 but he returned to see the excavations and kept a record of what he saw in a series of sketches rather as we would now capture a series of images on our mobile phones as souvenirs of our travels.

The Rev. Wallis was an enthusiastic amateur antiquarian with a deep knowledge of what we would now call the heritage sector and his sketches can be used to put the excavations at South Shields into context. Some of his drawings are preserved in Robert Blair's scrapbook and they show he was an accomplished artist with an eye for detail. Apparently completed on site on pages torn from a lined notebook, they captured some of the most interesting items found by the diggers during the early excavations: a large iron key, a bronze handle for carrying a soldier's helmet, a bronze lamp with three wicks, the blue enamelled fittings from a belt found with the remains of at least three swords and their scabbards. Such things were the detritus of everyday life in the fort, touched by the soldiers, administrators, traders, and ladies of the Roman Empire; lost, broken, thrown away, sometimes deliberately hidden and forgotten. Wallis also sketched the foundations of walls and buildings to document for himself the exciting discoveries that were being reported in the local, regional and even national newspapers: the steps down to the strong room, the south east corner of the wall, the enigmatic stone table and he also made a rough plan of the forum and sketched boats on the river when there was nothing else to captured his attention (see illustration on the next page).

Few of the visitors who flocked to the excavations on the Lawe in the spring of 1875 had travelled as far as the Rev. Wallis. He had been born at Westoe and was a member of an old South Shields family with an illustrious history, but now lived at Bucklebury near Newbury and he travelled back to his hometown, as a tourist on the railway which his family had helped to

Sketches and notes made by Rev. William Marshall Wallis, on his visit to the excavations on the Lawe in 1875 preserved in Robert Blair's Scrapbook

create, a new breed of traveler created by the railways which would play an important part in South Shields' future. The Wallis's were landowners, shipbuilders and shipowners who found fame and fortune as the founders of one of Shields' great industries. Sometime before 1720 according to legal records Robert Wallis started building and repairing ships at his yard at the end of what is now Baring Street on the Lawe in defiance of the charter giving the Corporation of Newcastle a monopoly of trade on the river. Shields tradition tells how an alderman who came to enforce Newcastle's rights was tipped into the Tyne for his trouble. There is no way of knowing if that story is true, but the records do show that Robert Wallis successfully fought off two legal actions from Newcastle attempting to close him down and his yard flourished.

The Reverend Wallis's father, who was also called William, was one of the promoters of the Stanhope and Tyne Railway when he leased land at Consett and entered into a partnership with Cuthbert Rippon and William Harrison to work coal at Medomsley and limestone at Stanhope and transport it on a wagonway to be loaded directly into ships at South Shields. The railway which opened in 1834 was engineered by Robert Stephenson and formed part of the route travelled by the first train from London Euston to Gateshead Greensfield on the 18th June 1844. That journey took around ten hours in 1844, but by 1875 took less than seven including a 25-minute stop for lunch at York. As the railways shrank the country it paradoxically also made local history, like the discovery of the fort on the Lawe, more important as towns tried to create their own unique identities and attract visitors interested in what we would now call heritage.

The Rev. Wallis was a man who knew about the latest advances in archaeology and kept himself up to date with new ideas in how museums could educate and inform the public about their history, something which was noticeably absent in the rather parochial outlook that shaped the excavations on the Lawe. He was one of the founder members of Newbury District Field Club in 1870, a society formed to promote the practical study of the natural history and antiquities of West Berkshire and North Hampshire, whose outings to places of historical or antiquarian interest were reported in great detail in the Newbury Weekly News as an example of local enterprise. The club's first outing on 21st June 1870 was a trip by private carriage to the Roman city of Silchester some twelve miles from

Upper image: A locomotive from the Stanhope and Tyne Railway which was promoted by Mr Marshall Wallis' father.
Middle image: Stanhope and Tyne Drops, the railway's terminus at South Shields.
Lower image: An express locomotive from 1875 when the national railway network was effectively complete.
Pictures reproduced by kind permission of South Tyneside Libraries

Newbury where they had lunch in a marquee and viewed the famous bronze eagle found on the 9th October 1866 and met its discoverer Reverend J G Joyce. The Rev. Joyce, Rector of Strathfieldsaye, entertained the group with a tour of the site and an account of the significance of the eagle as a symbol to the Roman legions. The publicity attracted many others to join them and on later outings large groups travelled by private train on the Great Western Railway to Salisbury and Dorchester to visit the cathedrals, churches, great houses and museums. The Rev. Wallis himself even hosted the club when they visited Bucklebury to view its historic church and picturesque avenue of ancient oak trees said to have been planted by Elizabeth I; he also provided lunch for the party, and gave an authoritative lecture on the history of the area.

The main line of the Great Western Railway bypassed Newbury, which was served by a small branch from Reading and, as a result, it was thought to be something of a backwater so one of the main aims of the Field Club was to use history to promote the town. After much debate they decided to commemorate the first battle of Newbury fought on 20th September 1643. The battle, which marked a turning point in the English Civil War with a decisive victory for the Parliamentary Army, was not an obvious choice with Queen Victoria in residence in nearby Windsor but the club raised the money by public subscription, with a plan that might have won the Queen's wholehearted approval. The monument would commemorate the losses on the Royalist side in general and the death of Lucius Carey, the second Viscount Falkland, and the King's Secretary of State in particular. The thirty three foot high obelisk of Cornish granite with inscriptions in Greek and Latin, unveiled on Monday 9th September 1878 in front of a large and enthusiastic crowd (some of whom later appeared in court charged with being drunk and disorderly) had unexpected consequences as it reignited old Civil War divisions being loudly denounced from the pulpit of the local Primitive Methodist Chapel. History had been written, as it had at South Shields with an eye to the future.

The Rev. Wallis who was a member of the Newbury Club's committee for over thirty years was not in favour of such political gestures. In a letter to the Newbury Weekly News published under the pseudonym of Garibaldian (Garibaldi is believed to have been in South Shields for a month in 1854 where he was enthusiastically welcomed by local working men) he

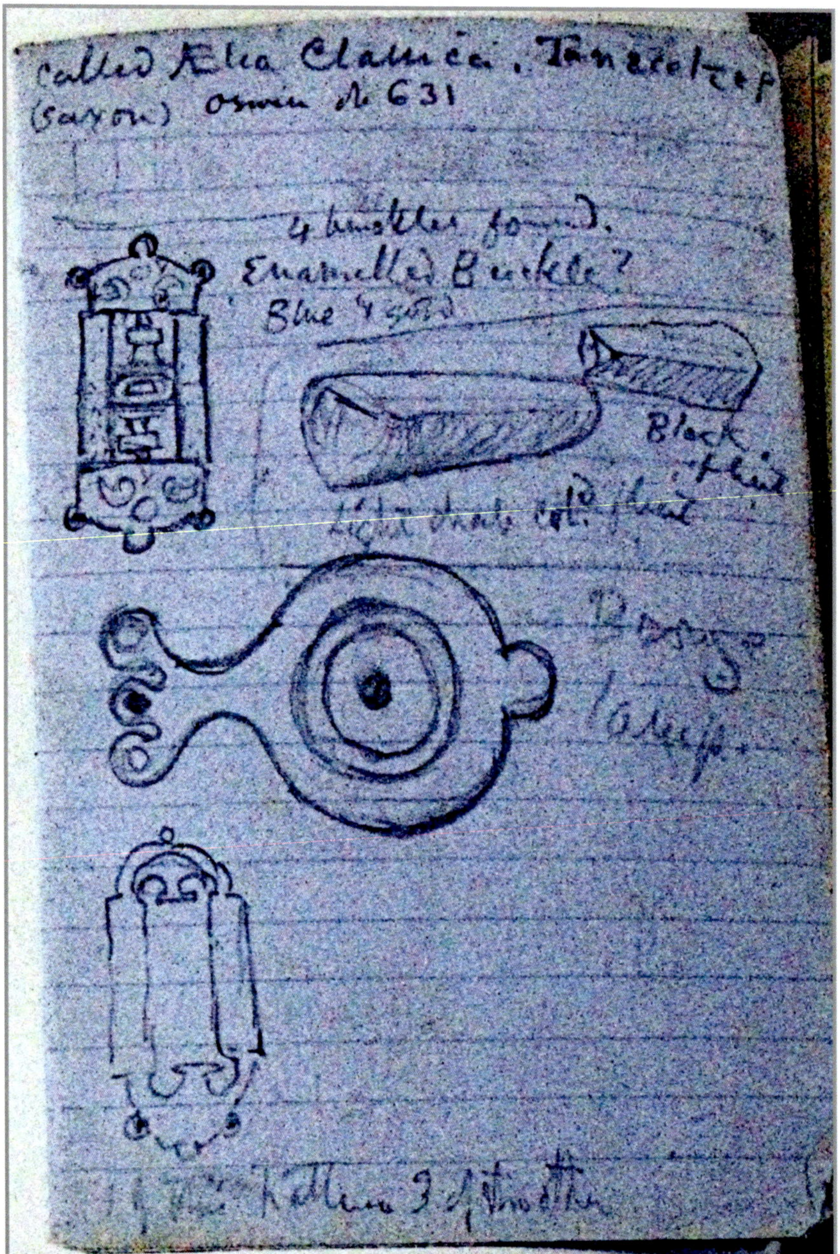

Sketches of finds drawn by Rev. William Marshall Wallis on the Lawe in 1875.
Blair Scrapbook; courtesy of South Tyneside Libraries.

The drawings that Robert Blair made of this oil lamp and buckle and present day photographs of them can be see on pages 154 and 176

complained that the memorial should have commemorated the dead, around 3,000, of both sides and suggested that the subscribers were misled when they contributed to something that was not an accurate commemoration of the battle but local politics were more important than historical accuracy.

Wallis had an interesting background and his arrival in Bucklebury was the result of an unusual combination of events. He was educated at the Percy Street Academy of John Collingwood Bruce and then went to Durham University where he was an assistant to the eminent chemist James Finlay Weir Johnson, who was reader in minerology and chemistry at the new university. Johnson was the leader in his field and an advocate of the application of science to agriculture but unfortunately little is known about Wallis's academic career, although his obituary in the Newbury Weekly News in 1901 says that he lectured on Chemistry, in the absence of Johnson who was based in Edinburgh. Wallis moved to Bucklebury on his marriage in 1858 to Anna Masterman (another famous Shields name as Lydia Masterman was the mother of Thomas Winterbottom, founder of the Marine School) when he inherited Roselands, an elegant house on Bucklebury Common at the end of the iconic avenue of oaks. He was never a professional clergyman despite being ordained as a voluntary curate in 1870, in recognition of his service to the church and he is still remembered in Bucklebury as the builder of the iron church where he preached, a tin chapel of ease opened on Bucklebury Common which survived until 1972, after being rebuilt in 1902 by his family as a memorial to him after his death. It served parishioners unable to reach the ancient parish church from that part of the village.

Newbury Field Club was a witness to the revolution that would shape British Museums in the middle of the nineteenth century which had one of its centres in the nearby City of Salisbury. Although it had little impact in the organization of the museum in Ocean Road in the obscure northern town of South Shields. The Rev Wallis visited Salisbury with the Newbury Field Club on 4th August 1875 after his return from South Shields.

It wasn't his first visit as the city was a regular destination for Field Club outings, but it was one of the Club's most ambitious and was reported at length in the local newspapers. One hundred ladies and gentlemen travelled first class on the Great Western Railway by special train in grand style. Club

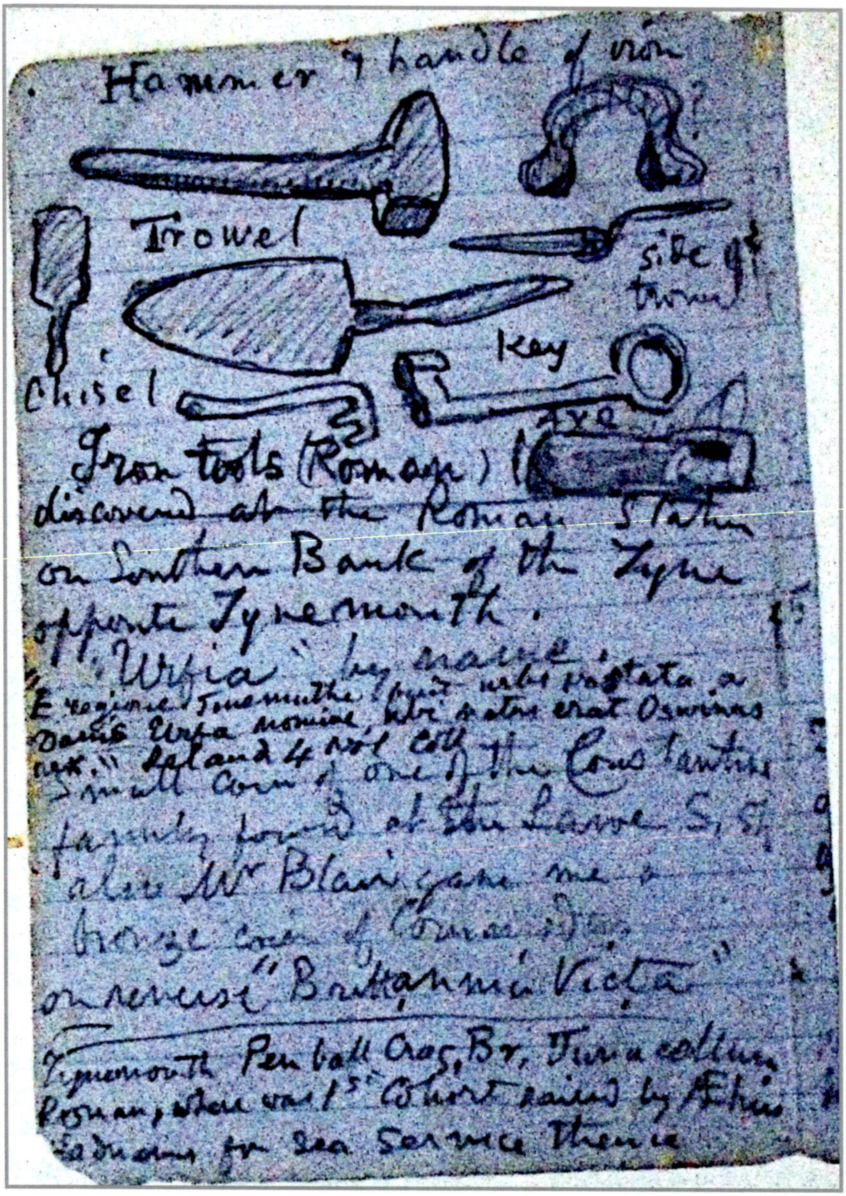

Sketches and notes made by Rev. William Marshall Wallis on the Lawe in 1875.

members toured the cathedral and visited the Blackmore Museum which was an outstanding example of the new approach to displaying items from the past. They were taken round the museum by the curator Mr. Stevens who explained, in an address printed in full in the Newbury Weekly Press, that the exhibits were grouped in cultures which linked the artefacts on display to the people who used them. The museum's collections came from all around the world and went back to the dawn of mankind in Britain. This approach contrasted, he said, with that of Col. Lane Fox, the pioneer archaeologist better known now as Augustus Pitt-Rivers, the first inspector of ancient monuments in Britain, whose collections were then on display at the Bethnal Green Museum in London. Col. Lane-Fox organised artifacts to show their development from simple to more complex forms, an approach which mirrored Victorian Britain's view of its own history and which reinforced its opinion that Britain represented the pinnacle of human progress. The Blackmore Museum which opened in 1867 was a philanthropic venture by William Blackmore a lawyer, who made his fortune as a financial adviser promoting investments in the American west. It grew out of Blackmore's interest in Native American culture, to be, in the words of one US academic (George Amos Dorsey Professor of Anthropology University of Chicago 1907-15), *'one of the best selected and arranged collections of man's prehistoric relics that I have ever seen'*. According to its founding charter the museum, had to be open to the public without charge for at least four days a week and was to be maintained at the expense of its founder. South Shields museum where the exhibits were chaotically presented with inscribed stones and monuments under tables, used neither approach and it is a pity that the opportunity for an exhibition that properly reflected the discoveries of the excavations was missed.

While the excavations attracted the crowds at Easter 1875 reports of spectacular finds from an obscure northern industrial town worried some archaeologists. Robert Blair, who as secretary was the public face of the excavation committee, was an unknown thirty-one-year-old solicitor without a formal academic background so understandably questions were raised about the quality of the excavation. As building work continued around the exposed remains that were later to be preserved in *The People's Roman Remains Park*, reminders of the Roman occupation of the Lawe continued to be found and brought to Blair's office in King Street or he

Below are drawings of finds from Robert Blair's scrapbook.
Note T J Bell's name at the bottom of the page; these pieces probably came from his collection. The earthenware oil lamp with 5 wicks is now in the Great North Museum:Hancock, Newcastle.
Page from Blair Scrapbook; courtesy of South Tyneside Libraries.
Photograph of the lamp by courtesy of Tyne & Wear Archives & Museums.

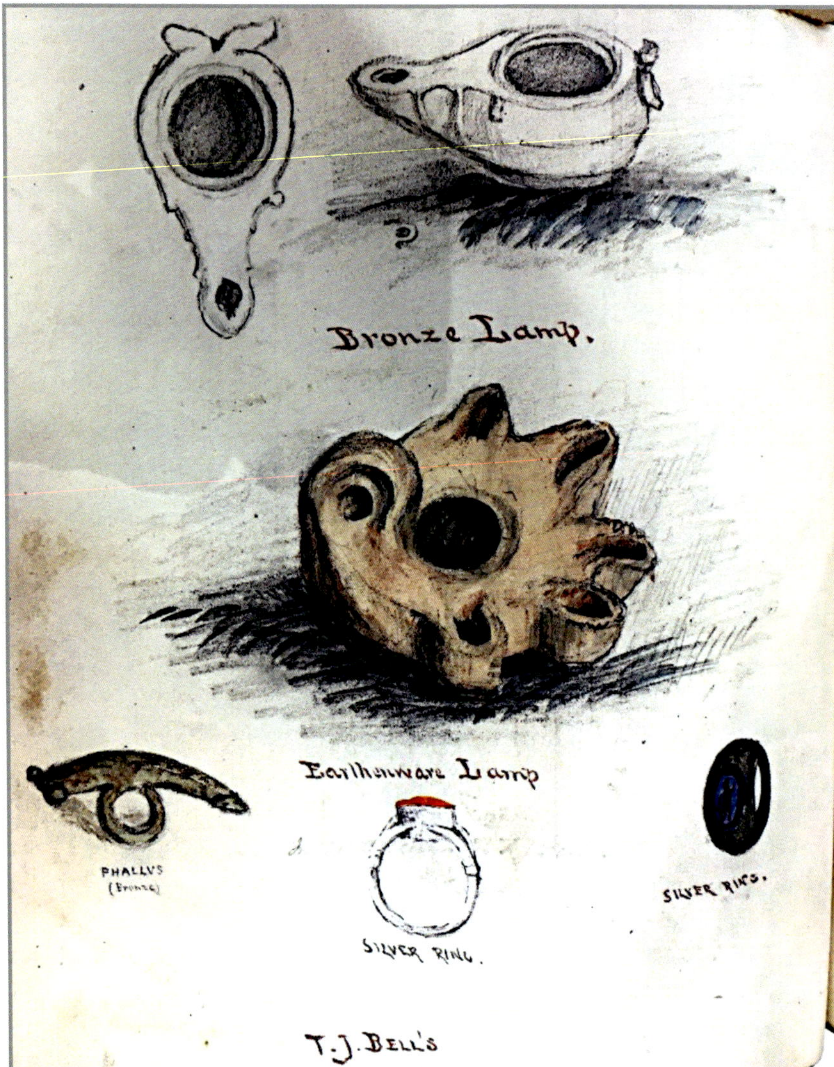

would be summoned to inspect the site of the latest discovery. The largest, like the monuments to Regina and Victor, quickly came to the attention of academic archaeologists and were discussed in detail in learned papers while the smaller finds often passed unnoticed - keys, bracelets, brooches, combs, needles, broken pottery, lamps, fashionable jet jewellery, the stuff of everyday life – and gave some cause for concern when they were produced at meetings of learned societies. Such was the quality and variety of finds, from what seemed at first to be an unpromising location, that some antiquarians found it difficult to accept that all were genuine or all came from the same site, a belief reinforced when Robert Blair brought a carved figure exposed as a forgery to a meeting of the British Archaeological Association in London on 5th February 1875. Part of the problem was the lack of control over the site – the original agreement with the church commissioners specified that finds should be deposited in South Shields museum but on an open site with ongoing building work, objects became the property of their finders if they were found outside of the formal excavation with disastrous results for the archaeology. Robert Blair bought items from the fort on what became a flourishing market in Roman antiquities in South Shields; in 1877 he obtained a beautiful Indian sardonyx cameo carved with the image of a bear from a treasure hunter who found it on the "site of the Roman Amphitheatre" on the Lawe, while the origin of the fine ivory clasp knife in his collection carved with the representation of a gladiator is unknown. A few of the objects in his collection could even have come from abroad, picked up by sailors on their travels and brought home as souvenirs, only to be sold when money was short. So the provenance of the delicate blue glass vase in the shape of a negro head is uncertain and it might not even be from South Shields.

The result was that the finds were split into two distinct groups: the objects from the excavation which came into the hands of the Corporation under the terms of the original excavation agreement and were displayed at South Shields Museum, and the private collections of other interested parties the largest of which belonged to Robert Blair. Blair's collection passed into the hands of the Society of Antiquaries of Newcastle-upon-Tyne after his death and many of the items are now displayed in the Great North Museum Newcastle. Looking at the treasures from his collection on display at the museum it is possible to share his delight in the contemplation of the

A photograph from 1902 of a portion of *The People's Roman Remain Park.* ***Note how close the houses are to the remains. The site is much larger now.*** *Photograph courtesy of South Tyneside Libraries.*

remains of a lost civilisation and understand a little of its lost glory but to appreciate his life's work you have to go to South Shields.

As a campaigner for the preservation and restoration of the site for most of his adult life, Blair would be overjoyed to see the fort as it is now with the rebuilt west gate, courtyard house and barrack block and purpose built museum; an enterprise nearly one hundred and fifty years in the making now very much a part of the identity of his beloved home town and his lasting memorial.

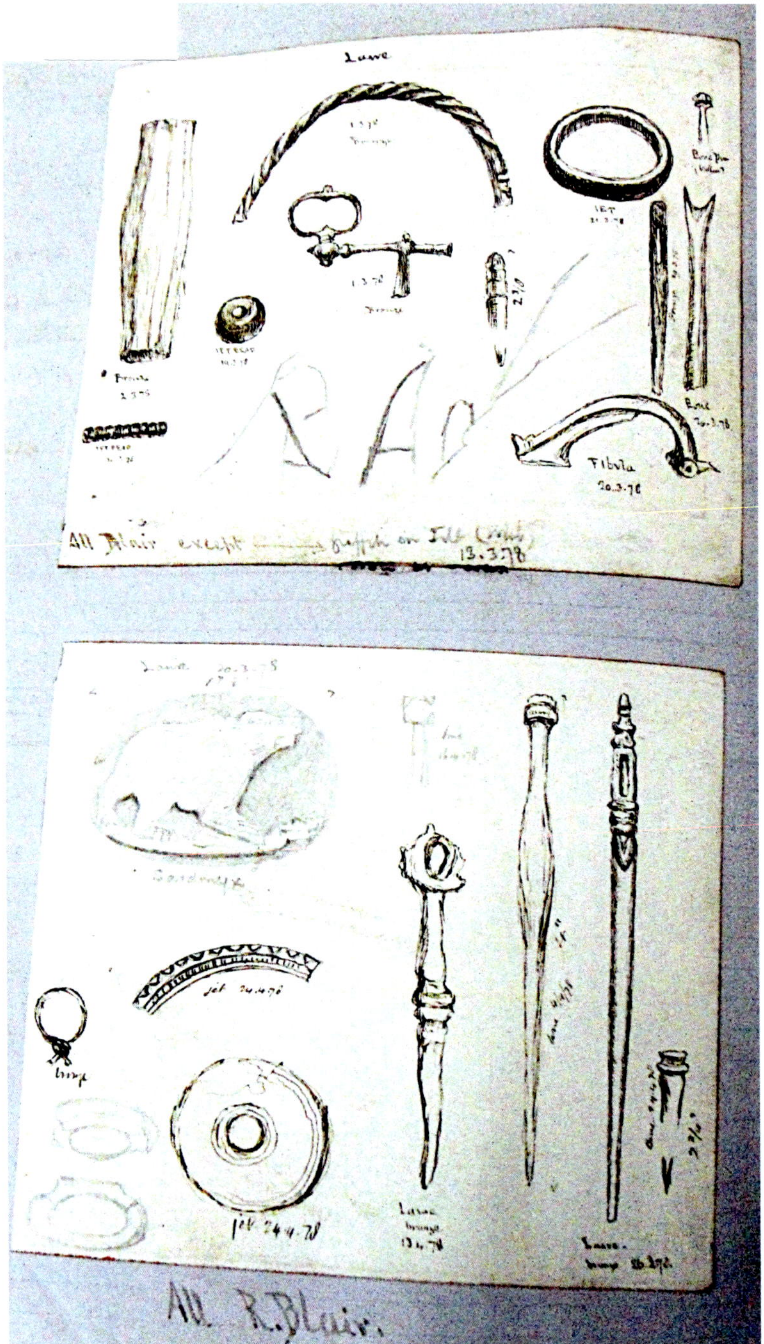

Page showing objects in Blair's collection.
Blair Scrapbook; courtesy of South Tyneside Libraries.

Index
Bibliography
Places to Visit

Drawing by Robert Blair.
Reproduced by kind permission of
Northumberland Archives, Woodhorn.

Index

Altar found 1682 77-79
Altar Table 93
Amulet, The book by Edith Nesbit 115
Bones Found
Human 89
Stag 89
Whale 89
British Archaeological Association 197
Brooch 137
Cameo with carving of a bear 114-115, 162-164, 219
Cemetery
Graves Found 18/2/76 181
Graves Found 10/6/76 181
Regina 117, 121, 125, 190
Victor Top Found 130, 131, 133
Victor Bottom Found 130, 131, 133
Civil war
Sconce on the Lawe 15
Siege of Newcastle 16
Siege of South Shields Fort 15
Cleadon Waterworks 36
Coins
AD 250 -350 97
Gold Coin found by Nicholas Fairles 25
Fairles Nicholas Excavations on Lawe 25
Corporation South Shields 186-187
Courtyard House Reconstruction 76, 221
Dodecahedron 205
Drain 96
Excavation
Drain 96
Forum Arch Keystone Bull's Head 100
Forum Columns 48, 85
Forum Fallen Wall 91
Forum Guard Chamber: 99
Forum Paving 99
Forum Plan 94-95
Forum Statue Torso of Male 99-100
Forum Stone Table 91
Forum Streets 105
Forum Treasure Chamber 75-76, 106-108
Ramparts Eastern 97
Ramparts Southern Gate found 105
Ramparts Western 81
Ramparts Western Gate Found 89

Time Team visit 11
Treasure Chamber 75-76, 106-108
Visitors Easter 97
Visitors Tyneside Naturalists Field Club 109, 111
Vandalism 197
Excavation fund subscribers
Baring, J T Bishop of Durham 56
Clayton, John 58
George, Henry 3rd Earl Grey (declined) 62
Palmer, Charles Mark (declined) 64
Percy, A G 7th Duke of Northumberland 60
Figures
Jupiter, small bronze 31
Minerva, steelyard weight 67
Priestess, small bronze 1
Forum
Arch Keystone Bull's Head 100
Columns 48, 85
Fallen Wall 91
Guard Chamber 99
Paving 99
Plan 94-95
Statue Torso of Male 99-100
Stone Table 91
Streets 105
Treasure Chamber 75-76, 106-108
Fundraising to continue the excavations 65, 167, 169
Garrison
Fifth Cohort of Gauls 77, 79, 99, 111
Gladiators 127-129
Goblet 183
Golden Lion Hotel 166
Head Vase in shape of gladiator 128, 129
Helmet Cheek Piece 126
Hypocaust 101
Inscriptions
Altar 77-79
Water Supply Dedication Stone 120
Regina monument 117
Imperial Seal 118
Jewellery
Crossbow Broach 9
Keys
Door 196
Finger ring key 113
Knife carved in the shape of a gladiator 128
Lamps
Blair drawing 154, 218

Lamps Bronze 99, 155
Earthenware 218
Photographs 154, 218
Letters
Blair, Robert; Case for excavation 47
Blair, Robert; invitation to opening of new museum 188
British Archaeological Association; preservation of remains 197
Bruce, J C, Outline of London lecture 170-173
Ecclesiastical Commissioners permission for excavation 63
Hooppell, Rev. Robert Eli; To Robert Blair re campaign 44-45
Lincoln, T; Case for preservation of remains 21/9/75 193-195
Society of Antiquaries London:
thanks to Blair for exhibiting finds 175
Scrutator (pseud. R E Hooppell); Case for excavation 40-43
Lifeboat
Identity of South Shields 16-17, 186-187
Lawe House Competition 21
Lifeboat Memorial 186
Northumberland Prize 19
Providence Disaster 17-18
St Hilda's Church Model 20
St Stephen's Church 17
Wouldhave and Greathead controversy 23
Maps
Lawe; Fairles 26
Lawe; Fryer 1773 10
Lawe; Richardson 1786 10
Roman Empire 116
Roman Remains Park 198
South Shields 1801 12
South Shields 1849 38
South Shields Alhambra 1875 3
Shields Heugh 1856 22
Marine School, South Shields 32-33
Finds kept in grounds 48
Hooppell, Headmaster of the Marine School 33
Meetings
Mayor permission to excavate 49
Notice of public meeting 50
Public Meeting forms a committee 53, 55
Muckble, Mohammed seaman's boarding house 116-117
Museum, South Shields 48, 184, 187-189
Name of Fort
Caer Urfa 11-12
Lugudunum 77-79
Tunocelum 89
New Town Hall South Shields 185-186

Objects
Altar found 1682 77-79
Brooch 137
Buckle 176-178
Cameo with carving of a bear 114-115, 162-164, 219
Coins AD 250-350 97
Coin gold found by Nicholas Fairles 25
Dodecahedron 205
Figures Jupiter, small bronze 31
Figures Minerva, steelyard weight 67
Figures Priestess, small bronze 1
Goblet 183
Head Vase in shape of gladiator 128-129
Helmet Cheek Piece 126
Imperial Sealing 118
Jewellery Crossbow Broach 9
Keys Door 196
Keys Finger ring key 113
Knife carved in the shape of a gladiator 128
Lamps Bronze 99, 155
Lamps Earthenware 218
Pine Cone Sculpture 46
Pottery Potter's Marks 66, 156
Pottery Samian Ware 153
Shield Boss 126
Tiles, COH V G 107
Tiles, Letters AC found 86-88

People

Alexander Severus Roman emperor
Assassination 121
Life 121
Name removed from water stone 121

Blair, Robert solicitor, antiquarian, secretary of excavation committee
Appointed to museum management committee 193
Appointed secretary by public meeting 53
Campaigns for water stone to go to museum 193
Controversy over forged finds 217, 219
Drawings 144, 146-149, 151-152, 154, 157-158, 162-163, 176, 182, 196, 204, 218
Early life and Education 139
Home (Harton lodge) 140, 141
Hon Secretary of Excavation Committee 49, 65
Letter advocating excavation 47
Obituary 143
Private collection 195, 217, 219
Picture 140
Society of Antiquaries 141-142, 195, 219
Solicitor 141

Broughton J Mayor of South Shields and agent for Ecclesiastical Commissioners
Appointed President of excavation committee 53
Grants access to site to excavation committee 49
Opinion on museum 187
Presides over public meeting 53
Bruce, John Collingwood antiquarian, writer of first guide to Roman Wall
Lecture to London Antiquarian Society 170-173, 179-180
Reputation 69, 71
Speech at opening of museum 187
Speech at public meeting 59
Speech to Tyneside Naturalists Field Club
Tomb Newcastle Cathedral 70
Caracalla, joint emperor son of Severus
Assassination 121
At South Shields 119
Coin 118
Family portrait 120
Murder of Geta 119
Named on altar 79
Sealing 118
Charles, John photographer Station Road South Shields, takes pictures of local curiosities and people, business closed 8th March 1878 when equipment sold by auction for unpaid rent.
Photographs excavations 74
Wet Plate photography 110
Clayton, John Antiquarian and Town clerk of Newcastle
Centurion in Scott painting 72
Chesters Roman fort 73
Development of Newcastle 72-73
Subscribes to fund 58
Visits excavation 92
Ellison, Ralph Carr landowner and antiquarian
Appointed the excavation committee by public meeting 53
Letter advocating excavation 40
Visits excavations 91-92
Visits excavations with John Clayton
Fairles, Nicholas tenant of Lawe Estate and magistrate murdered by Ralph Armstrong during 1832 miner's strike for which crime William Jobling was executed under law of *common purpose*.
Excavations on the Lawe 25
Field House 27-29
Gentlemen of Lawe House 25
Gold coin found 25
Lifeboat 21
Map of Lawe excavations 26
Murder 27
Gardiner, Ralph writer 39

Geta, Joint emperor son of Severus
At South Shields 119
Coin 118
Murdered 119
Named on altar 79
Removed from family portrait 120
Sealing 118
Hooppell, Rev. Robert Eli Headmaster of Marine School later rector of Byers Green and excavator of Roman Fort at Binchester, Bishop Auckland
Campaigns for preservation of remains 197
Contagious diseases Act 35, 37
Headmaster of the Marine School 33
Joint Hon. Secretary of excavation committee 49
Leads visit of Tyneside Naturalists Club 109, 111, 166-167
Letter to Robert Blair re campaign tactics 44, 45
Letter as "scrutator" advocating excavation 40-43
Moves to Binchester 65
Picture 32
Speech at public meeting 10/3/75
Visits Roman Remains Park for newspaper 199, 201, 203
Julia Domna wife of Severus
Suicide 121
Murder of Geta 119
Portrait with family 120
Leland, John Henry VIII's Antiquarian
Names fort Caer Urfa 11
Oswin King of Northumbria born at Fort 13
Visits Tynemouth 11
Lincoln T antiquarian
Appointed to excavation committee 55
Letter advocating preservation of remains 194
Meets mayor to get permission for excavations 49
Oswin King of Northumbria
Born at South Shields 13
Burials at Tynemouth 13
Site of Shrine 13
Oswald, Joseph architect and surveyor of 32 Mosley Street Newcastle
Surveys excavations 75, 103
Regina freedwoman wife of Barates
Aramaic inscription 117
Fashion 123
Jewel Box 123
Key 123
Monument illustration 122, 124
Monument Discovered 117, 125
Slavery 121, 123, 129, 131
Victor freedman of Numerianus
Discovery of monument 130, 131
Life 135
Slavery 121, 123, 129, 131

Scott, William Bell Artist
Coal and Iron painting 70
The Romans cause a wall to be built painting 72
Severus, Septimius Roman emperor
Coin 118
Death at York 119
Life 119
Scottish campaign 119
Sealings 118
Siddall, Samuel proprietor of Alhambra Amphitheatre, Mill Dam South Shields
Alhambra Theatre description 3
Alhambra Theatre fire 7
Stages performance of Julius Caesar 2, 5
Smith, Ecroyd antiquarian
Lectures in Free Library 102-103, 168
Wallis, William Marshall Clergyman, antiquarian, artist
Family background 211
Newbury Field Club 215-216
Newbury History 213, 215
Sketches excavations 209-210, 214, 216
Visits excavations 209
Places
Binchester
Hooppell excavates 63
Roman Fort 63
Lawe Top
Empress Terraces 6
Civil War Sconce 15
Field House 27-29
Lawe House 24-25
Roman Street Names 209
St Stephen's Church 17-18
Mill Dam
Alhambra theatre 3, 7
Customs House 38
Segedunum (Wallsend)
Reconstructed Bath House 206
Roman names on metro station 207
Tyne Dock
Opening 36-37
Significance 39
Pine Cone Sculpture 46
Plans
Forum 94-95
Fort 1875 104
Roman Remains Park 198
Port 135

Pottery
Blair drawings 148, 150, 152
Potter's Marks 66, 156
Samian Ware 153
Ramparts found
Eastern 97
Southern Gate found 105
Western 81
Western Gate found 89
Regina Memorial
Aramaic inscription 117
Discovery 117, 124-125
Illustration 121
Roman Army 127, 131
Roman Remains Park
Antiquary's description 200-201, 203
New Museum on site 202
Origin 199
Panorama 220-221
Plan 198
Postcard 198
West Gate reconstructed 202
St Hilda's Church South Shields
Foundation and History 15
Lifeboat model 20
Salt Manufacture at South Shields 15
Sealings
Imperial 118
Shield Boss 126
Slavery 121, 123,
Society of Antiquaries of Newcastle upon Tyne 51,141-142, 195, 219
Stanhope and Tyne Railway 39, 212
Statues
Male torso 161
Tiles
COH V G found 107
Floor found 89
Letters AC found 86- 88
Time Team visit 11
Trade 23
Trams 185-186, 207-208
Treasure Chamber 75-76, 106-108
Visitors on Site
Easter 97
Tyneside Naturalists Field Club 109, 111
Wallington Hall 69-71
Vandalism 197

Victor the Moor 130-133, 135
Volunteers used in excavation 89
Walls and Chambers found 81
Water Stone
Alexander's name removed 120
Controversy over preservation 191
Found 120, 191
Picture 192
Weapons and Armour
Buckle 176-178
Helmet cheek piece 126

The Tyne entrance from the end of the Herd Sand Groyne. The red lighthouse is the leading light for ships entering the Tyne, the low and high lights at North Shields are to be seen on the right, and the low hill of the Lawe is in the middle behind the lighthouse. The shield boss and helmet cheek-piece were found near here leading some archaeologists to suggest there may be a Roman shipwreck on the sands.

Select Bibliography

Allason-Jones, Lindsay (ed) (2011):
Artefacts in Roman Britain, their purpose and use,
Cambridge University Press.
Has many references to objects found at South Shields.

Allason-Jones, Lindsay & Miket, Roger (1984):
The Catalogue of Small Finds from South Shields Roman Fort,
Society of Antiquaries of Newcastle upon Tyne, Newcastle.
Essential reference book for finds from the fort with a history of the site.

Blair, Robert, undated:
unpublished Scrapbook relating to South Shields Roman Fort,
copy in The Word, South Shields.

Breeze, David J (2006*):*
J Collingwood Bruce's Handbook to the Roman Wall,
Society of Antiquaries of Newcastle upon Tyne, Newcastle.
Historic handbook to the Roman Wall including the fort at South Shields once edited by Robert Blair.

Hodgson, George B (1903):
The Borough of South Shields: From the Earliest Period to the Close of the Nineteenth Century,
Andrew Reid & Co, Newcastle.
The standard history of South Shields written by the editor of the Shields Gazette at a time when the rise of the town seemed irresistible and it needed to find its history. Available online as an ebook.

Hooppell, Rev. Robert Eli (1891):
Vinovia, a buried Roman City in the County of Durham,
Whiting & Co., London.
Historic account of Rev. Hooppell's excavations at Binchester which he began after leaving South Shields in 1875; has detailed plans and architectural drawings of the remains which shows advances from methods used on the Lawe, copy in Durham University Palace Green Library.

Places to Visit

Arbeia, South Shields Roman Fort:
Expanded site includes the object People's Roman Remains Park, spectacular reconstructions of the west gate, a barrack block, and a courtyard house, while the museum has Regina and Victor memorials and much more. Not to be missed. Normally open Easter to October.

Great North Museum: Hancock Newcastle-upon-Tyne:
Displays items from Robert Blair's private collection of Roman artifacts which were donated by Blair to the Society of Antiquaries of Newcastle of Tyne. Robert Blair was secretary of the Society and editor of its journal for many years and the objects include a helmet cheek piece, and bronze patera found on Herd Sand together with the bear cameo, ivory knife Handle carved in the shape of a gladiator and the blue glass vase in the shape of a Negro head. The provenance of the vase is unknown but the collection is made up of objects purchased by Blair from '*prospectors*' or given to him by their finders because of his prominent role in the 1875 excavations and has many items discovered during building works on the Lawe after completion of the object excavation of the site. It was a condition of the 1875 excavation that all finds were placed in South Shields Free Library Museum, so all finds from this period are now in the collections of the Arbeia, South Shields Roman Fort. Great North Museum: Hancock normally open all the year.

South Shields Museum (formerly the Free Library):
Objects from the 1875 excavation and the monuments to Regina and Victor were displayed here before the Arbeia Museum was built in the 1950s. Now much changed but well worth a visit for an insight into the history of South Shields. Normally open all the year.

Vinovia (Binchester) Roman Fort:
Site near Bishop Auckland originally excavated by Rev. Dr. Hooppell after he was appointed Rector of Binchester in 1875. Well worth visiting for the spectacular bath house and the ongoing excavations on the site. only a fraction of which has been investigated. Normally open Easter to October.

Segedunum (Wallsend) Roman Fort:

Excavated fort previously covered by housing in the 19th century well worth a visit for reconstructed bath house and spectacular viewing tower. If you arrive by train lookout for the Roman names and Latin notices on the metro station, a modern echo of South Shields promotion of its Roman past.. Normally open all year.

***The twenty first century entrance to the museum building at Arbeia South Shields Roman Fort, previously known as** The People's Roman Remains Park.*